Robotic Process and Cognitive Automation
The Next Phase

Robotic Process and Cognitive Automation
The Next Phase

Mary C. Lacity
and
Leslie P. Willcocks

SB Publishing
United Kingdom

A 'SB Publishing' book
www.sbpublishing.org

Cover design:
Nick Sample
www.nicksample.com

Cover images:
Balancement (a.k.a *Swinging*) by Wassily Kandinsky, 1866 - 1944
1925, oil on board
By kind permission of Tate Modern, Bankside, London SE1 9TG, UK

Authors:
Mary C. Lacity and Leslie P. Willcocks

Published in 2018 by:
SB Publishing
60 Loxley Road
Stratford-upon-Avon
Warwickshire CV37 7DR
Tel: +44(0)1789 267124

A CIP catalogue record for this book is available from the British Library
ISBN ISBN 978-0-995682-01-6

Printed and bound in Malta by Latitude Press Ltd.

Contents

Contents

Contents

Figures

8

Tables

Preface

Automation is poised to have a profound impact on the global economy. The number of organisations catching onto the productivity and cost-savings offered by 'robot workers' is swelling year-on-year. Indeed, ISG's 2017 Automation Index found that nearly three quarters of all enterprises will leverage automation in some form by 2019. This will have a transformational effect on back office and customer service functions, as we know them today.

We are riding the crest of a wave. Where in the past clients could expect to receive a five to ten percent productivity boost as a result of their IT outsourcing contracts after two years, we now see examples in which enterprises are realising improvements of between 40 percent and 140 percent over the same time period. What's more, our data shows that Robotic Process Automation (RPA) is helping organisations to perform tasks effectively with less than two thirds of the resources they had previously needed. This has only been made possible through automation.

We are seeing these opportunities in our own work. Our job as advisers is to help our clients to better understand their own needs, clarify their vision, and to match this to products and services available in the marketplace. We've been pleased to see that, over the last 12 months, RPA has moved from being perceived and executed as a cost-saving tactic to being recognised as a strategic necessity. This is to be encouraged, as the consequences of automation align so closely with organisational priorities around transforming services, improving productivity and controlling cost.

Talk of automation is everywhere. While some commentators extoll its benefits, others fret about job losses. In nearly every scenario we analysed for the ISG Automation Index, we found no evidence of human redundancy – still, the debate around the redeployment of resource is an important one, and something that is examined in the final chapters of this book. Yet what are often missing from the conversation are details about what is actually happening today. This book fills that gap.

Robotic Process and Cognitive Automation: The Next Phase presents the reader with a compelling picture of the attributes, markets, adoption and success rates of automation. As in previous volumes, Mary Lacity and Leslie Willcocks demonstrate their leading authority in this field. The new data presented here, as well as a fresh analysis of existing research, reveal a thriving sector with tremendous growth potential. The case studies contained within these chapters provide insights into the results that can be achieved through automation, as well as the valuable learning from organisations that are well along their automation journey. Coupled with Mary and Leslie's incisive commentary, this book should be received as the CIO's ultimate guide to automation.

Barry Matthews - Head of UK, Ireland and Netherlands at ISG

Endorsements

"Process automation is real and here to stay, with modern enterprises starting to dip their toes into the cognitive systems space. Lacity and Willcocks show you how generate business value in real world examples. If you weren't sure if Intelligent Process Automation was real, grab a coffee and find out where the field is heading, how companies are using it, and how to deliver real business value."

Lee Coulter, CEO Ascension Shared Services

"Lacity and Willcocks have written the next chapter on the most disruptive phenomenon to impact business operations since offshore outsourcing two decades ago: automation technology advancements and smart cognitive applications that bridge the chasm between man and machine in the enterprise. This book describes how the cognitive era is creating the human middleware of the future!"

Phil Fersht, CEO and Chief Analyst, HfS Research

"What makes this book so ground-breaking is the way it debunks and dispels much of the hype and fear surrounding automation and AI. Mary Lacity and Leslie Willcocks look at the impact these technologies are having through real world examples and the customer experience. Analysis and insights are derived from the people driving the most significant digital transformations of our time. The result is a must read for anyone interested in the future of work."

Alastair Bathgate, Group CEO of Blue Prism

"Professors Lacity and Willcocks' analysis of real cognitive deployments provides essential advice for senior executives leading the company's digital transformation. Their comprehensive understanding of the intersection between business and strategy allows them to pinpoint the key learning in each case study which has a direct impact on outcomes."

Chetan Dube, CEO and Founder, IPsoft

"Based on insightful case studies of early adopters and innovative developers, this book will help prepare companies to take advantage of powerful new technologies. Lacity and Willcocks do a masterful job of distinguishing the hype from the reality."

Dr. Jeanne Ross, Principal Research Scientist, MIT Center for Information Systems Research

"Lacity and Willcocks have long been the experts on robotic process automation, but now they're focusing their attention on more intelligent machines. If you care about the impact of cognitive technologies on your organization you should start here."

Thomas H. Davenport, Distinguished Professor, Babson College and Research Fellow, MIT; Author of *Competing on Analytics* and *Only Humans Need Apply*

"This is the most insightful coverage yet of the use of the emerging cognitive tools. In addition, the interesting and original analysis of the value of RPA follows on nicely from the previous books. The authors demonstrate excellently the recognized value of RPA when done properly, as well as the challenges faced by the uninitiated."

David Poole, CEO of Symphony Ventures - the leading independent RPA advisory firm

"This is a well-researched, well-written and important book. Mary and Leslie are uniquely qualified to take on one of today's most rapidly growing industry trends. Anyone who really cares about how organizations are maturing and integrating technologies to deliver wins for shareholders, customers and employees should read this book."

Debi Hamill, CEO, IAOP

About the Authors

Dr. Mary C. Lacity is Curators' Distinguished Professor at the University of Missouri-St. Louis and a Visiting Scholar at MIT CISR. She has held visiting positions at the London School of Economics, Washington University, and Oxford University. She is a Certified Outsourcing Professional®, Industry Advisor for Symphony, and Senior Editor of *MIS Quarterly Executive*. She has given keynote speeches and executive seminars worldwide and has served as an expert witness for the US Congress. Mary was inducted into the IAOP's Outsourcing Hall of Fame in 2014 – one of only three academics to ever achieve this. She has published 26 books – most recently Robotic *Process Automation and Risk Mitigation: The Definitive Guide* (2017) and *Service Automation: Robots and the Future of Work* (2016) – both with SB Publishing, UK, co-author Leslie Willcocks. Mary's publications have appeared in the *Harvard Business Review, Sloan Management Review, MIS Quarterly, IEEE Computer, Communications of the ACM*, and many other academic and practitioner outlets. **Email: Mary.Lacity@umsl.edu**

Dr. Leslie P. Willcocks has an international reputation for his work on automation, global management, outsourcing, e-business, information management, IT evaluation, strategic IT and organisational change. He is Professor in Technology Work and Globalisation at the Department of Management at London School of Economics and Political Science.

He also heads the LSE's Outsourcing Unit, and, for the last 28 years, has been Editor-in-Chief of the *Journal of Information Technology*. Leslie is co-author of 55 books including *Nine Keys To World Class BPO* (2015), *Moving to The Cloud Corporation* (2014), and *The Rise of Legal Services Outsourcing* (2014) and has published over 230 refereed papers in journals such as *Harvard Business Review, Sloan Management Review, California Management Review, MIS Quarterly* and *MISQ Executive*. He has delivered company executive programmes worldwide, is a regular keynote speaker at international practitioner and academic conferences, and has been retained as adviser and expert witness by major corporations and government institutions. Forthcoming books include *Global Outsourcing Discourse: Exploring Modes of IT Governance* (Palgrave, 2018). Leslie's research into the management of cloud business services appears as *Cloud and The Future of Business: From Cost to Innovation* (www.outsourcingunit.org).

Email: l.p.willcocks@lse.ac.uk

About Chapter Co-Authors

Andrew Craig has been visiting Senior Research Fellow at the London School of Economics and Political Science UK where he helped set up the Outsourcing Unit. He heads the IT leadership and governance stream of Rame Associates and is also a director of Board Coaching Ltd. He has coached executives, teams and boards in the Defence Procurement Agency, the UK Border Agency, the leisure industry, Balfour Beatty, HSBC and finance and fund management companies. Andrew is co-author of T*he Outsourcing Enterprise: From Cost Management to Collaborative Innovation* (Palgrave Macmillan, 2011). In his professional British Army career, as Brigadier, he directed the recruiting operation - an annual requirement of 16,000 people - and was responsible for Human Resource planning for a workforce of 120,000. He commanded engineering operations worldwide, including the first Gulf War and Bosnia, and led the UK's planned military response to nuclear, biological and chemical terrorism. Andrew received an OBE in 1992.

Gero Gunkel is the cognitive automation program manager at Zurich Insurance. As part of Zurich`s Business Development and Innovation team, he manages Zurich`s artificial intelligence portfolio since 2015, driving the adoption of AI solutions across the whole insurance value chain. Previously he worked for Zurich`s internal consulting team as a senior consultant. Before joining Zurich, Gero worked on the launch of an innovation consultancy in London. He holds a BA in Economics from the University of Heidelberg and a Masters in Management from the London School of Economics and Political Science.

Dr. Rens Scheepers is chair of Information Systems and Business Analytics at Deakin University, Australia. His research focuses on how organisations derive business value returns from the application of information and communication technologies. He has conducted research in Europe, Africa and Australia in sectors such as manufacturing, telecommunications, hospitality, healthcare, aged care, policing, and banking. Rens' publications have appeared in the *European Journal of Information Systems,* the *Journal of Information Technology*, the *Information Systems Journal* and the *Journal of the Association of Information Systems.* He currently serves on the editorial boards of the *Journal of Information Technology*, and the *Journal of Strategic Information Systems.*

Authors' Introduction and Acknowledgements

This research was conducted with the support and funding of the Outsourcing Unit at the London School of Economics and Political Science, Blue Prism, Redwood, IPsoft, and the Information Systems Group. Once again, our research has been massively dependent on the kindness and the sharing of valuable knowledge and experience by literally hundreds of people working in organisations at every level. An immense thank you to all of them for the conversations, interviews, information and guidance, without which a book like this just would not have been possible. Our continuing thanks go to colleagues at the LSE, University of Missouri-St. Louis, MIT and Deakin University. Their support, patience, and constructive words were highly valued as we progressed this project. As ever we thank family and friends for their understanding and wisdom over long periods of time, and our publishers, SB Publishing, for their creativity, superb skill, time management and anticipating just about every problem.

We would also like to thank Tate Modern for giving us permission to use the marvellous painting, *Balancement* (1925), by Wassily Kandinsky, on the book cover. If you are passing through London you can see this painting for yourself. 'Balancement' can mean rocking, swaying, oscillating, the act or result of balancing or adjusting, equipoise, an even adjustment of forces. Kandinsky once said: *"Just ask yourself whether the work has enabled you to 'walk about' into a hitherto unknown world."* Balancement is a powerful concept for approaching the next phase of automation – moving from an undue focus on technology, to working through how so many things can be orchestrated and made to move together in a balanced and dynamic manner. Despite the increasing abstraction of his work, Kandinsky maintained a profound sense of how vital it is to remain fundamentally human – experiencing, feeling, learning, moralising, designing and sense-making – attributes we really are going to need as we move ourselves through the next phase of automation and beyond.

Chapter 1

Service Automation: Overview

By Mary Lacity and Leslie Willcocks

> *"Today, we can say that robotic process automation takes the robot out of the human; cognitive automation complements and amplifies both the human, and RPA. Service automation technologies can deliver a triple-win of value for shareholders, customers and employees – but only if managed well."*[1]

Leslie Willcocks and Mary Lacity

1.1. Introduction

Welcome to the third book in our service automation library collection. We started out in late 2014 with the limited ambition to research a promising area that was being called Robotic Process Automation (RPA), but we soon got overtaken by a high profile debate and media attention focusing on automation and the future of work. The debate and anxieties had featured several times already in the twentieth century, usually in times of recession or very low economic growth, but reignited throughout 2015. As a result, our research has been framed in this much bigger context, and looks at a time-line from 2016 to 2027, and in our final chapter, as far as 2065.

Our initial, limited ambition with RPA was to discover if there was any 'there' really there, and if so, to what it could amount. We limited our focus to software robots, rather than physical robots, and to service applications, which unlike industrial settings and physical robots, were very under-studied.

Over 60 years combined experience with, and research into, computing and digital technologies told us that new hardware and software went through a hype and fear stage, followed by hard learning as good and bad experiences and usage emerged. There then followed a period of maturation and control and more considered – even strategic – use of the technology, and a limited few leaders moved to a further stage of leveraging the technology to achieve business results well above average for their industry. Throughout the last thirty-five years of engagement with advancing information and communications technologies, we also noticed that time and again, success and disappointment were much less products of the technologies themselves, than of management decisions and actions, capabilities and incapabilities. We made the assumption – correct as it turned out – that something similar would happen with robotic process automation.

Our first book, *Service Automation: Robots and The Future of Work*, had only a limited number of RPA adoptions to draw upon. At the time RPA was a very small market, but fortunately several organisations had been evolving their RPA usage over three to six years, were mature adopters, and provided many lessons from which we, and also newer adopters, were able to learn. As we shall see in the next chapter, and in the cases throughout the book, these lessons have proven robust across time, in different applications and often in different contexts. The book stressed that successes were being achieved, and identified some 25 management 'action principles' that underpinned positive business outcomes. Our second book, *Robotic Process Automation and Risk Mitigation: The Definitive Guide*, updated the findings from February 2016 to early 2017. As the market grew exponentially, more cases became available, and our research began to discover risk factors and less easy deployments than we were finding in the earlier period. We identified 41 risks experienced across the automation life cycle, and expanded the action principles to 30 in order to mitigate these risks. These are detailed in Chapter 2, along with recent additional RPA cases.

This present book catches RPA in transition as organisations scale, find further uses, and also trial and see how far cognitive automation tools have advanced, can complement RPA, and expand the service automation repertoire. In this chapter we lay down some introductions to the area. Firstly, we outline the research base we draw upon. Secondly, we map the service automation landscape. Thirdly, we look at the size of the RPA and cognitive automation markets, which were growing exponentially during 2017, and into 2018. We then report on our survey evidence on service automation adoption rates, the impact on jobs in client and provider organisations, and success rates.

1.2. The Research Base

We conducted empirical research on service automation to answer three questions:

1. Why are clients adopting service automation?
2. What outcomes are they achieving?
3. What practices distinguish service automation outcomes?

To answer these questions, we conducted three surveys of outsourcing professionals attending the International Association of Outsourcing Professionals world summits in 2015, 2016, and 2017 and conducted interviews with service automation adopters, software providers, and management consultants across the major business sectors. In the course of our research, we collected 23 detailed service automation adoption stories and some 33 case vignettes.

Depending on the subjects' availability and preferences, we conducted interviews in person, over the telephone, and through email. We posed a number of questions pertaining to their service automation adoption, the business value delivered, and lessons learned. We also interviewed software provider representatives to discuss their companies' automation capabilities, challenges they help their clients overcome, and the future they envisioned for service automation. We asked advisors questions pertaining to client service automation adoption, effects on outsourcing, automation tool capabilities, and the future of work as a consequence of automation.

Of the 23 research sites on which we gave detailed focus, seven had their headquarters in the United Kingdom, six in the United States, three in Germany, two in Switzerland and one each in France, The Netherlands, South Africa, Sweden, and Russia. Adding in the 33 case vignettes we developed, the organisations studied inhabit many sectors, including healthcare; pharmaceuticals; agriculture; energy; telecommunications; hi-tech; manufacturing; media; management consulting; business processing and IT services; financial and accounting services; retail; insurance; higher education; and transportation. This demonstrates that service automation is affecting a broad range of industries.

1.3. Mapping the Service Automation Landscape

Service automation includes a variety of tools and platforms with various capabilities, and we wanted to ask clients, providers, and advisors to comment on specific automation tools within the broad service automation landscape. To help make sense of this landscape, we consider two broad classes of service automation tools: Robotic Process Automation (RPA) and Cognitive Automation (CA). Each class of tools is designed to deal with specific types of data and processes (see Figure 1.1).

We conceive of the realm of RPA as occupying the part of the service automation landscape that handles structured data and rule-based processes. As such, we define RPA as *'using software to automate tasks previously performed by humans that use **rules** to process **structured data** to produce deterministic outcomes.'* Most RPA tools connect to existing software (like enterprise resource planning systems) by assigning the software 'robot' a logon ID and password – including RPA platforms. People who configure RPA tools do not need programming experience, but rather use RPA's friendly graphical user interfaces to configure robots to execute processes. Within the realm of RPA, there is a lot of variety, including RPA tools that focus on desktop deployment, enterprise server deployment, or cloud deployment. Popular companies in the RPA realm include Blue Prism, Automation Anywhere, and UiPath. The number of suppliers listing their products as 'RPA' was over 45 by mid-2017, and rising still further as we entered into early 2018.

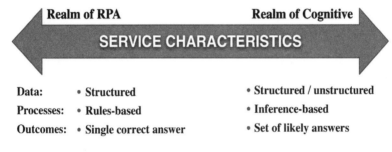

Figure 1.1: The service automation landscape

The IEEE distinguishes between robotic desktop automation and robotic process automation. The IEEE's *Guide on Terms and Concepts in Intelligent Automation* was approved and published in 2017. Here are the definitions:

> "**Robotic Desktop Automation (RDA)**: *Computer application that makes available to a human operator a suite of predefined activity choreography to complete the execution of processes, activities, transactions, and tasks in one or more unrelated software systems to deliver a result or service in the course of human initiated or managed workflow. **Synonyms**: agent-assist automation, assistive automation, in-line automation.*"[2]

> "**Robotic Process Automation (RPA)**: *Preconfigured software instance that uses business rules and predefined activity choreography to complete the autonomous execution of a combination of processes, activities, transactions, and tasks in one*

25

or more unrelated software systems to deliver a result or service with human exception management."[3]

We conceive of the realm of cognitive automation as occupying the part of the service automation landscape that handles unstructured data and is capable of inference-based processing. We define **cognitive automation** as *"using software to automate or augment tasks that use inference-based algorithms to process unstructured and structured data to produce probabilistic outcomes"*. The new set of tools, including IPsoft's Amelia and IBM's Watson, use natural language interfaces to read, build patterns and relationships among data, and apply knowledge to solve problems, or to pose additional pertinent questions. Some of these tools also claim emotional intelligence, the ability to assess another human being's sentiment or state of arousal. The IEEE offers a more thorough definition:

> *"***Cognitive automation:*** The identification, assessment and application of available machine learning algorithms for the purpose of leveraging domain knowledge and reasoning to further automate the machine learning already present in a manner that may be thought of as cognitive. It results in the system performing corrective actions driven by knowledge of the underlying analytics tool itself, iterating its own automation approaches and algorithms for more expansive or more thorough analysis enabling it to fulfill its purpose. The automation of the cognitive process refines itself, dynamically generating novel hypotheses that it can likewise assess against its existing corpus and other information resources."*[4]

By late 2017 there were more than 120 providers claiming to be offering CA and even Artificial Intelligence (AI) products. Amongst the well-known providers are IBM Watson, Workfusion, IPsoft, Expert System, Nuance and Digital Reasoning. Artificial Intelligence is a widely used term to refer ostensibly to the area of cognitive automation, but has quickly become almost an umbrella market term for the whole area of robotic process and cognitive automation. As a leading AI researcher, Margaret Boden says: *"AI seeks to make computers do the sorts of things that minds can do. Some of these (e.g. reasoning) are normally described as 'intelligent'. Others (e.g. vision) aren't. But all involve psychological skills – such as perception, association, prediction, planning, motor control – that enable humans and animals to attain their goals".*[5] The term AI is used when a machine mimics 'cognitive' functions that humans associate with human minds – for example learning and problem solving – but, as leading AI researcher Igor Aleksander points out, intelligence in the context of robots addresses an 'algorithmic' category of processes, needing a human designer, and cannot be compared to 'intelligence' in human beings.[6] For Aleksander, robots and AI can be neither conscious nor mindful. He regrets the descriptor AI – *"smart computing would have done"* – and comments that after 60 years of intense scientific effort the intelligent robot vying with the intelligence of a human being is proving to be much more elusive than the predictions of many futurologists.

Despite these sorts of severe qualifications, the rhetoric has run way ahead of the reality and, during 2017, unfortunately, an academic research term had been permanently hijacked to often misrepresent, and certainly to add glamour to, product offerings. For these reasons we tend not to use the term AI in this book unless it refers to technologies that do, indeed, seek to make computers do the sorts of things that minds can do.

1.4. Size of RPA and CA Markets

Research firms estimate the size of markets by summing the revenues generated from companies who sell service automation products and services. The RPA market is easier to size than the CA market because the software and service providers are easier to identify. The main RPA providers include Automation Anywhere, Blue Prism, Jidoka, Kofax Kapow, Leo Kryon Systems, Pega/ Openspan, Redwood, UiPath and WorkFusion. Advisors in the RPA space include Symphony Ventures, ISG, KPMG, E&Y, and Accenture, among others. Sizing the cognitive automation market is thornier, as many providers, like IBM, seem to count many tools as 'CA'. For example, IBM reported $4.6 billion in revenues from its 'Cognitive Solutions'[7], yet the entire CA market has been sized around $1 billion to $2.4 billion by research firms. It's difficult to reconcile the estimates, but here we go ...

RPA Market. Across estimates, the RPA market is still small but growing rapidly. Forrester, for example, estimated the RPA market at $250 million in 2016, and predicted it would grow to $2.9 billion in 2021.[8] HfS Research sized the RPA market at $443 million in 2017 and predicted it would reach $1.2 billion by 2021.[9] Looking over a longer term, Grand View Research expected the market to reach $8.75 billion by 2024.[10] The predicted annual growth rates across firms ranged from 38 percent by HfS, to 100 percent by the Everest Group.[11]

CA Market. As with the RPA market, statistics for CA are variable, reflecting different data sources, definitions and methodologies. Tractica estimated CA market revenues at just over $1 billion in 2018, rising to over $11 billion in 2024. By that date the North American market would account for some $3 billion, Western Europe some $2 billion, and Asia Pacific some $4.2 billion. Statista's estimates for what they call the 'Artificial Intelligence' market are higher – some $4.1 billion in 2018 rising to $46.5 billion in 2024 and $59.7 billion in 2025.[12] Allied Market Research (2016)[13] suggests that the Artificial Intelligence market size will reach $19 billion by 2022, growing at a CAGR of 45.4 percent from 2016 to 2022. Looking across studies, estimates of market revenue growth rates hover between 40 percent and 60 percent per annum.

Despite the massive attention given to service automation since 2016, and its impact on the future of work, these relatively low market figures are surprising. In Chapter 9 we discuss in detail the many factors that may well slow service automation adoption. These factors will also emerge from the many case studies we discuss through the other chapters in the book. But for the moment, let's turn to the more immediate adoption rates.

1.5. Service Automation Adoption Rates

Each year at the Outsourcing World Summit (OWS), we partner with the IAOP to administer a survey during the client-only and provider/advisor-only networking sessions. In 2015, 2016, and 2017, the survey focused on service automation, defined as 'using software to perform tasks, processes, or entire services that were previously performed by humans.' Detailed results from each survey may be found in *Pulse Magazine*.[14] Here we summarise the most recent findings. For the 2017 survey, we also partnered with Dr. Ron Babin, Associate Professor at Ryerson University, and we collected responses from 68 clients and 59 providers. We first present what clients reported.

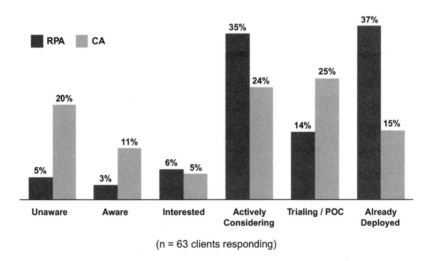

(n = 63 clients responding)

**Figure 1.2: Client organisational adoption of
service automation technologies**

We asked clients to indicate the adoption stages for RPA and CA in their organisations. ***Among the clients who responded to the survey, 37 percent indicated that their organisations had already deployed RPA*** (see Figure 1.2). Certainly we saw a rapid maturing of RPA capabilities over just one year. In contrast, as at February 2017, only 15 percent of client organisations had already deployed cognitive automation. In our case study research, we were finding that cognitive automation projects would increasingly go to market in late 2017, which is supported by the survey: *25 percent of client organisations were primed to deploy cognitive automation services 'soon'*, as they were currently doing trials or proofs-of-concepts (POC) for cognitive technologies.

We next asked clients which sourcing approach they typically used for service automation programs. *Clients most commonly reported that they relied on their current service providers to automate services for them* (see Figure 1.3). This is good news for service providers that have developed significant automation capabilities. For clients, the benefits of engaging a traditional Business Process Outsourcing (BPO) provider include a full suite of integrated services that combine labour arbitrage, process excellence, change management maturity and technology expertise.

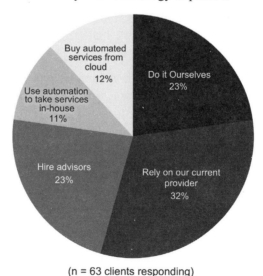

(n = 63 clients responding)

**Figure 1.3: Client organisational approach to
service automation**

30

Advisors will also be pleased to learn that 23 percent of clients said they hire advisors to help with service automation. In the past few years, we have seen advisors quickly building service automation practices in response to increased client demand. Advisory firms track the service automation landscape and help clients with their service automation journeys. Credible advisors need to master a variety of tools to be 'tool agnostic' and they must understand which tools are best suited to meet a client's needs. Advisors are building capabilities by a variety of means. These include: adopting tools to automate their own internal services, hiring pioneers from early enterprise adopters, and sending analysts through the software provider's training certification programs.

About a quarter of clients were managing automation programs themselves, without outside help from providers or advisors. With insourcing, client organisations bear all the risks of service automation themselves, but earn all the benefits – if managed well. For this 'do-it-yourself' (DIY) model to pay off, clients need to invest significant resources in building internal service automation skills. In our first service automation book, *Service Automation: Robots and the Future of Work,* (2016), we described how client organisations can build a Center of Excellence for RPA. In our second service automation book, *Robotic Process Automation and Risk Mitigation: The Definitive Guide,* (2017), we described how to elevate RPA to a service automation capability that integrates automation tools under one strategic unit.

Finally, a smaller percentage of client organisations were using service automation to bring services back in-house (11 percent) or beginning to buy cloud services (12 percent). The cloud deployment is a particularly interesting trend to watch, as our case study research found that organisations in some industries – like healthcare and financial services – avoided cloud RPA in 2016 because of regulatory concerns.

We also wondered: Who do clients think benefit the most from service automation for outsourced services – the providers or themselves? The answer surprised us: ***Nearly half the client respondents indicated that benefits from service automation were shared with their providers.*** A further 40 percent indicated that they, i.e. the client, benefited the most. Only 12 percent of clients reported that providers were the primary beneficiaries. These findings indicate a significant change since 2016. In that year, our original research found clients complaining that their BPO providers had little incentive to automate services because any FTE (Full-Time Equivalent) savings generated from automation would reduce the provider's revenues. We argued in our 2016 book that if a BPO contract is based on FTE rate cards, like so many were at the time, clients and providers would need to negotiate a gainsharing allocation of the FTE savings generated from automation.[15] Clearly, clients and providers are learning to share the benefits, or perhaps stiff competition is forcing the providers to respond.

We now turn to the BPO providers. For the provider community, we sought a richer picture of their service automation deployments. We wanted to know whether they were deploying RPA and CA in their service offerings and, if so, were they buying RPA solutions off-the-shelf (OTS) or building their own bespoke, proprietary software? ***Among the 59 providers who responded to the survey, 44 percent indicated that their organisations had already deployed bespoke RPA solutions and 25 percent had already deployed OTS RPA-enabled services for their external clients*** (see Figure 1.4). This data suggests that providers were ahead of clients as far as RPA deployments, which may add further insight as to why clients frequently rely on providers to deliver automation programs. A higher percentage of providers built their own RPA solutions than bought OTS, indicating that they likely perceived RPA as a unique competitive advantage. Another possible interpretation is that some providers may modify, integrate and rebrand third-party RPA tools as proprietary.

Twenty percent of providers reported that they have already deployed cognitive automation tools externally to clients using both OTS and bespoke tools. For providers, we see plenty of growth opportunities for services to be augmented with cognitive technologies. Based on our studies of CA adoptions, the real stumbling block has been training the CA tools. If a provider takes on that intensive machine-learning overhead for a specific domain area, then surely they could provide more value-added services that customers could not afford to replicate in-house.

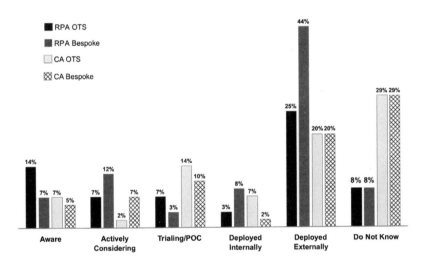

Figure 1.4: Provider organisational adoption of service automation technologies

1.6. Automation and Jobs in Client and Provider Organisations

Amidst the fears that automation could lead to a 'jobless future', we have always answered the question, *"Does service automation lead to massive layoffs?"* with empirical data. On the OWS 2017 survey, we asked respondents: *"What does your organisation do with the FTE savings generated from automation?"*

For the 68 clients who responded to this question (see Figure 1.5), the most common responses were redeploying employees within the unit (49 percent) and redeploying employees to other work units within the company (32 percent). For the 56 providers who answered this question, the majority redeploy employees to other parts of the company (54 percent) or redeploy employees within the work unit (47 percent), and use FTE savings to take on more work without adding headcount (50 percent). *For two years, our case study research has repeatedly found that service automation technologies were used to free up employees from dreary, repetitive work so that they can focus on more value-added tasks. Our OWS survey certainly corroborates that finding.*

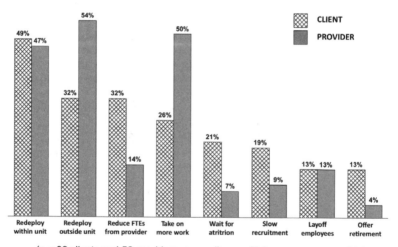

(n = 68 clients and 56 providers responding; multiple responses possible)

**Figure 1.5: Destination of FTE savings
generated from automation**

Clients also reported that they reduced FTEs from the provider organisation (32 percent) as a consequence of automation. Given that clients most frequently relied on service providers for automation (see Figure 1.3), it also makes sense that such a high percentage of respondents removed FTEs from their outsourcing relationships. What else did client organisations do with the FTE savings generated from service automation? Over a quarter of them took on more work without adding more headcount; clients also ratcheted down headcount gradually by either waiting for natural attrition (21 percent) or by slowing recruitment (19 percent). Only 13 percent of clients indicated that their organisations lay-off employees or offered early retirement as a consequence of automation. Providers rarely used attrition, retirements, or slow recruiting. Like clients, only 13 percent of providers laid off any employees. The issue of automation, jobs and work receive detailed treatment in Chapter 9 of this book.

1.7. Service Automation Success Rates and Outcomes

On automation success rates, there have been many surveys, but these give varying results. HfS Research found 51 percent 'satisfied', 33 percent 'neutral' and 16 percent 'dissatisfied' with the business value from RPA deployment. On cost savings, 52 percent were 'satisfied', 37 percent 'neutral', and 10 percent 'dissatisfied'.[16] In their June 2017 Automation and AI survey, ISG Group found 75 percent of clients rating automation and AI as strategic differentiators, critical to delivering products and services, and also freeing up staff to do more value-added work. But around one third were finding four major challenges, namely: lack of budget; organisational resistance to change; governance; risk or compliance concerns; and security issues. What causes such differences in outcomes?

Our case study findings show that action principles are the difference between success and failure. Many of our case study organisations have achieved the triple-win for shareholders, customers, and most surprising of all – employees. Our first book, *Service Automation: Robots and the Future of Work*[17] covered the triple-wins at the Associated Press, Telefónica O2, Xchanging, and many other companies. Our second book, *Robotic Process Automation and Risk Mitigation: The Definitive Guide*[18], found other companies also achieving the triple-win with RPA. In this newest book, we not only add to the RPA evidence base, but also cover, for the first time, evidence of organisations achieving a triple-win with cognitive automation. Aggregating these findings, we have listed the specific benefits and sources of shareholder, customer, and employee value that RPA and CA has delivered across case study companies (see Figure 1.6). What is interesting is that we are finding some organisations experiencing not just one or two but multiple business benefits from their service automation investments. However, as the surveys warn, success is not guaranteed and requires managers to enact a number of principles identified in this book.

SHAREHOLDER VALUE	CUSTOMER VALUE	EMPLOYEE VALUE
♠ Operational efficiencies	♠ Enhanced customer journeys	♠ Learned new skills
♠ Positive ROIs	♠ Improved service quality	♠ Increased employee
♠ Increased scalability	♠ Fewer Errors	satisfaction
♠ Increased agility	♠ Round-the-clock service	♠ Focus on more critical tasks
♠ Increased compliance	delivery	♠ Help deal with demand
♠ Better content governance	♠ Improved service	volatility
♠ Workforce flexibility	consistency	♠ Raised awareness of the
♠ Improved competitive	♠ Faster service resolution	potential of service
positioning	♠ Faster access to crtitcal	automation
♠ Raised brand awareness	human assistance	♠ Enhanced reputation as an
	♠ Increased response accuracy	innovator
	♠ New services online quickly	
	♠ Multi-channel delivery	

**Figure 1.6: The potential 'triple-win' for RPA
and cognitive automation**

1.8. Conclusion: The Journeys You Are On

This chapter has laid down foundations for an understanding of service automation in terms of attributes, markets, adoption and success rates. But this forms just a prelude to a series of chapters that document the work-in-progress that is service automation in so many organisations.

Potentially you are on three journeys:

1. First, there is the journey of reading this book.
2. Second, there is the journey of deploying RPA and CA, now and in the near future.
3. Third, you, with us, are on a journey into an uncertain but heavily technologised future in which service automation will play a rising, and potentially massive role.

The First Journey. In Chapter 2 we provide an in-depth update on RPA's direction of travel, looking at the journeys of multiple organisations and the lessons from their experiences. Chapter 3 begins our in-depth examination of developments in cognitive automation. Here, in an overview, we use the metaphor of 'cogs and wrenches' to explain the roles of machine learning, image processing, and natural language processing (cogs), and the wrenches we are uncovering that hinder progress, specifically, the 'data wrench', the 'algorithm wrench' and the 'technology embeddedness wrench'. The chapter also provides detailed backgrounds on IBM Watson, IPsoft's Amelia, and Expert Systems as important CA technologies that our case studies used.

The cognitive automation use case studies start with KPMG in Chapter 4. By early 2017, KPMG's cognitive capabilities included a tracking service of well over 100 cognitive technologies, development of many IBM Watson use cases and use cases in other CA products – most notably Microsoft's Cortana Intelligence Suite. In Chapter 5 our exploration of CA continues by examining how cognitive automation, in particular IBM Watson, has been used at Deakin University as part of a strategic reimagining of university education and its delivery through digital technologies over the next five years. Chapter 6 changes context to financial services, and the use of IPsoft's Amelia as a cognitive virtual agent at SEB - a Nordic corporate bank. In Chapter 7 we change setting again, and examine Zurich Insurance's application of cognitive automation to an injury claims process, taking this through from the prototype to full implementation. Chapter 8 brings together all our case learning on cognitive automation. We identify 32 CA 'action principles', 19 of which are unique to CA as compared to the RPA action principles tested and derived in Chapter 2. Our last chapter revisits the 'automation and future of work' debate and presents composite evidence that leads us to qualify heavily the accepted equation of automation and massive job loss. We produce a much more complex and nuanced picture of what we know, and what could happen.

The Second Journey. The second journey you will be probably on, as a practitioner, is the present or future deployment of RPA and CA technologies. We have devised Chapters 2 and 8 specifically to support this work. We can add that to the Feeny Technology Navigation framework, which is particularly useful to bear in mind and apply to these technologies. Our colleague David Feeny[19] suggests that managers need to navigate through four digital technology types and agenda: Hype, Capability, Useful and Strategic. Media, consultants, and suppliers generate 'Hype' – and one can see how AI has become already over-hyped as the market has become tired of just 'RPA'. 'Capability' is technology that can actually perform, but is invariably a technical solution in search of a business problem. This is usually the technologist's agenda. 'Useful' service automation tools could be quite dangerous. User demand and agendas could lead to a plethora of tools, all with cost/benefit justifications but not joined up, or delivering much real value. Feeny suggests that the business agenda should be to look for strategic usage – the relatively few applications that give disproportionate payback, and even underpin strategic direction and differentiation. As a reader working through this book, you will see, we think, the abiding utility of this navigation framework when deploying service automation technologies.

The Third Journey. The third journey into the future we are on together – whether we like it or not. There is no doubt that robotics and the automation of knowledge work, along with what we identify as seven other digital technologies, will have massive impact on the world of work over the next 10 to 15 years. But what shape that takes is not pre-configured and already determined. Reviewing all the research, as we do in Chapter 9, one is struck by the tendency, especially in the earlier studies, to start with the assumption of a digital apocalypse and (reluctantly) work back. Our own direction of travel suggest that, in practice and condsidering the publicity, the RPA and CA, markets are actually surprisingly small. Even if they grow exponentially over the next ten years, will not add up to anything like the 'Work Automageddon' presented in the media and elsewhere. Our research for this book, at the organisational level, suggests many technical limitations, a much longer time-line, many challenges to deployment, and ironically, an existing and rising labour shortage in the requisite skills for automation. Meanwhile at the macro level, Chapter 9 suggests at least eight major qualifiers to the more extreme scenarios on job loss through automation. And of course, managerial mind-sets, strategies, and actions in major corporations and government agencies will shape how these and other technologies will be implemented in practice. This book can, amongst other things, shape those managerial mind-sets, strategies and actions. With that thought in mind, we turn to Chapter 2.

Citations

1. We coined the phrase *'RPA takes the robot out of the human'* for our first book, presented in February 2016 at the IAOP world summit Orlando. We acknowledge Margaret Boden's definition of AI from Boden M (2016) *AI: Its nature and future*, (Oxford University Press, UK).

2. Quoted from the *IEEE Guide for Terms and Concepts in Intelligent Process Automation*, July 2017.

3. Quoted from the *IEEE Guide for Terms and Concepts in Intelligent Process Automation*, July 2017.

4. Quoted from the *IEEE Guide for Terms and Concepts in Intelligent Process Automation*, July 2017.

5. Boden, M (2017) *AI – Its Nature and Future*. (Oxford University Press, UK).

6. Aleksander, I. (2017), 'Partners of Humans: A realistic assessment of the role of robots in the foreseeable future'. *Journal of Information Technology*, 32, 1-9.

7. IBM posts 21st straight revenue decline. Post by Brandy Betz, SA News Editor 18th July, 2017.

8. https://www.forrester.com/report/The+RPA+Market+Will+Reach+29+Billion+By+2021/-/E-RES137229.

9. Figures from HfS Research, 10th June 2017. HfS note that this covers software licenses and the direct services market, including implementation and consulting services focused on building RPA capabilities within an organisation. It does not include wider operational services like BPO, which may include RPA becoming increasingly embedded in its delivery. Taking these and other factors into account, we would estimate the market as over US$2 billion by end of 2017. HfS note that the broader market for what they call intelligent services automation is ten times the size of the RPA market.

10. http://www.grandviewresearch.com/press-release/global-robotic-process-automation-rpa-market.

11. http://www.grandviewresearch.com/press-release/global-robotic-process-automation-rpa-market.
https://www.forrester.com/report/The+RPA+Market+Will+Reach+29+Billion+By+2021/-/E-RES137229.
https://www.automation.com/automation-news/industry/it-robotic-automation-market-to-reach-498-bn-by-2020.
https://www.gartner.com/doc/3556834/forecast-snapshot-robotic-process-automation.
http://www.horsesforsources.com/RPA-marketsize-HfS_061017.

12. Retrieved from Techemergence.com and statistia.com websites, July 2017.

13. Allied Market Research (2016), *Artificial Intelligence Market Overview Report*, downloaded from Allied Market Research website, 11th August 2017.

14. The detailed survey results were initially published in *Pulse Magazine*: Lacity, M., Babin, R., and Willcocks, L. (2017), 'Research Center: Service Automation Trends Survey'. *Pulse Magazine,* Issue 28, pp. 40-44.; Lacity, M. and Willcocks, L. (2016), 'Speed of Automation Adoption Faster for Providers than Customers'. *Pulse Magazine*, May/June, pp. 10-17.; Lacity, M., Willcocks, L., and Yan, A. (2015), 'Are the robots really coming? Service Automation Survey Findings'. *Pulse Magazine,* Issue 17, pp. 14-21.

15. Willcocks, L. and Lacity, M. (2016), *Service Automation: Robots and the Future of Work*, (SB Publishing, UK). For sales contact info@sbpublishing.org. Available from http://sbpublishing.org/service_automation.html.

16. Fersht, P. (2017) *The Market Outlook for Robotic Process Automation.* Presentation, Blue Prism World conference, London, 21st June 2017.

17. Willcocks, L. and Lacity, M. (2016), *Service Automation: Robots and the Future of Work,* (SB Publishing, UK). For sales contact info@sbpublishing.org. Available from http://sbpublishing.org/service_automation.html.

18. Willcocks, L. and Lacity, M. (2017), *Robotic Process Automation and Risk Mitigation: A Definitive Guide*, (SB Publishing, UK). For sales contact info@ sbpublishing.org. Available from http://sbpublishing.org/risk.html.

19. See Willcocks, L. Sauer, C. and Associates (2000) *Moving To E-Business* (Random House, London), Introduction.

Chapter 2

Robotic Process Automation: The Next Phase

By Leslie Willcocks and Mary Lacity

> *"You have to plan for where this is going to be, not where it is now. You have to build a foundation for a tower block, not a bungalow."*

Patrick Geary, Chief Marketing Officer, Blue Prism

> *"You need to apply the same sort of big enterprise systems discipline to robotics automation tools as you do to anything else."*

Adrian Guttridge, Executive Director, Xchanging Insurance

2.1. Introduction

Robotic process automation (RPA) really took off during the 2016-2018 period. As we saw in Chapter 1, the market was sized at under $1 billion dollars in 2017, but with estimated market revenue growth rates up to 100 percent, per year. Why such rapid growth? RPA tools are general-purpose tools that can automate any task that uses rules to process structured data. As such, RPA is clearly primed to take off across all functions and industries, as every organisation has processes with these characteristics. Indeed, HfS Research has suggested that a third of major enterprises would make significant investments in RPA between 2017-2019 across industries such as hi-tech (51 percent) and banking and insurance (44 percent).[1] Our February 2017 survey found 51 percent of organisations across all industries were at proof-of-concept stage or already deploying RPA. To demonstrate the market's dynamism, by June 2017 ISG Group were reporting 50 percent of organisations surveyed deploying, and 30 percent piloting RPA projects.[2]

These figures give only some sense of the increasing pervasiveness of RPA across organisations and sectors, and the RPA scaling occurring within organisations. The evidence is that the next phase will see a continuation of this trend. But another, more worrying, trend emerged during 2017, with increasing reports of challenged RPA deployments. Our extended research for this book finds that RPA success is far from guaranteed and our most recent research has examined in detail successful and more problematic automation deployments. Service automation – like all organisational initiatives that try to scale – emerges as fraught with risk. We have been able to identify seven areas of risk, and also the management 'action principles' that lower risk and seize the opportunities inherent in the automation tools becoming available.[3] We point to these in the next section.

The rest of the chapter captures the further progress made in RPA adoption and learning, and the new directions in which organisations are taking RPA usage. First we provide an overview of recent developments, then, with illustrative cases, focus on the key emerging roles of service automation strategy, scaling, stakeholder buy-in, and using RPA and cognitive automation in complementary ways. Following this, we detail two case studies of effective RPA deployments – one in a more complex environment and one in harness with enterprise systems. These specific contexts are increasingly attaining higher profile as RPA adoption spreads beyond simple, high volume transactional and desktop environments.

2.2. Risks and Action Principles

In our previous work, *Robotic Process Automation and Risk Mitigation: The Definitive Guide*,[4] we identified 30 management practices, which we call 'action principles' for gaining business value from RPA (see Table 2.1).

Action principles are similar to 'best practices' in that both seek to share knowledge from prior experiences. But whereas best practices imply that mimicry will always produce similar results – that 'one-size-fits-all' – action principles recognise that four factors make a practice effective or otherwise. The usefulness of a practice depends on:

- The objectives the organisation is trying to achieve;
- The organisation's unique context;
- Whether the organisation has the retained capability to implement the practice effectively; and
- Timing – there are good and less good moments to apply a specific practice.

As social scientists, we view managers as thoughtful agents who scrutinise 'best practices' derived from other people's learnings to decide whether practices need to be modified, or perhaps discarded, within their organisations.

We reproduce the risks and action principles in Table 2.1 (below) as a template for assessing how well RPA is being managed. In practice we are finding that the best RPA performers – when getting triple-wins for shareholders, customers, and employees – applied over 80 percent of these action principles. This trend has continued across our latest researched cases. However, as we shall see, emerging trends have seen some organisations stumbling. A large part of this has been from not applying certain action principles altogether, or applying them thoughtlessly – regardless of objectives, context, resources, and timing. In the next section we discuss how these action principles have been applied most recently, and identify some standout key challenges and areas that need particular attention.

2.3. Developments

On the large scale, it is notable how quickly RPA is being adopted across industries, in particular banking, financial services, insurance, healthcare,

Risk Categories	41 Major Risks	Action Principles to Mitigate Risks
Strategy	1. Misunderstood or missed value 2. Lack of strategic intent and design for end-point 3. Under-resourcing RPA 4. Buried in a division, delegated too low 5. Thinking too small, and short-term 6. Damaging reputation if messaged as a way to cut jobs	1. Conceive of RPA as an enabler of a larger business strategy 2. Cultural adoption by the C-suite 3. Consider RPA for more than just cost savings 4. Decide who is best to 'own' the automation program
Sourcing Selection	7. Missed value or excessive costs by choosing the wrong sourcing model, or... 8. Wrong advisers/partners, or... 9. Right ones too late 10. Getting locked into tools or BPO providers	5. Use credible advisory firms to bridge gaps in client knowledge 6. Incentivize BPO providers to share the benefits of automation
Tool Selection	11. Choosing good tool(s) for the wrong tasks 12. Choosing bad tool(s) 13. Proliferation of tools 14. Tool lock-in	7. Match tool capabilities with strategic objectives 8. Consider overall value of tool capabilities, not just price 9. Have IT help vet the software 10. Test tool capabilities with a controlled contest 11. Select a software provider with sound financial position and stable customers
Stakeholder Buy-in	15. Stakeholders ignore, stall, resist or derail the automation program 16. IT not involved / uncooperative 17. Union or employee backlash 18. Lack of visible progress	12. Involve IT from the start 13. Communicate the value of automation to employees 14. Promise no layoffs as a consequence of service automation; ratchet down headcount gradually instead 15. Select 'rising stars' for service automation projects 16. Redesign employee scorecards
Automation Launch	19. Lack luster use cases 20. Pick wrong services to automate 21. Initial projects fail technically, financially or politically 22. Testing short-cuts 23. Incomplete process definitions documentation 24. Unrealistic estimates 25. Try to automate too much	17. Select 'wow' projects based on impact to customers and employee 18. Build realistic business cases 19. Redesign human work for robotic work 20. Consider Pareto's Principle
Operations/ Change Management	26. The robots stop working, or... 27. The robots do not function as intended 28. Business rules evolve or IT interfaces change 29. Not enough robots 30. Costly maintenance 31. Slow updates 32. Poor change control 33. Mismanaged communication 34. Insufficient training 35. Unclear roles	21. Make sure the robots are work-ready 22. Manage the robotic workforce 23. Assign clear boundaries of responsibility
Road to Maturity	36. Automation momentum stalls 37. Champions leave 38. Skills shortages 39. Under-utiliisng software robots 40. Re-inventing across automation islands 41. Integration issues emerge as new technologies are adopted	24. Establish a Center of RPA Excellence 25. Re-think talent development for skills needed for enterprise automation capabilities 26. Multi-skill the software robots 27. Reuse components to scale quickly and to reduce development costs 28. Continually improve existing automations 29. Integrate tools to automate services end-to-end 30. Establish a Center of Automation Excellence

Table 2.1: RPA risk mitigation framework

pharmaceuticals, telecommunications, media, and retail. RPA has also been spreading across functions, especially across contact centres, human resources, finance and accounting, and across processes as varied as front-office customer onboarding to back office claims processing.[5] BPO service providers have also been finding ways of incorporating RPA into their continually shifting business and operational models. This has resulted in RPA spreading from the UK and US, to developing markets in Western Europe, Scandinavia, Australia and New Zealand, and, by mid-2017, Japan. This momentum continued and stretched further into Asia Pacific and Latin America during 2017 and into 2018.

Also notable in this period has been the rapid adoption of RPA in shared services and global business services operations. As we observe in our study on the subject, shared services executives have a limited number of transformation levers they can pull. Looking across case examples such as Royal DSM (see below), Telefónica O2, Ascension Ministry Services Center, Siemens and Bosch, they have all variously used, and revisited centralisation, standardisation, IT enablement, offshoring (relocating to a lower cost location), and process optimisation. RPA is providing a sixth, quite powerful, lever. Centralisation may well give five to 10 percent performance improvement, standardising and optimising another 10 to 20 percent, and historically offshoring could give a 10 to 30 percent cost advantage.[6] But organisations run up against the limits to applying these management practices. Meanwhile they are finding that RPA may well provide another 30 percent or more improvement, plus many other positive business outcomes.

During early 2016 to late 2017, we researched many successful RPA implementations that were gaining multiple business benefits.[7] We also noted a swathe of emerging challenges (which we discuss below) and we pinpoint the major highlights here. Over the 2016-2018 period many organisations were failing to be strategic and ambitious enough with their RPA plans and actions. Quite a few organisations ran into problems when they tried to scale their RPA usage. Many also ran into later problems because they failed to secure enough stakeholder buy-in early enough. At the same time, another emerging trend saw an increasing number of client organisations using RPA and cognitive automation as complementary technologies. Below we discuss these challenges and trends in more detail.

2.3.1. Emerging challenges

As we saw in Chapter 1, HfS Research, reporting in mid-2017, found 51 percent clients 'satisfied', 33 percent 'neutral' and 16 percent 'dissatisfied' with the business value from RPA deployment.[8] ISG Group, also in mid-2017, reported around one third of organisations experiencing challenges such as underfunding, organisational resistance to change, lack of governance, and concerns with risk, compliance and security.[9]

More anecdotal evidence suggested a rise in deployment problems during 2017. For example McKinsey, *"in conversations with dozens of executives"*, discovered companies encountering challenges when trying to scale localised proofs of concept.[10] Ernst & Young reported that they had seen 30 to 50 percent of initial projects stalling, failing to scale, being abandoned or moving to other solutions.[11] Consistent with our own findings, this has not been because of the technology, but through common management mistakes.[12] They also report many successful projects. Management consultants, of course, are more likely to see the indifferent experiences, because a major part of their trade is helping clients when things go wrong.

Our ongoing qualitative research gives us further, more selective insights. RPA tools run into problems when clients attempt to scale (see below). Many clients do not put in place the necessary governance and often do not use tools that contain built-in technical controls. An RPA and cognitive skills shortage is already upon us. This means that retained capability and in-house teams are sometimes not strong enough, a situation exacerbated by sometimes skeptical senior management who under-resource automation initiatives and who fail to take a strategic approach. Consultants are also hit by skills shortages and cannot always provide the support necessary – likewise BPO service providers. In addition, we are finding that clients are often not giving stakeholder buy-in and change management nearly enough attention. RPA software providers have also been working very hard to meet the exponentially rising demand and often have been unable to provide the level of client support previously given as a matter of course.

In the wider marketplace, clients were finding it difficult to assess the actual capabilities and suitability of many tools, not least because of the high level of 'RPA washing' with some vendors claiming their tools have all the attributes of all other vendors' tools, and more besides. In practice, we observe quite a lot of RPA 'rebadging' of existing products to make them more marketable. There is also quite a lot of over-claiming about how far some RPA tools are adaptable enough to fit with enterprise systems, and with cognitive technologies. There are many over-claims on the ability to provide comprehensive cognitive automation as opposed to discrete tools that can fit with some RPA deployments. All this has not made tool selection an easy task, so many clients on tight budgets have found themselves locked into the wrong or bad tools, complicated by their organisation's growing ambitions and changing objectives for automation.

2.3.2. Automation strategy pre-empts many problems

The RPA evolution framework shown in Figure 2.1 is particularly pertinent to 2017-2018 developments. From its inception, RPA tended to be seen as a tactical, quick-win tool to achieve business benefits and bypass IT's long work queues. The early adopters – for example, Telefónica O2, RWE npower, and Xchanging – gradually moved to a more strategic understanding, especially where the tools had enterprise integration and not just desktop productivity capability. Basically, these organisations evolved over time through the first three phases, and some had, by late 2017, also moved to Phase 4.

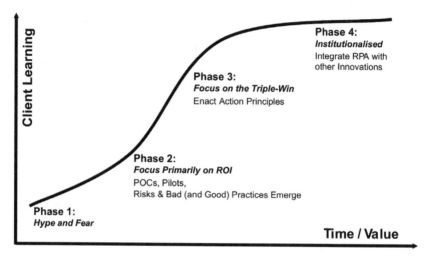

Figure 2.1: RPA evolution in organisations 2010-2018

We have been finding all too many, more recent, RPA adopters stuck in Phase 2, having been persuaded that there is something 'there' with RPA, in terms of business value and problem solutions. More recent adopters can accelerate success if they take on board the lessons and attempt to start as 'strategic' (i.e. at Phase 3 in Figure 2.1) from the start. Doing so lays down key foundations, and pre-empts many of the problems we saw emerging during 2017. In this context, being strategic means:

1. Understanding and planning for the mid-term and long-term endpoint
2. Aiming for 'triple-wins' for shareholders, customers, and employees
3. Resourcing RPA as a strategic business project
4. Ensuring the C-suite is completely on board with the strategic vision
5. Identifying and managing change and implementation challenges from the start
6. Centralising automation capability to accelerate scaling

We have seen more strategic behaviour in global companies like American Express, EMC, Siemens, BNY Mellon, Prudential, Raiffeisen Bank, Nokia,

Barclays Bank, and BPO service provider OpusCapita, as some examples. American Express is notable for its accelerated, strategic approach to rolling out RPA globally.

For its shared services, Siemens established a global RPA centre of excellence by mid 2017 to define a global approach, and set up other 'RPA factories' in selected regional delivery centres around the world.[13] It looked to integrate RPA with the Business Process Management/Operations platform and Enterprise Resource Planning (ERP) layer, globally. Siemens identified critical success factors as: integrating RPA into a larger automation strategy; alignment with process governance; C-level support with risk capital; and process optimisation being combined with RPA. Other critical success factors included: partnering with IT and external partners; developing analytical skills and expertise in automation and process optimisation; clear governance and comprehensive operating model; a centralised standards framework including for IT architecture and infrastructure; and stakeholder orientated communications and change management.

OpusCapita[14] is interesting as a BPO service provider, that, like Xchanging, first developed RPA to improve internal operations, then extended this to offering RPA services to clients as a point of competitive differentiation. The learning points were: use existing and new capabilities to offer RPA services to customers; facilitate a hybrid organisation structure; be willing to cannibalise sales from traditional BPO while moving to a hybrid model; and beware the client pressure to reduce service prices.[15]

This last case touches on a fundamental point most organisations were wrestling with across 2017. What is the end-point? One next step is to move to an automation strategy that embraces RPA and cognitive automation tools as they came on stream, and fits with other IT systems and capabilities (see Chapter 8). But a further, more transformational, step is to develop and integrate RPA, CA and digital technologies into a service automation strategy consistent with an organisation's strategic business goals of enhanced customer experience, and competitive differentiation. Many organisations are still waking up to the realisation that, what started as an RPA, may well become something altogether bigger, namely a service automation journey (see the RWE innogy case below).

2.3.3. Scaling can be problematic

We found many organisations running into problems when they tried to scale. Two main explanations were the tools they were using, and the degree to which they carried out preparatory work to facilitate scaling. Some RPA tools are not easily scalable, especially those based on a recording capability – what IEEE calls 'robotic desktop automation' – and do not fit easily with enterprise systems. Many RPA vendors offer their tools as a quick implementation, 'fast and cheap' process win, but here what is gained at the front end of the deployment process is eroded very quickly when clients try to scale for wider and more intensive organisational usage. Other 'RPA' vendors offer what is effectively a disguised form of 'software development kit'. This needs a lot more IT development by the in-house team than first imagined, and incurs additional –often unanticipated – expense, time and resource. Taken as a breed, RPA tools vary in the extent to which they ensure automation runs in a secure environment. Not all RPA tools are the same, including on the dimension of security.

Whatever the vendor, all RPA needs a lot of preparatory work if it is to be scalable and robust as an enterprise-strength integrated business tool across the enterprise. The only question is: do you do that work at the front end, or later, when the problems begin to emerge and the maintenance costs rise? In one interview, John Davis, IBM Distinguished Engineer, suggested that while vendors promote rapid content development, some RPA vendors also recommend applying development methodologies that actually take a lot of time and effort.[16] However, the reasons for taking a rigorous approach become obvious when you fail to do it, and run into serious, costly problems that could have been circumvented by up front analysis and design. He suggested that a screen scraping robot might take a half day to create and give, say, ten people some efficiency, while an enterprise robot might take several weeks to develop but can scale, deal with unexpected exceptions and be reused. The result is a much greater saving opportunity allowing more people to move on to higher value work, leaving a smaller number to deal with the robot-recognised exceptions.[17]

2.3.4. Early stakeholder buy-in is a must

As RPA gained profile in organisations and was scaled across 2016-2017, we found managers running into very similar problems that IT-enabled business projects had routinely been running into for many years. It became clear that it was all too easy to get deflected into technical issues, and the attractive potential business benefits RPA offered, and begin to neglect key change management issues. This meant that, as well as a strategic vision for RPA, there had to be in place a project sponsor, a project champion and project management capability. It also meant that a lot of time would be needed getting stakeholder buy-in and getting the right structures in place. It meant that RPA had to be treated as a business project, with multi-disciplinary teams, working to fulfill business goals. Another corollary was that business change projects, for many years, have tended to operate using a time-box philosophy, eschewing over-functionality and applying the 80/20 rule – focusing on the 20 percent that gave 80 percent of business value sought. Human resource and organisational change management also must come to the fore. This meant:

- Define clear endpoints and goals
- Fully resource change management capability
- Message the purpose and value of RPA to staff
- Ensure strategic alignment, new competencies and changes are institutionalised and embedded in work practices

Increasingly we discovered organisations implementing RPA and needing to build stakeholder buy-in and change management practices to make the transformation successful. Jon Theuerkauf, Managing Director and Group Head of Performance Excellence at BNY Mellon, reminded us of this in recounting how he and his team identified the need to get stakeholder buy-in very early on in order to get RPA implemented and scaled in the conservative banking culture in which he operates.

The bank's primary functions are managing and servicing the investments of institutions and high-net-worth individuals. BNY Mellon is the world's largest custodian bank. As of June 30th, 2017, BNY Mellon had $31.1 trillion in assets under custody and/or administration, and $1.8 trillion in assets under management. It operates in 35 countries in the Americas; Europe, the Middle East and Africa (EMEA); and Asia-Pacific, and employs over 50,000 people.

BNY Mellon began its RPA journey in early 2016. By June, they had multiple projects underway and had moved approximately fifty software robots into production. One key use case was reconciling unsettled trades on behalf of customers. Another use case was to automate the daily reconciliation of clients' assets held in custody to Investment Manager data. By March 2017, BNY Mellon could report results such as 100 percent accuracy in account-closure validations across five systems; 88 percent improvement in processing time; 66 percent improvement in trade entry turnaround time; and 20-second robotic trade settlements vs. 60 seconds by a human. Through 2017, the automation of processes noticeably accelerated as BNY Mellon gained the benefits of doing a great deal of preparation work during the start-up phase.

Jon Theuerkauf has been an effective Project Champion, and was fully supported and sponsored by his boss, the Head of Client Service Delivery – the bank's service operations unit. As the Project Sponsor, Jon's boss provided resources, 'air cover', and allowed a fail fast culture to exist in the RPA environment. The interesting dimension was how Jon and his team not only worked to gain stakeholder buy-in from the business people who would ultimately be using the technology, but also brought together control, audit, risk, legal and various technical SME's to help the RPA team build the infrastructure they believed was necessary to run fast and run safely.

Jon's belief was to *"begin with the end in mind"* and use all the available resources to get what you need in place first and then go. Keep learning, and *"change as you learn from what you are doing and from others, but don't get paralysed."* He also got agreement on governance rules and on how the projects would be run and managed. He set a goal to have projects delivered in 28 days using a combination of Waterfall and Agile software development methods called 'Wagile'.

BNY Mellon completed 40 RPA automation projects in 2016, with an average delivery time between 45 and 60 days and is now working to get that closer to the 28-day average. It was Jon's belief that in order to build and use automated processes fast, a whole support infrastructure is required to be in place first or you risk be slowed down or stopped later.

By mid-2017, BNY Mellon had over 200 robots in production. They had automated 100+ processes and were adopting machine learning, OCR technologies and other Intelligent Automation tools into their, now new, SmartTech Ecosystem. They will at some point move to explore and test further advances into cognitive automation. Jon commented:

> *"The existing environment today is at least three-to-five years out from a fully integrated automated operating environment leading the way to something resembling more akin to a more mature adult's cognitive capability. To get there, begin your automation efforts with the end in mind, and remain focused on a more structured data operating environment."*

2.3.5. RPA and CA are already complementary technologies

This leads into the other development we have seen while researching for this book. From late 2016 through 2017, we saw RPA and CA increasingly being used together.

Some examples: IBM's global IT outsourcing services business combined Blue Prism RPA software with components of IBM's Watson technology. In one service area – Global Technology Services Technology, Innovation & Automation – IBM has well over one thousand customers, and a range of automation tools, including 200 RPA software licenses run out of London and Amsterdam.

One use is in email ticket triage. Customers have email task IDs with which they can send a support request to IBM. The request (e.g. *"my printer is not working"* or *"I've forgotten my password"*) needs to be routed to the correct resolver group. The RPA robot can get the request and log it into the ticketing system, but it does not understand the content of the email, and so cannot engage the relevant resolver team. Enter the CA tool, which receives the information from the RPA robot, and then with a high degree of certainty (learned from reviewing historical tickets) can say, for example, *"this is a network support request"* or *"this is a telephony request"*. The RPA robot can then assign the ticket to the correct resolver group.

A similar process can be used for more general unresolved requests collected by help desks coming in many forms, not just email. Customers could be having problems with storage, networks or databases, for example. The emails, text messages, or telephone requests go into a pool of logged tickets. Each request will be quite specific and creates a dispatch problem. Who is best able to resolve the problem quickly? The RPA tool will bring Watson into play (see Figure 2.2). This has been educated to categorise the service request, search the database of past successful services, and extract the top ten employees in the world able to fulfill the request. This 'top ten' is then returned to the RPA tool, which searches the systems of record for candidate availability, assigns the work, and then notifies the client and service agent.

An extension of this is to actually do the work with automation, using RPA and CA in tandem. For example, for a network support problem about opening firewall ports, Watson capabilities enable the service to be equipped with full instructions on what to do to open firewall ports. These instructions can be communicated to the requester, and, if needed, also to the resolution person. Alternatively Watson Natural Language Understanding can be used to extract what it needs from the ticket and then trigger the appropriate automation tooling to go and actually execute the resolution of the request – resolving the problem efficiently without human intervention, thus enabling support teams to focus on other critical issues.[18]

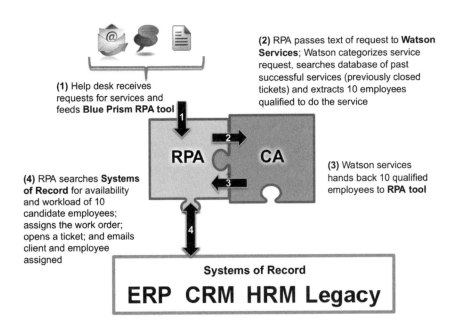

Figure 2.2: IBM example - RPA and CA as complementary technologies

Increasingly we have been seeing CA tools actually feed into RPA tools, especially in banking, insurance and financial service organisations. A bank, for example, will have an interactive chat bot at the front end in dialogue with customers, but will draw upon RPA to get the information it needs to be able to have a more fulfilling conversation with the end user – for example about a stolen credit card. RPA will log on to legacy systems to discover the card details and personal and account details, and pass these to the chatbot. The conversation will end in decisions being made (e.g. card cancelled, new card issued) then the Watson solution will instruct the RPA tool to execute the requirement (e.g. stopping the stolen credit card, issuing a letter to the customer, printing a new card, and updating the customer's account). Thus RPA is used to fulfill at the back-end everything that the front-end has promised to the customer.

Swiss Post Solutions provides another example where a customer is ordering a high speed Internet, fixed telephone and cable television service.[19] A cognitive automation tools collects, centrally, all incoming multi-channel data then extracts key information, categorises and prioritises requests. These requests are then passed to internal RPA robots set up to interact with enterprise systems and delivers on the follow-up process (e.g. record customer and request; set up customer profile and number; create the contract; set up direct debit; check warehouse inventory; coordinate delivery dates; and pass exceptions to human agents to resolve). The multi-channel platform then, through automation tools, communicates decisions and validations, and makes personal contact through preferred channels to fulfill delivery.

These are just examples of many cases we have seen currently – either operational or underway. As later chapters will reveal, while cognitive automation does different things from RPA, the two technologies can be highly synergistic; 2017 saw several organisations experimenting and being quite inventive about combining these technologies to optimise service performance.

2.4. Illustrative Case: RPA at innogy SE

Innogy SE is an established European energy company formed in April 2016, as a subsidiary of the German RWE group. The company has three business segments – Grid & Infrastructure; Retail; and Renewables – meeting the requirements of a modern decarbonised, decentralised and digitised energy world. The innogy brand name is a synthesis of innovation, energy and technology.

Npower Business Solutions is innogy's B2B energy supplier and services provider in the UK, and was formerly owned by the RWE parent. As one of three npower energy supply market segments – the other two were Residential and Small and Medium-sized Enterprises (SMEs) – Business Solutions became involved with RPA around 2014. Npower Residential had adopted Blue Prism software as early as 2009, as we documented in an earlier book.[20]

The Business Solutions (BS) division operates at the high-end part of the B2B energy market. Traditionally BS has been a B2B commodity energy supplier on long term contracts with some of the largest businesses in the UK – industrial customers like Tata Steel, multi-site retailers (like Sainsbury's supermarket and Marks & Spencer), telecoms, utilities, and some large public local authorities. BS has been number two in terms of the volume of electricity supplied to such businesses, and has been market leader in developing very complex risk management and trading products. Typically, customers have a framework agreement and can actually trade energy half-hourly to meet their requirements in real time. This is complex servicing, often with a very tight and bespoke service agreement with each customer.

2.4.1. The Business Context for RPA

Npower BS has been successful with its business model, but in the last few years has faced increasing market disruption from new competition. The market had some 40 suppliers by 2015, often without the same level of overheads, and able to squeeze margins more easily. BS has been facing increasing regulation, decarbonation and demand destruction, while customers are looking for ever-increasing energy cost efficiency and innovation. The BS imperative became to innovate and cut costs. The name 'npower Business Solutions' reflected the company's ambition to transform from a commodity supplier to an energy solutions partner. One result was diversification into new technical services areas, including, for example, a real time energy monitoring and management capability placed on customers' premises, controlled remotely. But such innovations were constrained by an ageing legacy architecture, multiple complex low-volume processes, and very high service costs. As one example, BS could be billing customers 300 million pounds a month through a green screen COBOL system on a mainframe which operated solidly and reliably, but could not provide a customer with an online copy invoice.

In this context, BS started to look at robotic solutions. However, the attractiveness of robotic solutions – and also outsourcing – is a function of the degree of scale, the volumes of transactions and their complexity. The domestic Residential business was at the most extreme scale of attractiveness for deploying robotics or outsourcing, dealing as it does with millions of standardised transactions, servicing five million domestic customer accounts in the UK. The Residential and Business Solutions segments both have about the same turnover – each about £3 billion a year – but whereas the Residential business has five million accounts, BS's revenue came from just 20,000 accounts. By 2014, Residential had already undertaken a significant amount of outsourcing and also had some 300 robots. The SME business was similar to Residential in terms of the simplicity of their products. It lacked large volumes but, under regulatory pressures, was quickly converging with the Residential area. Figure 2.3 shows the differences between the three npower businesses.

At the unattractive end of the volume / complexity continuum

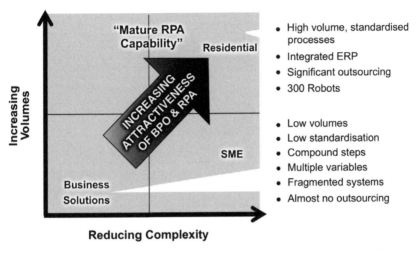

Figure 2.3: RWE npower – three businesses and RPA usage
(Source: Marshall, M. (2016))[21]

Business Solutions was at the wrong end of the scale of attractiveness, dealing with very low volumes, low standardisation, lots of regulation, very fragmented systems and with almost no outsourcing. Process complexity was considerable, as shown by Figure 2.4. BS was undertaking 650 different processes each made up of many activities. Only three processes were operated by more than a hundred people. Over half of processes had five or fewer people operating them and 20 percent of the processes only had one operator. A very challenging environment indeed. How could BS exploit robotic opportunities in such a low volume, highly complex environment?

Before doing so, BS spent some five years achieving a 20 percent productivity improvement using what Mick Marshall, Mid Market Service and Transformation Manager, called 'soft measures'. Job productivity was measured in terms of the numbers of energy meter points that can be managed by one full-time worker.

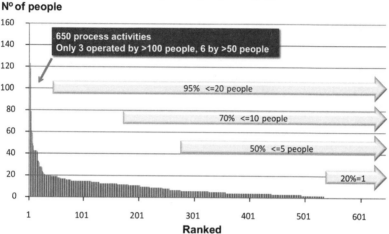

Figure 2.4: Business solutions – dominated by low volume, non-standard activities
(Source: Marshall, M. (2016))[22]

"Technology very definitely did not come first! We started looking at our performance waste initially understanding the productivity of our different employees and how we can get the least productive employees up to the best practice levels using coaching, development, training and so on. We looked at planning waste, where we're tracking what our people are doing with their time, and at all the different activities that they're undertaking so that we can make sure that we're allocating the right numbers of people at the right times for the right tasks. Only relatively late in the day did we start to look at process waste." **Mick Marshall, Mid Market Service and Transformation Manager**

Some success was achieved, but BS was fragmenting its processes into more and more activity, more and more specialisms and the inherent inefficiency of that was being masked by the fact that they were growing rapidly, taking on new customers. When growth ran out, the inefficiency became exposed and productivity took a down turn. At that point automation began to be considered as part of the answer.

> *"Most of our activities are in this long tail of relatively low-volume transactions, but what makes them automatable is that, although there's a low volume of transactions, all of those transactions have very high volumes of process steps – 'swivel chair' activities with lots of different, complex steps in order to achieve a process outcome. These are the kind of areas we have targeted."* **Mick Marshall, Mid Market Service and Transformation Manager**

2.4.2. Mid-2014: Beginning the RPA Journey

The drivers for using RPA were very much about flexibility and agility, and not just costs, in what was becoming a fast changing competitive market, with the need to respond rapidly to regulatory requirements and to dynamic customer requirements in the marketplace. At the same time, BS had to do this while lowering traditional project delivery costs and risks, and leverage more lifetime value from aging legacy systems. According to Mick Marshall:

> *"With tight restraints on capital investment across the company, we needed to leverage more value from our legacy architecture. And, in some cases, it wasn't just about automating existing processes, but considering completely new processes that didn't exist before or had long been in the 'too difficult', 'too expensive' pile."*

Business Solutions set up an operational agility team within the customer service unit as a business initiative. Initially it was seen as an opportunistic and tactical alternative to outsourcing, which had been introduced in the Residential and SME operations. Business Solutions lacked the scale and standardised processes necessary to outsource effectively, and automation looked a more viable alternative, already having a high and successful profile in the Residential division. In the end RPA did not need a very detailed business case.

The IT function was involved early on in order to demonstrate to them that BS was using non-invasive tools that fitted into the IT governance and security framework. This was made a lot easier because they were able to take on board all lessons, and a staff member, from the Residential business. BS pooled a team of six developers in a Centre of Excellence, using the Blue Prism software inherited from the domestic business. The operational agility team worked closely with business processing analysts to re-engineer processes incorporating robotic tools.

Right from the very outset, BS placed a very heavy focus on engaging employees and communicating what it was trying to achieve. This was managed through regular briefings, open days, and surgeries, where employees could see a robotic process operating and automated screen working.

2.4.3. Project Launches

Consistent within the overarching set of drivers, BS launched a number of specific projects, each justified on its own merits (see Figure 2.5). Labour reduction or avoidance figured in the rationales, as did better debt collection, and avoidance of regulatory sanctions – fines for failures in work systems could be millions of pounds. Quality was also a key criterion in terms of more accuracy, reduced rework and more dependable processes. Customer trust had also become a massive issue in the highly competitive UK energy industry, so it became vital to increase customer satisfaction and retention by being able to guarantee performance and service quality. Mick Marshall stressed that although a lot of the initiatives seem to be justified primarily on cost, the major drivers were not mainly labour savings, but were multi-faceted.

BS selected initial automation candidates from processes that were relatively labour intensive; repetitive; uninteresting to perform; prone to human error; where there were multiple legacy systems practices required; where business rules could be trained easily; and where the jobs often involved seasonal temporary work. In practice, BS sales were not spread evenly throughout the year, but clustered around April and October. Cash collection activity accelerated with the financial year-end in December, while some significant customer regulatory requirements had to be met in March-May. So BS had lots of seasonal and temporary work that, without automation, could only be met by agencies and temporary workers.

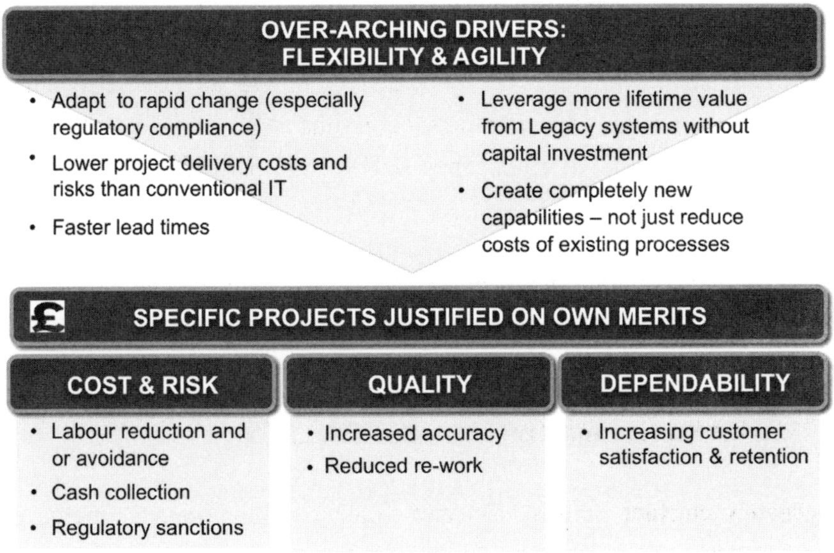

Figure 2.5: Business solutions - RPA drivers and business case
(Source: Marshall, M. (2016))[23]

BS were also looking for quick wins, with short lead times and fast payback. While the projects became almost self-selecting, with local managers eager to gain the benefits, there were significant constraints on what could be achieved. This was not a large-scale transformation effort, but taking away fractions of individuals' worktime rather than wholesale job displacement. The legacy systems, however, were a particular constraint on processing speed, and what could be achieved.

Let us look at some of the projects launched ...

Invoice statements. BS had a new regulatory requirement to provide customers with contract end-date and renewal details on their invoices. This was to stop automatic rollover renewals where the client had forgotten about contract end date. The manual process for this used a decision tree to select the narrative to apply to invoices, and this amounted to 20 minutes per transaction for some 20,000 customers. The IT department, using outsourced IT providers, was commissioned to provide a conventional IT delivery but the solution failed with the regulatory deadline looming. The BS Operational Agility team was given the challenge to deliver an RPA alternative within six weeks. It succeeded in reducing transaction time to 25 seconds, and resulted in avoiding taking on 21 more agency staff (£525k p.a.) and a potential two million pound fine:

> *"That was a really important project for us. Not just because of its business impact but because it opened the door, and gained credibility for the robotics team throughout the rest of the business. The requests for help started to pour in."* **Mick Marshall, Mid Market Service and Transformation Manager**

Emergency contact details. BS had a license obligation to provide gas customers with emergency contact details where the customer had not been in contact for over a year. The manual process involved lots of 'swivel chair' time, and data extracted from multiple systems to create a mail merge letter. The process took about 25 minutes per transaction. The Blue Prism RPA solution extracted the data, applied the same rules, added the letters to the queue – and took two to three minutes per transaction. This accomplished the work of four FTEs (£100k p.a.), avoided a two million pound fine and the risk that business customers with a gas leak would not know who to contact to prevent an explosion.

Missing contract renewals. BS had a critical outstanding business requirement to put out-of-contract customers on default rates or risk unbilled consumption and lost revenue. There was a manual process, which was not working very effectively, to match customers to their contract end dates, identify any missed renewals, generate new default contracts, and call them so they could be billed for the energy they were using. The RPA solution simulated the manual steps and led to an increase in capturing those kinds of details from 35 percent to 95 percent.

Success led to further examples. BS looked for other potential areas. One included automated data extracts to match payments to customers' outstanding bills, thus accelerating the rate at which reminders could be sent:

> *"Previously, we were waiting for customers to go into debt before we'd send a standard payment due reminder letter. We automated a process for sending advance reminders of payments due with a significant impact on speeding cash flow into the business whilst preventing customers going into debt. That was a really quick win for us."* **Mick Marshall, Mid Market Service and Transformation Manager**

Another example arose where BS had diversified into generation services. Customers like farmers, for example, might be putting up wind turbines on their land but they lack expertise on how to connect to the grid and trade their energy and renewables certificates in the market. At one point, about 20 people were providing that service and generating a third of the company's business emissions profit, but doing it on legacy IT, including spreadsheets. At their request, the operational agility team deployed RPA in order to collect data centrally and generate customer invoices, and this proved much more reliable.

2.4.4. Year One Deployment 2014-2015

In the first year, BS deployed ten robots and automated 17 processes, achieving an annualised rate of saving of about 40 FTEs. Of the processes automated, BS saved about 60 percent of the processing time, compared to purely manual operations. Overall, this contributed to an eight percent increase in productivity across the business as a whole, measured by the number of energy supply points per front-line worker. These results are summarised in Figure 2.6.

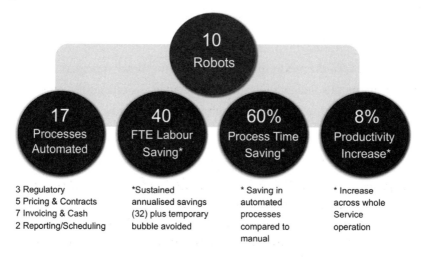

10 Robots			
17 Processes Automated	**40** FTE Labour Saving*	**60%** Process Time Saving*	**8%** Productivity Increase*
3 Regulatory	*Sustained	* Saving in	* Increase
5 Pricing & Contracts	annualised savings	automated	across whole
7 Invoicing & Cash	(32) plus temporary	processes	Service
2 Reporting/Scheduling	bubble avoided	compared to	operation
		manual	

Figure 2.6: Business solutions – RPA delivery in the first year
(Source: Marshall, M. (2016))[24]

2.4.5. Further Developments 2016-2018: Automation as a strategic enabler

During this journey, BS deployed robots tactically and opportunistically. But over the next two years, BS thinking has seen RPA and other automation tools become a part of the strategic landscape. Overriding pressures have not gone away. The business still faced some falling margins, increasing competition, more regulatory demands and the business still struggled to offset inherent efficiencies by growing demand and realising economies of scale where possible. Growth in the industry has been declining, however, with regulatory and environmental agendas eating into demand, and customers expecting ever-increasing energy efficiency and innovation. But this is also an opportunity with BS recognising that there is often more money to be made from working with customers to reduce their energy consumption than there is from supplying the energy in the first place.

Strategically, BS plans to get a slice of that market and be involved in a longer part of the value chain. This involves aggregating demand into larger process steps. Rather than having regimented lines of people operating in silos, BS has been bringing people together to work in bundled, multi-skilled ways, clustered around customer requirements. In this way BS can develop an ability to cope with greater demand diversity rather than creating multiple fragmented individual specialisms. Mick Marshall said:

> *"RPA has been a strategic enabler for that. It is helping us to reduce a lot of the manual process steps, eliminate the routine labouring tasks and improve overall quality and reliability. This has massive cultural impacts for our organisation in how you think about and imagine the content of labour, the kinds of people that we need in our business, how those people are managed, and the physical environment that they work in. So we are very much on a long journey now, moving away from a labour process which concentrated on having a functional division of labour – a very regimented, factory-type organisation – towards one where we have more blended, multi-skilled work processes."*

RPA is helping to move BS's work culture from one where people were very much separated from the results of their work, to one which is more engaging, where people understand the end-to-end processes better, and are working closer with customers. Training has been reorganised:

> *"Where previously we were training people basically to operate computers, now people are learning much more about how to develop, operate, understand and improve the processes on which they're working. Previously, customers probably had a very transactional experience, with nobody really understanding*

the full relationship that they have with us. It's now much more of a 'focus on relationship' management." **Mick Marshall, Mid Market Service and Transformation Manager**

At the same time the physical reorganisation of workspaces has changed to allow people to operate flexibly and form project teams as needed. There is a shift from a command and control model to a more engaging, participatory approach. In this respect robotics has moved into becoming a real enabler of these major shifts in business strategy and the operating model that underpins it. Mick Marshall summarises:

> *"What we're finding in our environment is very much that robotics have been augmenting human intelligence rather than artificial intelligence replacing human beings. They are very different kinds of journeys."*

2.4.6. Case Discussion and Lessons Learned

The case sees a mature user of RPA – formerly RWE npower – move from using automation for high volume, relatively simple transactions in its Residential business, to deploying RPA tools in its Business Solutions B2B division, representing a relatively low volume, complex process environment. As we detailed in a previous book, npower Residential had scaled RPA use to some 300 robots by 2014, and then moved on to automate 35 percent of its back office work by 2017. In Business Solutions, RPA was not the first expedient sought to solve problems of a dynamic changing market, more demanding customers, being serviced by legacy processes and technologies. BS first looked to improve on its performance and planning inefficiencies until it came to look at what it called its 'process waste'. Clearly, in this demanding environment, there were still plenty of challenges that needed addressing, and, running out of significant alternatives, BS turned to RPA as a potential new lever.

Automation can tap into real business problems and opportunities for improvement. As we found in other cases, RPA yielded multiple business benefits, rather than just reduced headcount and cost savings. The 'triple-win' for customers, shareholders and employees emerged as RPA was used to help deal with quality issues, regulatory compliance difficulties, customer dissatisfaction, labour shortages and widespread (expensive) use of temporary workers, as well as cost and process inefficiencies. At the same time, RPA gave Business Solutions more agility and flexibility while supporting opportunities to innovate in its own operating model, but also on the behalf of customers. In practice RPA was still constrained by legacy technologies, but at the same time, it was supporting process reengineering and a major shift in the business strategy and operating model. When people ask: *"Why RPA?"*, in case after case, we found the research answer to be that RPA provides a genuine, relatively cheap and quick solution to organisational challenges at a tactical level, and potentially a strategic level.

Organisational learning establishes sound action principles for RPA deployment. Business Solutions provides a controlled test case for the RPA action principles we detailed in our earlier npower case looking at the 2008-2016 period.[25] There we noted the following lessons leading to effective RPA deployment and strong business outcomes:

- Strategic RPA requires cultural adoption by the C-suite; this materialised eventually at BS.
- Let business operations lead RPA; this was clearly learned and followed in the BS case.
- Send the right messages to staff – again clearly learned and applied.
- Evolve the composition of RPA teams over time; BS has built its team along with ever increasing demand since 2016.
- Identify process and sub-process attributes ideally suited for automation; BS was very clear from the start on this, and made sure it had the process analysis capability needed.

71

- Prototype continually as RPA expands to new business contexts; BS adopted the prototyping, time-box practices from the start.
- Re-use components to scale quickly and to reduce development costs; this was inherited with the Blue Prism software capability derived from the Residential business.
- Bring IT on board early; IT was one of BS's first stakeholders to be called upon.
- Build a robust infrastructure; BS inherited quite a lot of legacy systems and infrastructure and from 2015 had to work within the resulting constraints as it scaled and automated more processes.
- Consider RPA as a complement to enterprise systems; like the Residential business, BS discovered that enterprise systems could not cover every requirement – RPA could automate processes not covered by the extant enterprise systems packages.

Review also Table 2.1, which lists 41 risks and 30 action principles, and recall that RWE npower Residential was amongst several mature users of RPA, upon whom we drew for learning that fed into these action principles. Npower Business Solutions clearly applied many additional lessons than the ones just delineated, and in many ways is almost a textbook example of applying at least 80 percent of the practices in Table 2.1 to very positive business effect. As just some examples we have not stressed so far: BS built its own team and automation capability; developed a centre of excellence; relied on internal and provider advisors; chose a well tried and tested tool compatible with its business environment and objectives; selected impactful projects; multi-skilled the robots and re-used components made sure the robots were work-ready; and managed the robot workforce well.

The RPA value proposition is real but different in a complex, low volume service environment. We are used to RPA being applied to high volume, standardised, relatively simple, repetitive tasks. However, the case indicates that it can be used also in complex service environments with much lower transaction volumes. In dynamic markets, RPA can help enhance capability and competitiveness through agility and flexibility, and not even be primarily about labour cost reductions. RPA can also support other, larger, changes in an organisation's process and operating models, not just eliminating repetitive manual tasks, and reducing FTEs, but also changing the content of labour, including upskilling and driving the focus from back office data processing into front office customer facing tasks, where the empathetic skills that humans possess are at a premium.

RPA can be a strategic enabler. We still continue to be surprised at how a relatively straightforward piece of configured RPA software can actually have strategic implications and consequences. But we found this in many other cases, including, for example, Gazprom Energy, Shop Direct, Xchanging, Leeds Building Society and Telefónica O2. Mick Marshall told us:

> *"Although we started off looking at RPA as a tactical, do-it-yourself alternative to outsourcing, the full value of robotics emerging for us is as an enabler of deep change within the business, because of its impact on the content of labour. And to that extent, our investment in robotics has definitely been investing in our people, rather than replacing them."*

The long-term strategic shift for BS, for market reasons, was moving from being a commodity energy supplier to an energy solutions partner (see Figure 2.7). This had the customer and market drivers of: reducing commodity margins, increasing competition (over 40 competitors by 2015), falling energy volumes and demand destruction. The operational model underpinning this had addressable challenges, but the solutions did not support the required strategic shift to becoming an energy solutions partner for customers. As Figure 2.7 shows, RPA and other automation tools provided a bridge that could improve the extant operational model, while moving to and underpinning the new one.

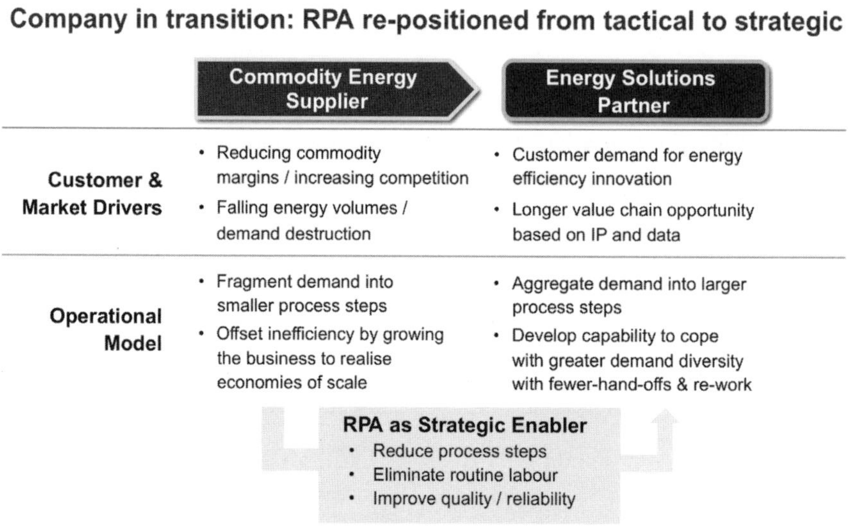

Company in transition: RPA re-positioned from tactical to strategic

	Commodity Energy Supplier	Energy Solutions Partner
Customer & Market Drivers	• Reducing commodity margins / increasing competition • Falling energy volumes / demand destruction	• Customer demand for energy efficiency innovation • Longer value chain opportunity based on IP and data
Operational Model	• Fragment demand into smaller process steps • Offset inefficiency by growing the business to realise economies of scale	• Aggregate demand into larger process steps • Develop capability to cope with greater demand diversity with fewer-hand-offs & re-work

RPA as Strategic Enabler
- Reduce process steps
- Eliminate routine labour
- Improve quality / reliability

Figure 2.7: RPA as strategic enabler
(Source: Marshall, M. (2016))[26]

2.5. Illustrative Case: Royal DSM Robotisation and Shared Services

In this case study, we describe DSM's successful implementation of RPA, using Redwood Software. Strictly speaking, the technology is different from that of other providers. Everest Group has called the technology and approach 'Accelerated Robotic Automation' (ARA).[27] To deliver scalability, resilience and security, Redwood's preferred method is to interact with core Enterprise Resource Planning (ERP) and other systems through Application Programming Interfaces (APIs) and other standard integration methods, or through desktop interfaces. To provide end users/subject matter experts with the easiest method for configuring robots, instead of using Information Technology (IT) programmers, Redwood's design allows robots to be fed with business parameters, which are external to the technical robot definitions themselves.[28]

By August 2016, DSM was deploying over 60 software 'process robots' to automate about 89 percent of the manual tasks associated with its financial close process (see Table 2.2). DSM earned a positive Return on Investment (ROI) within nine months. DSM shrank its financial close process from 15 to three days using RPA. Since then, through to 2017, DSM moved to automating other financial and accounting operations.

	Time Frame	% of Manual Tasks Automated	No. of Automated Processes	Scale	Results
Phase I	July to November 2015	89%	19	Migrated 3 business groups, comprising 60 company codes	• Faster financial close - from over 2 weeks to just 3 days • Increased accuracy and compliance
Phase II	February to August 2016	89%	25	Migrated 6 business groups, comprising 130 company codes	• 45 FTEs freed up for more valuable work • ROI in 9 months

Table 2.2: Royal DSM's initial RPA capabilities at a glance

2.5.1. Royal DSM - The Business Context for Robotisation

DSM is a multinational company operating in 50 counties and headquartered in Heerlen, in the Netherlands. It functions in three industries: health, nutrition and materials. The company produces vitamins, carotenoids, premixes for food and feeds, enzymes, minerals, cultures and yeasts, pharmaceuticals, bio-plastics, and coating resins – to name but a few of its products. DSM is recognised as an innovator in biomedical materials, advanced biofuels, bio-based chemicals, and solar systems.[29] In 2015, DSM earned profits of €88 million on €11.5 billion in sales. It employed 20,750 people worldwide, of which 23 percent worked in the Netherlands.[30] In August 2011, DSM announced the adjustment of its organisational and operating model, including the expansion of shared business services beyond IT and human resources, into financial services.

2.5.2. Financial Shared Services (FSS) launches in 2012

After considering several sourcing and location options, DSM rejected outsourcing and decided instead to have five regional business service offices and one large captive centre in Hyderabad, India. The captive centre would create the dual benefits of lower costs through labour arbitrage, while still keeping the employees engaged with and connected to DSM. The FSS plan called for all of DSM's business units to be migrated to the financial shared services within five years. Like most multinational companies, the main challenge was standardisation. DSM's history includes many mergers and acquisitions that brought along their legacy systems and processes. DSM, for example, had several ERP platforms, including 13 different SAP (Systems, Application and Products) implementations.

FSS decided to build a seamless gateway on top of the legacy systems rather than bear the expense of implementing one global instance of an ERP platform. This quickened implementation and FSS was able to migrate 130 company codes to which robotics were applied across Europe, Asia Pacific (including China) and the United States, by 2015. In 2015, the CEO requested that FSS speed up the remaining migrations. A new global improvement program was started. The Arjuna Project aimed to propel FSS to the top quartile of the world's best global shared services performers. DSM had room to improve; a recent benchmark indicated that its credit management was performing at the 45th percentile and its accounts payable and account to report services were performing at the 65th percentile. For example, DSM was taking 15 days for financial close when top performing companies were closing, on average, in 3.28 days. FSS's mantra became 'F for **First** time right, S for **Simplification**, and S for **Standardisation**.'

Theo de Haas, Senior Business Partner Group Services for FSS, and his senior staff established three top performer practices:

- Greater use of process and technology-related best practices.
- Move non-essential activities out of the critical path so they can be managed and resolved during the month.
- Automate many traditional, clerical manual tasks with Robotic Process Automation.[31]

In particular, RPA was being touted as a new breed of software robots, designed to be used by subject matter experts, and that it interacted with existing systems of record. But the FSS leadership had many questions: Is RPA secure? How long do RPA implementations take? How will RPA interact with its ERP systems? De Haas decided to assess the RPA concept, thus beginning DSM's robotisation journey.

2.5.3. Royal DSM's Robotisation Journey

Like most organisations, FSS began their RPA journey with a Proof-of -Concept (POC). This aimed to assess the financial and technical feasibility of RPA. The FSS leadership decided to examine the financial close process as the test case. There were an astounding 485,000 manual activities per month in the financial close process. Humans were not only doing the transactions, but also pausing to document each step to ensure compliance. De Haas and his team estimated that they could easily automate 60 percent of the manual tasks and achieve the target return on investment. Furthermore, the quality would improve because the software robots would follow all the rules.

Convinced of its financial value, de Haas approached the Chief Financial Officer (CFO) with the RPA proposal. She stressed that any RPA solution would require built-in controls and checkpoints to verify that the process ran correctly. FSS decided to build a test solution and turned to its existing software provider for help.

Redwood was an obvious fit with DSM. DSM's FSS was already using SAP Financial Closing Cockpit and Redwood had already helped to automate many system background tasks. Redwood also offered RPA tools. FSS valued the fact that Redwood was focused on financial services and had deep subject matter expertise. In contrast, according to Theo de Haas, many other RPA providers pitched the technical capabilities of their products instead of their ability to optimise financial processes. Redwood software is also fully implemented with SAP – a big advantage from FSS's perspective, given that they were running global financial services on 13 versions of SAP.

The technical feasibility of RPA was tested on the month end close process for one of DSM's business groups, Engineering Plastics. The POC team replicated a previous month's end close using Redwood's RoboFinance® solution, and found the software robots producing the exact same figures, but much quicker. The POC team proved the financial and technical feasibility of RPA and FSS launched a two-phased implementation plan.

2.5.4. Phase I: July to November 2015

Phase I aimed to automate financial close for three business groups. DSM created an RPA project team that comprised FSS and Redwood employees. FSS assigned three people: two business process experts and a program manager. Redwood assigned four people: three technical software experts and a financial expert. The financial expert from the Redwood team was to examine the proposed process redesign to ensure it would follow best practices and could be performed by the software robots.

Much of the initial work focused on documenting tasks performed by humans in enough detail to be specified as rules for the software. Humans can execute tasks with less detailed instructions than software robots because humans know how to fill in the gaps in instructions. For example, where there is an intercompany imbalance during a reconciliation process, from experience a user might instinctively know which companies have been incorrectly posted to. A robot, however, will have to be configured to trawl through all the companies to locate the incorrectly posted item. Despite this, the robot will process at a much faster speed than the user. Mohammad-Sajjad Hussain, Lead Business Process Expert for DSM Business Services, India explained:

> *"Existing documents are for users who unconsciously perform the activities and often they don't even refer to them. But when you are trying to implement robotics, you are asking a robot to do a task it will not understand based on documents [designed for humans]. So your documentation should be as detailed as possible, and of course, [embody] a clear understanding of what would be the impact before, and after, the task."*

The RPA team also had to redesign the process for automation, so that the robots and humans were not constantly passing steps to one another. This required re-sequencing some activities, pulling some processes out to be performed at another time, or eliminating inherited tasks from legacy processes that were no longer needed. On this, Redwood experts helped FSS understand industry best practices.

Just as FSS had done with Engineering Plastics, FSS closely involved the three business groups to verify that the software robots were executing tasks as expected. For this Phase, FSS included extra checkpoints in the software to build trust and to gain stakeholder buy-in.

By the end of Phase I, FSS had exceeded its business case by automating 89 percent of its manual tasks. Quality also improved. De Haas offered the example of booking journal entries: Prior to robotisation, journal entries came in on spreadsheets or emails to be processed by humans. After robotisation, journal entries were input directly into the software robots. The robots evaluate the entry, post it, and send it back to the business units without human intervention:

> *"Nobody's touching it. Everything is done automatically through the robot, which of course is good because of speed but also the quality. Previously we still had discussions like, 'Book a thousand*

Euros', and somebody else said, 'No, no, it was 10,000 Euros, you didn't hear me well.' Those kind of issues are gone now." **Theo de Haas, Senior Business Partner Group Services, FSS.**

Phase I was completed in November 2015. FSS focused on year-end close before beginning Phase II.

2.5.6. Phase II: February 2016 to August 2016

Phase II sought to bring six more business groups onto the RPA platform. In total, 130 country codes from across the business groups were to be migrated to RoboClose®, which added many more users to the RPA program. For this phase, FSS had learned enough about the software to take charge of implementing the business rules. The team built templates for three of the six business groups, configured the software and ran user acceptance tests by April 2016. Once again, the robots worked as expected and the three business groups went live the following month. As FSS's RPA team gained more experience, their ability to onboard new companies accelerated:

> *"We're now in a situation that we can do one whole company code per week. We will set the business rules, we'll test it, and we do a full production in one week, which is, if you look from an automation point of view, unheard of because it's not something you do with an SAP implementation. You don't do an SAP implementation in just one week."* **Theo de Haas, Senior Business Partner Group Services, FSS**

The remaining three business groups were migrated a few months later. Theo de Haas said:

> *"We went globally live for Europe, China, APAC, and for the USA. We didn't have any glitches. It worked like a charm."* **Theo de Haas, Senior Business Partner Group Services, FSS**

As highlighted in the introduction to the case (see Table 2.2), DSM achieved multiple business benefits from automation, including FTE savings and faster delivery of financial close from 15 to three days. In total, about 45 fewer FTEs were needed to complete the process. The human work that remained was shifted away from doing transactions to more value-added monitoring, auditing and judging the results.

2.5.7. What's next for RPA 2016-2018?

FSS had both near-term and long-term plans for automation. In the near-term, DSM's Latin America business units, which used Oracle as their ERP system, were migrated to the RPA platform for financial close. Eliminating some of the extra checkpoints that were put in to build confidence during the startup phase, also further optimised the financial close automation. Theo de Haas, Senior Business Partner Group Services, FSS said:

> *"We can start optimising by taking some controls out. We now trust how it works."*

Up to mid-2016, automation had been applied to the tasks performed by the captive centre in India, where 80 percent of the financial close processes took place. But FSS also had regional business centres performing the other 20 percent of activities. Mohammad-Sajjad Hussain, Lead Business Process Expert for DSM Business Services India said:

> *"We would then require the involvement of the business and make sure that all the businesses performed the activities similarly."*

Beyond financial close, FSS also applied RPA to accounts payable, accounts receivable, and credit management. As Theo de Haas explained:

> *"RPA is here to stay, so it's not something that will go away. It's not hype, it's not something that will pass in three or four months."*

2.5.8. Case Discussion and Lessons Learned

What might other organisations considering RPA learn from DSM? We discuss four lessons pertaining to *project management* – managing the phases of the automation program, and four lessons pertaining to *change management* – managing the stakeholders affected by change including senior executives, business groups, employees working in shared services, and the IT function. We see project management as *'doing the thing right'* and change management as *'doing the right thing.'*[32]

Best practices for project management include:

1. Letting business operations lead RPA
2. Picking the right automation approach
3. Selecting the right implementation provider
4. Redesigning processes to maximise the benefits and minimise the risks of automation

(1) Let business operations lead RPA. Potential service automation adopters often ask, *"Where is service automation launched – in business operations, IT or in outsourcing provider firms?"* Across our RPA client adoption stories, it was the business operations groups, including shared services groups, which led most automation programs, and only two were led by IT. RPA's appeal is that the tools are designed to be used by subject matter experts rather than by IT programmers. RPA recognises that it is cheaper, better, and faster to train subject matter experts to do their own automations rather than have them explain their deep domain understanding to an IT software developer who then explains it to a team of IT coders. Because RPA tools are designed for subject matter experts, RPA adoptions are primarily initiated and led by business operations. At DSM, Theo de Haas, Senior Business Partner Group Services, explained why FSS led the project:

> *"It's not an IT project, it's a business project with a small IT component. Ninety-nine percent of the project is about business*

rules; it's about making sure that the processes work so we did it with business process experts."

(2) Pick the right RPA approach: Screen automation vs. process automation. Providers have very different approaches to automation. Some offer quick and cheap solutions that are deployed on desktops. These tools are suited for organisations that want to democratise the workforce and allow individuals to control the automation of their own work. Other RPA providers, including Redwood, aim to automate enterprise transactions on a platform that is secure, available, and controlled. For DSM, this latter approach fit their needs because they aimed to automate financial close – an extremely important process to control and secure.

Prospective RPA buyers need to consider the total cost of ownership, not just the cost of the RPA software license. Screen automation software is typically cheaper and easier to learn than process automation software, but total costs of automation need to consider the full development and long-term maintenance costs. Theo de Haas explained:

> *"A lot of RPA vendors are really just doing screen scraping, which requires a lot of maintenance if you want to change it. I think the biggest advantage that we have with Redwood is that everything is controlled by business rules. So my advice to companies who really want to do this, is that you should do process automation and not screen automation. If you do this at the screen level, you'll probably wind up be having even more problems that erode into your savings because you have huge maintenance on your hands."*

Neil Kinson, Chief of Staff for Redwood, concurred and said that screen automation tools could result in:

> *"... a plethora of point solutions dealing with individual micro-process or meta-robots that becomes unmanageable. If you roll*

out a new version of ERP, suddenly you'll break all of your robots, or at least you have to retrain them. And more importantly, it's very difficult for the IT function to quantify and define and control those changes."

This is something we have also observed in several case studies examined in our new research between 2016-2018.

(3) Select the right implementation partner. Once organisations pick an RPA approach, they also have to pick an RPA tool and an implementation partner – which may or may not be one and the same. Picking the tool is actually the easy part. A number of advisory firms now have RPA practices to advise clients on technical capabilities and total cost of ownership for the more established RPA tools. The harder part is picking the right implementation partner. The right partner needs real subject matter expertise and enough excess talent to devote FTEs with those rare skills, to the client organisation for the entire engagement. Implementation partners also need prior experience with the tool and they should be willing to help the client build a mature RPA capability so the client can function independently after the engagement.

If real estate success is all about, 'location, location, location', then RPA success is all about 'subject matter experts ... (repeat twice more!)', included by the implementation partner. Research has shown that the risks of provider opportunism can be mediated with strong contractual governance, but rigorous contract negotiations and contract monitoring increase transaction costs.[33] Another way to mitigate opportunism is to invest in strong relational governance based on mutual obligations, trust, and co-commitment.[34] DSM credits the good relationship with Redwood, in part – because of its prior relationship – but also to the fact that Redwood's RPA sales team was also part of the RPA delivery team. This ensured that the sales people did not over-sell, over-promise, or over-commit. DSM interviewees also praised Redwood's subject matter expertise and cooperation. Mohammad-Sajjad

Hussain, Lead Business Process Expert, DSM Business Services India said:

"The engagement with them was excellent. They had very good expert knowledge and they were very patient and....we partnered with them very well, and, even though it was a virtual team, we never felt that we are distant from them or that we don't understand each other."

(4) Redesign work. FSS, like other companies we have studied, had to figure out the best way to design steps in an end-to-end process that would make automation worthwhile. If a human has to intervene at too many points, end-to-end processing time may not be significantly reduced. FSS discovered that some steps could be taken out of the critical path and completed at another time. For example, intercompany reconciliations could be done all the time with robotics rather than just at month end. FSS also discovered that some steps could be eliminated altogether – they were just legacy tasks because *"we've always done it this way"*. Taking, for example, asset depreciation, DSS found that it was best to batch the tasks that involved unstructured data and needed human judgment, so as not to interrupt automated processing. Meanwhile some tasks were eliminated altogether, and others reserved for another time. The secret was to optimise the sequence of steps in an end-to-end process.

Next we address *change management*, and how best to address the concerns of senior executives and business unit leaders, the employees working in shared services, and the IT function.

Best practices for change management include:

1. Letting senior managers see RPA capabilities
2. Prepare employees
3. Ease transition for redundancies
4. Bring IT onboard early

(1) Show RPA's capabilities to senior managers and business units.
Decades of research identify senior management support as a critical factor
for project success.[35] Automation programs are no different – in our study, the
client organisations with C-suite support achieved the most strategic benefits
from service automation. At DSM, the Director of FSS was quick to gain the
support of the Chief Financial Officer during the Proof-of-Concept phase.
The CFO's major concern was that any automation needed to have built-
in audit trails to show exactly what the software robots was doing at each
step in the process. Similarly, the business units also wanted confirmation of
compliance by any work being done by software robots.

While the RPA program team quickly became convinced that the robots
would not go rogue, senior managers and business unit managers needed
more sustained evidence before trusting the software robots. Theo de Haas,
Senior Business Partner Group Services for FSS explained:

> *"Because trust is one of the key things you need when you do RPA,
> it cannot be a black box. It's really necessary for people to build the
> trust that the robot is not making mistakes or screwing up figures."*

Mohammad-Sajjad Hussain, Lead Business Process Expert, DSM Business
Services India, added that building up this trust delayed the project a bit, but
that this aided user acceptance:

> *"People had to test them and certify that they are comfortable that
> the robot is doing exactly what they would do manually. So it took
> some weeks for them to understand what the robot is doing."*

(2) Prepare retained employees. Like all our RPA case studies, FSS had
to define what the new organisation would look like after robotisation. The
immediate task was to define which tasks software robots would do and
which tasks remaining employees would do. Furthermore, the employees
needed to be trained on how to work with robots. In general, the employees
working with the software robots welcomed automation. Mohammad-Sajjad

Hussain, Lead Business Process Expert, DSM Business Services India, said:

> *"It's about working with the new tools so that it's something exciting for people who are just used to doing the activities manually."*

Neil Kinson, Chief of Staff for Redwood added:

> *"So RPA is not just about taking FTEs out, it was about raising the level from pure transactional to more rewarding work – creating a higher quality of work."*

(3) Ease transition for redundant employees. Across our RPA cases, the topic of redundancy was always sensitive. Organisations like to share the stories of upgrading the skills of the retained employees or taking on more work without adding more headcount. The reality is that, as RPA scales, many companies need fewer employees. Companies need to develop plans for redundant employees. Across our cases, organisations either waited for natural attrition to gradually ratchet down headcount; offered early retirement; or offered career counseling for redundant employees that could not be deployed to other jobs within the organisation. At DSM, the majority of people were reassigned to higher value tasks such as reporting and redesigning processes. Theo de Haas, Senior Business Partner Group Services for FSS, explained:

> *"People want to do that [take on more challenging work] but also of course, we assess them to also make sure that they really can make that step. We also give them the chance of doing it."*

Some redundant people – mostly middle managers – were offered professional career counseling and used the opportunity to pursue lifelong ambitions. The long-term challenge for an organisation like DSM is to figure out the career paths in shared services for the next decade.

(4) Bring IT on board early. Across many of our RPA cases, business operations questioned when or if to bring in the IT department. Some RPA champions initially excluded IT at the onset for two reasons: (1) service automation was seen as a business operations program since it required process and subject matter expertise, not IT programming skills, and (2) fears that IT would beleaguer the adoption with bureaucracy. In most such instances, however, clients found, in hindsight, that IT has an important role to play. Clients learned the importance of involving the IT department from the beginning so IT can help validate the RPA software as enterprise-worthy, manage how software robots access existing systems, and manage the infrastructure so it is available, secure and scalable.[36]

At DSM, FSS informed the Global IT Leadership Team only after the robots were in production during May 2016. FSS gave the IT leaders a demonstration of the product, explained how it worked, and showed them the business results in terms of cost savings and quality improvement. According to de Haas, the CIO was very impressed with the speed of project delivery and the results. Why didn't FSS bring IT in the loop earlier? Redwood took the lead for educating DSM's IT department because Redwood was in a better position to explain the technical requirements of the software than FSS. Edwin Klijsen, Director of Financial Transformation for Redwood, explained the role of IT in RPA:

> *"It's an IT solution in the end, so there needs to be maintenance and support and input also from IT side...When considering enterprise-grade robotic solutions, then collaboration with IT is a must. Any enterprise-class robotic system needs to meet the IT security and governance requirements of the organisation."*

2.5.9. Summary

The Royal DSM-Redwood case demonstrates the challenges, implementation lessons and multiple organisational benefits possible from RPA. It also demonstrates how some tools enable scaling to enterprise level. The DSM case makes clear, however, that, when it comes to achieving business benefits, good management – amplified by new technology – really does make the difference. We identified eight effective actions in the case. At DSM these formed the strong foundation for growing and scaling service robotisation in the enterprise globally. These findings gel very well with our findings in previous shared service cases.

The Royal DSM case also demonstrates that RPA is best treated as a strategic long-term investment and not as a one-off tactical initiative. Strategically this brings to the fore several challenges. Strategic use of RPA requires careful thought, much pre-emptive focus on future work design, change management, and the skills implications and human-machine balance for the emerging workforce. Our wider evidence so far, documented in our recent book and many papers,[37] is that service automation, applied strategically to scale across multiple processes, will reshape how work is achieved, its location, and the human skills mix needed – against a context of ever rising information workloads for organisations. These were certainly the major issues as Royal DSM moved into further robotisation of the global financial shared service operations.

2.6. Conclusion

This chapter establishes that robotic process automation is alive and well – in fact growing exponentially in terms of corporate use. It comes in many forms, but an increasing number of management challenges have to be addressed if strategic, rather than incremental business value, is to be gained. Along with market growth, the 2016-2018 phase has seen growing challenges when organisations seek to scale their RPA deployments. The action principles we have developed mitigate these risks, but along with scaling and higher corporate profile, RPA needs to be treated additionally, as part of a major business transformation project, with all the management practices this entails. We also point to the importance of incorporating RPA into corporate strategic thinking; linking, then integrating RPA with service automation strategy; digital developments; and business strategic intent. Through case vignettes and two detailed cases, we demonstrated how organisations were endeavoring to deliver on this remit.

We pointed to a small, but definite, development in 2017 – namely the increasing number of organisations seeking to utilise RPA and cognitive automation tools as complementary technologies. We see this as prelude to major developments in automation strategy and cognitive automation use during the 2018-2020 period. Our next chapter provides a comprehensive introduction to cognitive automation. This is followed by detailed cognitive automation cases studies, culminating in Chapter 8, which summarises the CA action principles emerging from our research, as a complement to the RPA action principles discussed in this chapter.

Citations

1. HfS Research (2017), *Five Things Companies Must Get Right With RPA*. HFS Research, Cambridge, June.

2. See Grandview Research quoted in chapter 1. http://www.grandviewresearch. com/press-release/global-robotic-process-automation-rpa-market. The Everest Group regularly quote much lower figures than this, for example predicting an $800 million market by 2018, but they are generally counting license fees of RPA vendors (see Everest Group webinar on 28th March 2017 on RPA Market and Technology Trends 2017). Different reports include different factors, make different assumptions and are constructed with different degrees of rigor. For example, it is not clear how far cognitive automation fees, consultancy, systems integrator and IT automation earnings, and RPA fees from BPO outsourcing contracts are included in statistics.

3. A full account appears in Lacity, M. and Willcocks, L. (2017) *Robotic Process Automation and Risk Mitigation: The Definitive Guide*, (SB Publishing, UK). March. For sales contact info@sbpublishing.org. Available from http:// sbpublishing.org/risk.html.

4. Lacity, M. and Willcocks, L. (2017), *Robotic Process Automation and Risk Mitigation: The Definitive Guide*, (SB Publishing, UK). March. For sales contact info@sbpublishing.org. Available from http://sbpublishing.org/risk. html.

5. Everest Group (2017) RPA Market and Technology Trends in 2017. Everest Group webinar presentation by Sarah Burnett, 28th March.

6. See Lacity, M. and Willcocks, L. (2016) *Robotic Process Automation: The next transformation lever for shared services*. LSE working paper 16.1, January.

7. In mid-2017 we surveyed over 100 clients actively using RPA tools from over 10 major vendors. Clients were recognizing business value and were recording general satisfaction. Over 50 percent were recording 6/7 out of 7 on business value, and on several other measures, including scalability, compliance, agility, security, employee and customer/user satisfaction, service quality, ease of learning and deployment speed. Theses results are based on preliminary data, and the sample and survey were extended in late 2017 to gain further insight.

8. Fersht, P. (2017) *The Market Outlook for Robotic Process Automation*. Presentation at the Blue Prism World conference, London, 21st June 2017.

9. ISG Group. (2017) RPA and AI Survey Report. ISG, London, June.

10. Edlich, A. and Sohoni, V. (2017), *The bots: Why robotic automation is stumbling*. Downloaded from McKinsey site, 24th May 2017.

11. See Fersht, P. (2017) Gartner: *"96% of customers are getting real value from RPA" – Really?* www.Hfsresearch.com, 25th May blog. See also Edlich, E. and Sohoni, V. (2017), *Burned by the bots: why robotic automation is stumbling*, 2nd June, www.McKinsey.com. Ernst & Young (2016), *Get Ready For Robots: Why planning makes the difference between success and disappointment*, (www.ey.com/Publications), December.

12. Ernst & Young (2016), *Get Ready For The Robots: Why planning makes the difference between success and disappointment*. Report, December.

13. Westhauser, N. and Unger, T. (2017) *Establishing an RPA Center of Excellence by Siemens*. Presentation at RPA conference in Dusseldorf, 28-30th June.

14. See Hallilkainen, P., Bekkhus., R. and Pan, S. (2017), 'Extending Internal RPA Adoption to Offering Services for Clients: Journey of OpusCapita', *MISQ Executive*.

15. Asatiani, A. & Penttinen, E. (2016), 'Turning robotic process automation into commercial success – Case OpusCapita'. *Journal of Information Technology, Teaching Cases*, 6(2), pp. 67-74.

16. Interview with John Davis, IBM, 14th August 2017.

17. Ricardo Badillo, (2017), *Benefits of the RPA CofE at Western Union*. Presentation at the Blue Prism World Summit, New York, 7th June.

18. These IBM examples are from an interview with John Davis of IBM 21st August 2017.

19. The example is from SPS (2017), *Intelligent Automation: The evolution of automated business processes.* SPS, Switzerland.

20. See Willcocks and Lacity (2016) op. cit.

21. Mick Marshall (2016), *Robotic Automation as Enabler for The Future `Operating Model – Experience at npower business solutions.* Presentation at the RPA and AI European Roadshow, 21st-22nd September, Dublin, Ireland.

22. Mick Marshall (2016), *Robotic Automation as Enabler for The Future `Operating Model – Experience at npower business solutions.* Presentation at the RPA and AI European Roadshow, 21st-22nd September, Dublin, Ireland.

23. Mick Marshall (2016), *Robotic Automation as Enabler for The Future `Operating Model – Experience at npower business solutions.* Presentation at the RPA and AI European Roadshow, 21st-22nd September, Dublin, Ireland.

24. Mick Marshall (2016), *Robotic Automation as Enabler for The Future `Operating Model – Experience at npower business solutions.* Presentation at the RPA and AI European Roadshow, 21st-22nd September, Dublin, Ireland.

25. See Willcocks and Lacity (2016) op. cit. Chapter 5.

26. Mick Marshall (2016), *Robotic Automation as Enabler for The Future `Operating Model – Experience at npower business solutions.* Presentation at the RPA and AI European Roadshow, 21st-22nd September, Dublin, Ireland.

27. Burnett, S. and Modi, A. (2017) *Pushing The Dial on Business Process Automation.* Everest Group, USA

28. Examples of business parameters include time zone, period, year, company code, account selection, cost centers, allowed deviations, exchange rate type (month end rate, month average rate), rules for provisions – basically any parameter which comprises part of the process that the specific robot needs to perform.

29. Source: de Haas, T. (2016) *Robotization in Shared Services.* Presentation at First European Innovation Summit, Wiesbaden, 27th-28th June

30. https://en.wikipedia.org/wiki/DSM_(company)

31. Source: de Haas, T. (2016) *Robotization in Shared Services.* Presentation at First European Innovation Summit, Wiesbaden, 27th-28th June.

32. Lacity, M. (editor), (2008), Editor's Introduction, in *Major Currents in Information Systems: The Management of Information Systems*, Volume 4 (series editors: Willcocks, L., and Lee, A.), Sage, London, viii-xxxiii.

33. For example, Williamson argues that contractual governance can mitigate the risks of vendor opportunism. Sources: Williamson, O., 1979. 'Transaction cost economics: the governance of contractual relations'. *Journal of Law*

and Economics 22, 233–261; Williamson, O., 1991. 'Comparative economic organization: the analysis of discrete structural alternatives'. *Administrative Science Quarterly* 36 (2), 269–296.

34. For a review of the empirical research on relational governance, see: Lacity, M., Khan, S., and Yan, A (2016), 'Review of the Empirical Business Services Sourcing Literature: An Update and Future Directions'. *Journal of Information Technology*, 31(2), 1-60.

35. These references show years of research tying senior management support to project success: Standish Group Chaos Report: https://www.infoq.com/articles/standish-chaos-2015; Sabherwal, R., Jeyaraj, A. and Chowa, C. (2006). *Information System Success: Individual and Organizational Determinants, Management Science*, 52 (12): 1849-1864; Lacity, M. (editor), (2008), *Major Currents in Information Systems: The Management of Information Systems*, Volume 4 (series editors: Willcocks, L., and Lee, A.), Sage, London; Nelson, R., (2007), 'IT Project Management: Infamous Failure, Classic Mistakes, and Best Practices'. *MIS Quarterly Executive*, 6, 2: 67-78.

36. *CIO Magazine* interview, 'Should CIOs be chief robot wranglers?' 26th July, 2016.

37. See Willcocks, L. and Lacity, M. (2016) *Service Automation, Robots and The Future of Work*, (SB Publishing, UK), especially chapter 10. Also Willcocks, L. (2016), 'How Organisations Can embrace Automation', *European Business Review*, April, europeanbusinessreview.com; Lacity, M. and Willcocks, L. (2016) 'Robotic Process Automation at Telefónica O2'. *MISQ Executive*, March, 15-1, 21-36.

Chapter 3

The Cogs and Wrenches of Cognitive Automation

By Mary Lacity

> *"Artificial intelligence is one of 50 things that Watson does. There is also machine learning, text-to-speech, speech-to-text, and different analytical engines – they're like little Lego bricks. You can put intelligence in any product or any process you have."*[1]

Ginni Rometty, CEO of IBM

> *"The bottom line can be put in the form of a four-word sentence: Symbols are not meanings. Of course, Watson is much faster than me. But speed doesn't add understanding...Literally speaking, there is no such thing as computer understanding. There is only simulation."*[2]

John Searle, Professor Emeritus at University of California, Berkeley

3.1. Introduction

There are opposing views, as illustrated by the opening quotes, as to whether software applications like IBM's Watson are actually 'intelligent'. We have never embraced the term 'artificial intelligence' because it too often imposes, on machines, human characteristics they simply do not possess. The term artificial intelligence mystifies what computers are actually doing, and escalates expectations about their performance. More short term, it conflates aspirations in research labs with what is commercially usable. We have always preferred the term 'Cognitive Automation' (CA).

As noted in Chapter 1, we define cognitive automation as *"a software tool that analyses unstructured and structured data using inference-based algorithms to produce probabilistic outcomes."*[3] In this chapter, we unpack this definition. We chose the metaphor of 'cogs and wrenches' to explain major concepts in a manner comprehensible to general managers. We will explain the biggest **cogs** – machine learning, image processing, natural language processing, and fast computers. Essentially, machine-learning techniques are the 'inference-based algorithms' to process images and natural language (i.e. 'unstructured data'). These are the 'so whats' about CA tools. These so-called 'recent' advances often have roots dating back decades; it is just that we finally have enough computational power to execute them. Computing techniques like Hadoop[4] and specialised hardware, like Google's Tensor Processing Unit (TPU)[5], provide the horsepower we lacked a decade ago.

We also discuss the **wrenches** that hinder progress. CA tools need colossal quantities of good data to perform well (i.e. the 'data wrench') and better algorithms are needed to expand functionality (i.e. the 'algorithm wrench'). Endemic to all technologies, CA tools are embedded in political, organisational, regulatory, social, economic, and physical systems (i.e. the 'technology embeddedness' wrench).

After explaining the cogs and wrenches of CA, we describe three specific CA tools – IBM Watson, IPsoft Amelia, and Expert System's Cogito. Several of the organisations we studied for this book adopted these tools, so it is worth understanding their functionality. The detailed organisational adoption journeys are the subjects of subsequent chapters.

3.2. The Cogs of Cognitive Automation

For our research context of business applications, the most relevant CA capabilities, which we call '**cogs**' in our metaphor, are machine learning, image processing, and natural language processing, and super-fast processors (see Figure 3.1). We will cover three machine learning concepts: deep learning, unsupervised learning, and supervised learning. These algorithms help computers interpret images and natural language text very quickly – so quickly, in fact, that they enable technologies like driverless cars. We then look at five ways in which machine learning algorithms process natural language to extract data, classify data, generate text, translate language, and convert text-to-speech or speech-to-text. Our CA overview is not comprehensive; there are hundreds of types of machine learning algorithms, but this introduction will be enough to understand how operational cognitive automation tools like IBM Watson, IPsoft Amelia, ad Expert System Cogito, work.

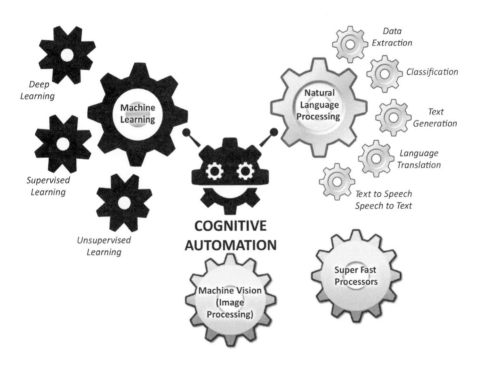

Figure 3.1: The 'cogs' of cognitive automation

3.2.1. Machine learning

"A computer program is said to learn from experience E, with respect to some class of tasks T and performance measure P, if its performance at tasks in T, as measured by P, improves with experience E."[6] **Professor Thomas Mitchell, Carnegie Mellon University**

Machine learning is a way to program computers so that computers perform tasks competently based on prior examples, not just based on logic rules. We cover three important machine learning concepts: supervised, unsupervised and deep learning. With ***supervised machine learning***, the inputs to the computer include data labels for each example. When the computer is input with new data it has not encountered before, the algorithm[7] instructs the computer to match the new input to the closest pattern.[8] Supervised machine learning makes it easier for the computer to perform well, but it may be prohibitively expensive to label all examples. With ***unsupervised machine learning***, there are no data labels. Instead, a machine learning algorithm extracts patterns based on the data. Unsupervised machine learning algorithms[9] typically need massive amounts of examples, i.e. data, to perform competently.[10]

Within this general class of supervised and unsupervised machine learning, there are hundreds of commonly used algorithms (see Figure 3.2). Here we cover ***deep learning algorithms***. These algorithms build a hierarchy of equations for processing the data inputs, which may or may not be labeled.

Deep learning, or deep neural nets as it is sometimes called, has quite a long history. But as any historian will attest, it is folly to identify a single event or person to mark the true beginning of an idea. We will arbitrarily begin in the 1940s, with the work of Warren McCulloch and Walter Pitts.[11] These researchers wrote a seminal paper that attempted to model the brain. Specifically, they attempted *"to record the behaviour of complicated [neural] nets in the notation of the symbolic logic of propositions. The 'all-or-none' law of nervous activity is sufficient to insure that the activity of any neuron may be represented as a proposition.*" McCulloch and Pitts recognised that either a neuron fires or it doesn't. The firing of a particular neuron will depend if and when the other neurons connected to it fire, thus creating a layered network of neurons. This idea from McCulloch and Pitts is applied today as deep neural networks or deep machine learning. The firing of a neuron can be represented with a '1' and the lack of firing with a '0' – something the digital computer is ideally suited to model. Think of a deep learning model as a one-way hierarchical structure[12] (see Figure 3.3), where inputs affect the behaviour in the next layer, which effects the behaviour in the next layer, until the output layer is revealed. The input data might be labeled (supervised learning) or not labeled (unsupervised learning). To see how machine learning works, we need to bring input data into the conversation, beginning with images.

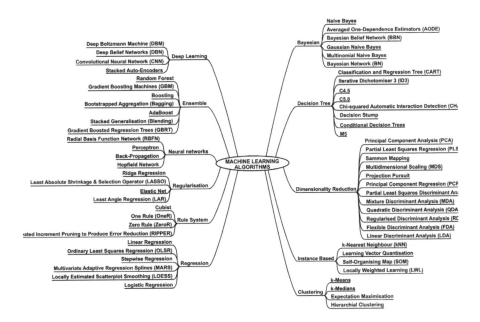

Figure 3.2: Examples of machine learning algorithms

(*Source: https://jixta.files.wordpress.com/2015/11/machinelearningalgorithms.png*)

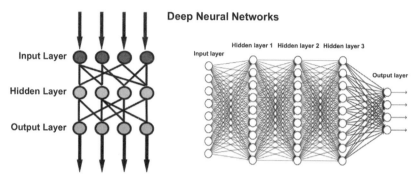

Figure 3.3(a): A simple deep neural net with one hidden layer[13]

Figure 3.3(b): A deep neural net with three hidden layers[14]

3.2.2. Image Processing

To demonstrate how machine learning works, let us examine the context of programming a computer to recognise alphabetic characters. It is very difficult to write logic rules to instruct a computer to recognise the letters of the alphabet because there are too many font types (see Figure 3.4 for some examples), and too much variety across human handwriting. With machine learning, a programmer inputs many examples of each letter of the alphabet into the computer. If the programmer uses supervised machine learning, a label would accompany each instance of a letter. For example, each instance of the letter 'a' would be accompanied with the label 'this is an a'; each instance of the letter 'b' would be labeled, 'this is a b', etc.[15]

Of course it's more complicated than this. Underneath the covers, each image is decomposed into tiny boxes (called pixels) and the colour of each pixel is coded as an array of numbers the computer can read as input. The output of the machine learning algorithm would be in the form of possible interpretations with associated probabilities. Figure 3.5 provides an example of a pixel array for the letter 'a' in the Arial font. Assuming the input was accompanied with a label, 'this is an a', the output would be a '1' with 100 percent probability that the image represents the letter 'a', and a '0' with zero percent probability that the image does not represent the letter 'a'.

100

Figure 3.4: Some examples of the different variations for the letter 'a'
(*Source: Text Coding Initiative*)[16]

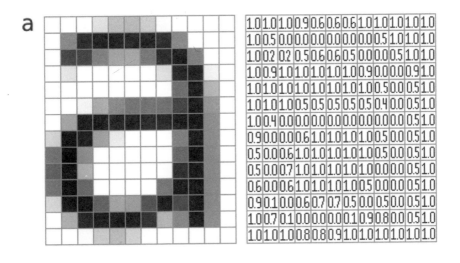

**Figure 3.5: An image of the letter 'a' in Arial font
and its associated pixel map**[17]

After supervised training, the computer uses the 'ground-truth' to interpret any new data that is unlabeled. For example, when a letter is inputted in a font the computer has not accessed before, it will find the pattern that matches it the closest and assign a probability to indicate its confidence in the output.[18] Programmers may set a threshold probability that triggers an exception for human review.

Figure 3.6: The Challenge Of Image Interpretation -
'Find all instances of the letter 'a' in an image'

Now let's escalate the complexity by asking the computer to correctly identify all the instances of the letter 'a' within a larger image. Figure 3.6 is an image from the signing of our first robotic process automation (RPA) book at the Outsourcing World Summit in February 2016. Finding all the instances of the letter 'a' within the image is no trivial task. The letter 'a' appears in multiple sizes and in multiple directions, including horizontal, vertical, sideways and upside down. Now multiply that task by programming a computer to recognise the table, each book, each sign, each stack of paper, the parts of three hands, a forearm, and one begins to appreciate why machine learning requires a massive amount of training data and computing power before it becomes proficient.

Now let's really ramp up complexity. Consider the task if the algorithm uses unsupervised machine learning, where each instance of a letter has no label. The algorithm will instruct the computer to categorise the data by finding patterns among the elements, perhaps by using cluster analysis or principle component analysis.[19] This requires massive amounts of data to extract patterns and distinguish letters – upwards of tens of thousands of examples.

Natural language processing is another breakthrough component of CA.

3.2.3. Natural language processing

Programming a computer to interpret natural language is even more complex than programming it to interpret images. Here we are not just talking about identifying a letter, (from the example above), but about extracting the semantic intent of text or speech from the relationships among words and sentences.

Algorithms that process natural language have been around for over 50 years. We will arbitrarily begin the discussion of natural language processing in the 1960s with Professor Joseph Weizenbaum at the MIT Artificial Intelligence Laboratory. He created one of the first computer programs with a natural language interface called ELIZA (see Figure 3.7). One of the ELIZA applications simulated a Rogerian psychotherapist using keyword searches and word substitutions. A response to *"My mother hates me"* was *"Who else in your family hates you?"*[20] The program used explicitly written rules. Weizenbaum was astonished that lay people thought his computer program actually understood them. His book, *Computer Power and Human Reason: From Judgment to Calculation*, is a response to lay people's reaction to ELIZA. In the book, he argued that computers should be programmed to

```
   EEEEEEEE  L            IIIIIII  ZZZZZZZ      AAA
   E         L               I          Z      A   A
   E         L               I         Z       A   A
   EEEEE     L               I        Z        A   A
   E         L               I       Z         AAAAAAA
   E         L               I      Z          A     A
   EEEEEEEE  LLLLLLLL     IIIIIII  ZZZZZ        A     A
```

```
ELIZA > (PLEASE TYPE IN ALL CAPS) WHAT'S YOUR NAME DEAR ?
AMIT
ELIZA > HI, I'M ELIZA. WHAT DO YOU WANT TO TALK ABOUT ?
AMIT > CAN I TALK ABOUT MY PROBLEM ?
ELIZA > SURE...!
AMIT > DUE TO ON GOING EXAMS IN COLLEGE, I HAVE A LOT OF STRESS.
ELIZA > PLEASE RELAX A LITTLE. SLEEP WELL.
AMIT > THANKS FOR YOUR ADVICE.
ELIZA > NO MENTION.
AMIT > BYE
ELIZA > BYE AND KEEP IN TOUCH...
```

Figure 3.7: Sample conversation with ELIZA
(Source: Afflictor.com)[21]

decide, but never to judge. Many other hand-written, rules-based NLP programs were written over the next two decades.

In the 1980s, machine learning algorithms drastically improved NLP. As discussed above, machine learning algorithms used statistics to interpret natural language. Beginning with the use of decision tree algorithms, current NLP software is based on sophisticated statistical inferences. If NLP machine learning has been around since the 1980s, why did it take so long before we had the likes of Apple's Siri or Amazon's Alexa? One doesn't just build an algorithm – an entire system must be constructed to meet requirements for speed, accuracy, security, and scalability.

Siri actually began as a US Defense Advanced Research Projects Agency (DARPA) project in 2003 (DARPA being the same agency that funded the invention of ARPANET, the precursor to the Internet). Five years later, the Siri project was spun off as Siri International (SI). SI raised nearly $25 million and improved the many parts of Siri, such as voice-to-text, text-to-voice, and processing against dictionaries/ontologies (see Figure 3.8). The system requires vast amounts of data, multiple algorithms and super-fast processing. Apple launched 'Siri Digital Assistant' on the App Store in 2010.[22]

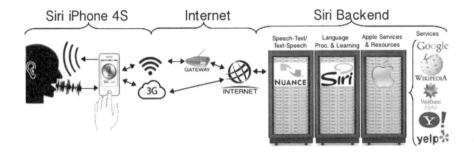

Figure 3.8: Apple's Siri system
(Source: http://www.venturewerks.com/blog-siriprimer.html)

For all their impressiveness, Siri and its competitors are still chatbots, producing one output for every input. They do not follow conversations. In contrast, advanced cognitive tools, like IPsoft Amelia, follow conversations, which requires considerable more algorithmic power. Matt Tomlinson, Global Director of Innovation for the video gaming company, Electronic Arts, described the differences between chatbots and CA tools as follows:

> *"My team spent a year reading white papers and testing different AI products. It comes down to this: two tier vs. three tier approaches (see Figure 3.9). A traditional chatbot has two tiers. In the chatbot world, the input layer processes natural language into various categories; the output uses business logic rules to come up with canned responses. Siri, Cortana, Alexa, and Google Home work this way. If you ask Siri to turn the temperature up one degree, Siri will say, 'I do not know what thermostat you are talking about.' You cannot just answer back, 'The one upstairs'. You have to rephrase the entire command to, 'raise the living room thermostat by one degree.' It's a simple input; a simple output. There's no*

memory, no context. It's not following a process. With the more advanced approach, the inputs are more sophisticated because they understand the sentiment and emotion. Also, the business logic layer tracks a complicated non-linear process that understands that the first utterance is just the beginning of a conversation. The most advanced thing I've seen with my tests of Amelia is the natural language generation. Amelia sounds human. Emulating the sentiment and emotion of the player is a core approach for us."

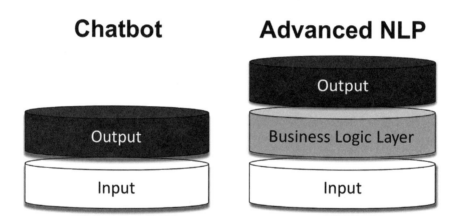

Figure 3.9: Chatbots vs. advanced NLP
(*Source: Adapted from Matt Tomlinson*)[23]

Functionally, organisations use advanced NLP for data extraction, classification, text generation, language translation, text-to-speech, and speech-to-text. Here are some examples from our research:

Data Extraction. Data extraction is a common organisational use for cognitive automation tools. Organisations need structured data to execute most business processes in their legacy systems such as Enterprise Resource Planning (ERP), Customer Relationship Management (CRM), Human Resource Management (HRM) and other systems of record. However, much of the data at the front end of a process comes in as natural language text, such as requests for products or services. Optical Character Recognition (OCR) is designed to extract data from such documents, but they only work so well. Increasingly, a CA tool complements an OCR tool to maximise data extraction. For example, we describe in Chapter 7 how Zurich Insurance uses a CA tool to extract data from medical reports – which are written in natural language – for claims processing.

Classification. Many organisational processes also need data classification. This is the tagging of data for process routing. In our first RPA book[24], we described how Virgin Trains, a train operating company based in the United Kingdom, used a CA tool to classify incoming customer requests. As Virgin Trains grew as a company, a tsunami of customer emails and social media activity ensued, stretching the existing staff beyond its limits. The staff spent too much time filtering incoming correspondence, categorising it, and then routing it for resolution. Virgin Trains adopted a CA tool by Celaton called inSTREAM™. The CA tool receives all the correspondence, filters it, categorises it to over 470 types and routes it. The staff then focused on more value-added tasks, such as spending more time with customers and with business operations folks working on the frontlines. The daily email processing time was reduced from 32 man-hours per day to four. Over the course of a week, by our estimate, that amounts to freeing up nearly six full-time equivalents (FTEs) for more value-added work such as dealing with difficult complaints, queries, and exceptions.[25]

Text Generation. Producing computer-generated responses requires different algorithms from those for interpreting natural language inputs. Ehud Reiter and Robert Dale usefully explain the difference. According to these authors, the former involves hypothesis testing and inference based statistics, whereas the latter involves *choice*: which text should be selected?[26] Many organisational processes require responses that are written in naturally-sounding text. As noted above by Matt Tomlinson, Global Director of Innovation for Electronic

Arts, advanced NLP tools alter outputs by considering the human's sentiments and emotions. In Chapters 5 and 6, we cover the examples of IBM Watson and IPsoft Amelia generating natural language, text based-responses to student queries at Deakin University, and customer queries at SEB.

Language Translation. Language translation software has significantly improved over the last few years. For example, Google's translation feature is remarkably competent (and it's free to use!). The algorithm driving it is based on deep machine learning, as described above. As a casual user, one might be left with the impression that language translation is a conquered domain in computing, but this is premature. Many organisational adopters report that language translation is still a difficult challenge in making CA tools proficient.

At the Digital Workforce Summit held in NYC in May 2017, Nicholas Moch, Head of Information Strategy and Architecture at SEB, said it took three months to get IPsoft Amelia to be functionally competent in Swedish, while it only a few weeks to train it to execute banking processes. Similarly, Junichi Kudo, Head of Applications and Content at NTT Communications reported that training Amelia to learn Japanese was the biggest challenge it faced. The Japanese language is written with no spaces between words, is structured differently than English, and omits parts of speech. He provided the following example: In English, one might ask, *"Did you go anywhere this summer?"* In Japanese, it would be asked, *"Did go this summer?"* The pronoun *'you'* and the object *'anywhere'* would be inferred from the context. NTT integrated Amelia with its own natural language processing tool to boost its competency.

Text-to-speech, speech-to-text. We have yet to discuss audio input. The challenges of speech recognition include the variety of pronunciations, accents, and tempo of audio signals, i.e. analogue signals, that need to be translated into digital signals (see Figure 3.10). Modern general-purpose speech recognition systems are based on Hidden Markov Models (HMM), that generate output probabilities, such as the likelihood that a human's utterance of the word, '*hello*' was correctly processed by the algorithm as '*hello*'. Again, algorithmic-based statistics are the foundation of machine learning. As far as our case studies, none of the organisational adopters have applied text-to-speech or speech-to-text yet. Rather, all inputs by humans and outputs by the computer are text-based. However, speech capabilities can be incorporated into CA tools by calling on an Application Programming Interface (API).

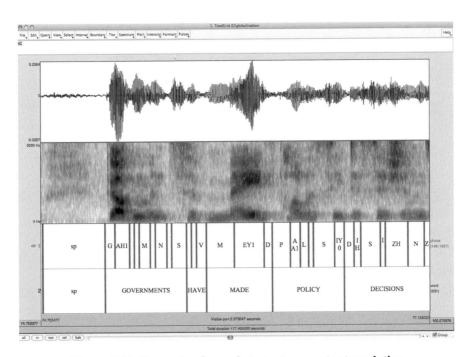

Figure 3.10: Example of speech-to-text computer translation
(Source: Sergio Grau Puerto (2012))[27]

Having covered cognitive automation's impressive capabilities that use machine learning algorithms to process images, natural language text and speech, we now turn to the current challenges.

3.3. The Wrenches

For all the marvelous advances in cognitive automation technologies, there are several obstacles, which we call '**wrenches**', that prevent these technologies from performing better, or from being more widely adopted:

The *'data wrench'* addresses the issues experienced with input data.

The *'algorithm wrench'* addresses the limitations of programming.

The *'technology embeddedness wrench'*, endemic to all technologies, refers to factors in the real world that inevitably slow adoption (see Figure 3.11).

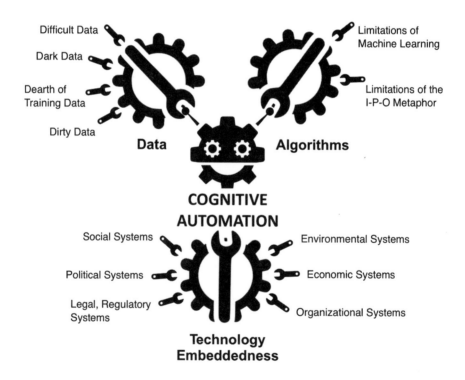

Figure 3.11: The 'wrenches' of cognitive automation

3.3.1. The Data Wrench

"Today's supervised learning software has an Achilles' heel: It requires a huge amount of data... Building a photo-tagger requires anywhere from tens of thousands of pictures as well as labels, or tags, telling you if there are people in them. Building a speech recognition system requires tens of thousands of hours of audio together with the transcript." **Andrew Ng, Founder of Google's Brain Deep Learning Project**[28]

"Forget artificial intelligence – in the brave new world of big data, it's artificial idiocy we should be looking out for." **Dr. Tom Chatfield, author**

In Ginni Rometty's[29] keynote address at the 2016 IBM World of Watson conference, she acknowledged four main lessons/challenges for Watson applications based on input from 700 Watson clients. The first lesson was 'better data, better outcome', or what long-time computers programmers might call, 'garbage in, garbage out'. The data challenge for CA ingestion can be enormous.

Organisational adopters of CA tools have to deal with ***difficult data***, which we define as accurate and valid data that is hard for a machine to read, like a fuzzy image, unexpected data types, or sophisticated natural language text. As to images, traditional OCR software is getting better at converting images to text with time, but it is still not 100 percent accurate. According to Cvision, a typical OCR accuracy rate is about 98 percent on a good quality image,[30] which means that there will still be about 200 errors on a 10,000 word document (about 30 pages). OCR accuracy rates increase when the software is enhanced with a good, supervised machine-learning algorithm. Advanced OCR tools (or OCR tools paired with a new CA tool) can further automate the extraction of data from images such as faxes, paper documents, and PDFs, into structured digital formats. For example, if an OCR tool has already learned to find a vendor number by extracting phrases from images like 'vendor #', 'vendor number', 'vendor ID', it would generate an exception check for human review when it encountered, for the first time, another version of the field, say for example, 'ven num'. A human would confirm that this is indeed another valid extraction of the vendor number field. The software would not need human intervention next time it reads it. Some versions of OCR also give weight to its 'guess', and humans can decide, based on the accuracy needs of the context, what the threshold weight for human review should be.

As much as 80 percent of an organisation's data is likely to be dark data that is un-locatable, untapped, or untagged.[31] Dark data typically includes data in text messages, documents, emails, videos, audios, and images. Cognitive automation tools, designed to perform a business function, like answering customer queries, might need another front-end CA tool – such as Lattice Data – to first 'illuminate' the dark data.[32]

CA tools require many good examples to establish a reliable ground-truth to serve as the tool's reference model. For example, Google DeepMind's AlphaGo program was trained with over 30 million moves and used 1,920 CPUs and 280 GPUs.[33] As of 2013, IBM Watson's corpus of knowledge in healthcare had 1.5 million patient records and *'600,000 pieces of medical evidence, two million pages of text from 42 medical journals and clinical trials in the area of oncology research'*[34] Organisations seeking to build their own CA applications may have only a ***dearth of good training data*** to instruct the tool. Among our case studies, SEB had to weed out human agent conversations that were suboptimal for training IPsoft's Amelia (see Chapter 6). Deakin University had to create its own corpus of 2000 question-answer pairs (see Chapter 5).

Finally, organisations have to clean up ***dirty data*** that is missing, duplicate, incorrect, inconsistent or outdated. In our CA cases, much of this work was done by tedious human review. Yet organisations have been dealing with dirty data for decades – might another approach be available? For example, might the Extract, Transform, and Load (ETL) processes – used to prepare data for data warehouses – be useful for loading data into CA?

3.3.2. The Algorithm Wrench

"Current machine learning approaches will not get us to real AI, the kind that can truly understand you, and learn new knowledge and skills by itself – like humans do."[35] **Peter Voss, Entrepreneur**

Limitations of today's Machine Learning Algorithms. We can certainly marvel at all the progress made in building machine learning algorithms. But what are the limitations of today's algorithms? Oxford University Professor Nick Bostrom, author of *SuperIntelligence: Paths, Dangers, Strategies*, summarised challenges of machine learning in his 2017 keynote speech at the Digital Workforce Summit.[36] He pointed out that we still do not know how to build algorithms for 'one-shot' learning. Whereas humans are innately adept at functioning well in entirely new situations, machines still need massive amounts of data to function well. Humans can readily transfer learning from one domain to another, but machines can only be programmed to function in specific domains. Even the Deep-Q program – which learned how to master 49 different Atari games by reading pixel data from previously played games, and applying deep learning and reinforced learning algorithms – operates in the limited world of Atari games that use joysticks.[37] Humans can readily explain the reasoning behind decisions. In contrast, machine algorithms can produce outputs based on millions of data points and millions of computations without explanation. How can we trust the output if we cannot audit the trail? Humans are still superior at understanding subtle and contextually rich natural language. And as far as big picture thinking, humans can conceive long-term goals and plan how to achieve them, whereas the most sophisticated, deep, hierarchical, reinforcement learning and planning algorithms still can't.

113

Peter Voss offered the following list of machine learning limitations:

- Each narrow application needs to be specially trained
- Require large amounts of hand-crafted, structured training data
- Learning must generally be supervised: Training data must be tagged
- Require lengthy offline / batch training
- Do not learn incrementally or interactively, in real time
- Poor transfer learning ability, re-usability of modules, and integration
- Systems are opaque, making them very hard to debug
- Performance cannot be audited or guaranteed at the 'long tail'
- Only encode correlation, not causation or ontological relationships
- Do not encode entities, or spatial relationships between entities
- Only handle very narrow aspects of natural language
- Not well suited for high-level, symbolic reasoning or planning[38]

What will it take to realise Ray Kurzweil's prediction that the 'singularity'[39] will happen by 2045? Do we just need more time for Moore's Law[40] and Metcalf's law[41] to get us there? Nick Bostrom described five possible paths to SuperIntelligence: artificial intelligence; whole brain emulation; biological cognition; networks and organisations; and brain-computer interfaces.[42] He clearly thinks SuperIntelligence is inevitable, but is uncertain as to which pathway will succeed and he is uncertain on the timeframe. Others argue that all AI research is based on the flawed 'Input-Output-Process' metaphor of the human brain. Let's look at this more closely …

Limitations of the Input-Output-Process Metaphor. Robert Epstein, a senior research psychologist at the American Institute for Behavioral Research and Technology and former editor-in-chief of *Psychology Today*, wrote one of the most interesting essays on this topic. He argues that we have the wrong metaphor for how the human brain works, and thus the wrong metaphor for artificial intelligence. The human brain does not function as suggested by the Input-Process-Output metaphor. He wrote:

"Your brain does not process information, retrieve knowledge or store memories. In short: your brain is not a computer."[43]

Recent work in neurobiology suggests that humans and animals do not simply retrieve memories; rather, humans and animals re-create them from various parts of the brain. So where did the Input-Output-Process metaphor originate? Epstein wrote:

"Our shoddy thinking about the brain has deep historical roots, but the invention of computers in the 1940s got us especially confused. For more than half a century now, psychologists, linguists, neuroscientists, and other experts on human behaviour have been asserting that the human brain is like a computer."[44]

Others might credit the Dartmouth Conference, where the future leaders of AI gathered during the summer of 1956 by invitation of John McCarthy. Among the 20 attendees, John McCarthy, Marvin Minsky, Nathanial Rochester, and Claude Shannon are credited with the term 'artificial intelligence'. The team set an agenda to search for artificial intelligence at the symbolic, rather than biologic level of human intelligence. They proposed to focus on deductive rather than inductive systems, and thought progress would be made quicker if focused on limited domains rather than general domains.[45] More often than not, people did not bother to dig deeper than the sound bites coming out of the AI labs that followed the conference. For example, the quote below by John von Neumann is rarely followed up with the rest of his essay, where he conjectured that the brain might work on a completely different architecture, perhaps a hybrid between analog and digital.

"The most immediate observation regarding the nervous system is that its functioning is prima facie digital."[46] **Professor John von Neumann, Polymath**

3.3.3. The Technology Embeddedness Wrench

Finally, we address the inescapable issue of technology embeddedness. Technology is never neutral, but rather technologies are developed and deployed in a dynamic political, organisational, regulatory, social, economic, and physical world. Scientists have to compete for attention and funding from governments and investors. Organisations have to earn returns on their CA investments – which exceeded $5 billion in 2016 according to *CB Insights*[47] – and make tough decisions on which CA technologies to develop. Governments also issue regulations and taxation that can strain or enable CA innovation, or simply perplex us: For example, The European Parliament proposed, in 2017, that robots with AI capabilities be granted 'personhood' status.[48] Societies worry about the effects of CA on jobs and on the quality of human life. The economy is both effected by our machine algorithms (think about the 2010 Flashcrash[49]) and effects technology choices. Computers consume physical resources, generate heat, and have other environmental impacts. It is technology embeddedness that makes predictions about technology largely speculative.

We have thus unpacked the definition of cognitive automation, and explained both the cogs and wrenches of the current state of technology. With this basic understanding, we can now better comprehend how major CA tools work. To illustrate cognitive automation further, we next take three major suppliers – IBM, IPsoft, and Expert System – that provided the tools in four of our case studies. We give insight into their market positioning, product offerings and how they are applied in workplaces.

3.4. IBM Watson

> *"What is Watson? IBM Watson is a technology platform that uses natural language processing and machine learning to reveal insights from large amounts of unstructured data."* **IBM Website (as of August 2016)**[50]

International Business Machines (IBM) is a global technology company headquartered in Armonk, New York. IBM operates in over 170 countries and has over 380,000 employees worldwide. In 2016, the company generated nearly $11 billion in net income on $80 billion in sales. IBM manufactures and markets computer hardware, middleware and software, and its services include cloud hosting and consulting services. As of 2017, IBM holds the record for most patents generated by a business – a record it has held for a quarter of a century. Inventions by IBM include the automated teller machine (ATM); the floppy disk; the hard disk drive; the magnetic stripe card; the relational database; Structured Query Language (SQL); the Universal Product Code (UPC) barcode; and Dynamic Random-Access Memory (DRAM).[51] IBM also built 'Deep Blue', the chess-playing computer, and of course 'Watson', is named after IBM's founder, Thomas Watson, who served as its CEO for 42 years.

3.4.1. IBM Challenge: Build a *Jeopardy*! champion

IBM is known for its splashy grand challenges. For nearly 50 years, computer scientists had been trying to build a computer to play competitive chess, and IBM finally did so in May 1997, when IBM's Deep Blue computer beat the world chess champion, Garry Kasparov. Deep Blue was able to assess 200 million chess positions per second – a great feat indeed – but one that operated in a structured, speechless, and contained domain.[52] Of course there is more to this story – Gary Kasparov recently co-wrote a book describing events from his perspective called *Deep Thinking: Where Machine Intelligence Ends and Human Creativity Begins*. Kasparov points to some limitations in the Deep Blue achievement. For IBM Watson, we think it's worth looking at its development in some detail. If nothing else, it is a story of human persistence and ingenuity.

Since Deep Blue, IBM had been searching for its next grand challenge. In 2004, Charles Lickel, IBM's research manager, pitched the idea of building a computer that could play *Jeopardy!*, a US game show, where humans compete to ask trivia questions after they are presented with the clues. The game is much more complex than chess; it requires fast (under one second) processing of unstructured, natural language. Clues posed to contestants are culturally rich, containing innuendos, double entendres, metaphors, and puns. Answers are organised within categories that give the contestants clues on how to interpret the answer. For example, in the 851th show that aired on April 25, 1988, a category was called 'Alphabet Soup' and the contestants were presented with the clue, *"To access this company's long distance lines, dial 10, then spell out the company's name by dialing 299."* The contestant, Ed Levin, buzzed in first and correctly responded, *"What is A-T-T?"*[53] To answer this question, the contestant had to understand that the question would require letters from the alphabet as indicated by the category name, and make the cultural connection as to how people use a phone to make a long distance call (by dialing 10). The contestant also had to understand that a rotary phone dial has both numbers and letters, and that '2' on the dial also contains the letters A, B, and C. So, how did IBM researchers build Watson to learn such a complicated game?

First, IBM knew it had to build a massively fast computer that could analyse a vast amount of seemingly trivial data. IBM built Watson using a cluster of ninety servers and 16 terabytes of random access memory.[54] Its initial size was close to ten standard US refrigerators.[55] Watson was loaded with encyclopedias, dictionaries, thesauri, movie databases, newswire articles, and literary works.[56] Watson could process the equivalent of a million books per second. So Watson was fast – but was it accurate?

Initially, IBM tried to train Watson using vast amounts of data, rules, and statistics. Watson's performance was poor compared to humans. On average, *Jeopardy!* champions buzz in ahead of two other competitors about 50 percent of the time, and answer correctly about 90 percent of the time. At the beginning of Watson's development, only 10 percent of its responses were accurate. IBM knew that it could not program all the possible rules for Watson to interpret the clues to answer correctly, so IBM decided to incorporate **supervised machine learning** into Watson's design.

Watson was loaded with every previous *Jeopardy!* clue / answer pair – over 10,000 of them. Watson hunted through the pairs to extract patterns about correct clues-answers as well as the evidence to support the correct answers. Watson used statistics to weight the importance of evidence in a clue. For example, one *Jeopardy!* Clue was: *"Keanu Reeves had a Nokia phone, but it took a land line to slip in and out of this, the title of a 1999 sci-fi flick."* Watson recognised based on patterns of previous questions to heavily weight the evidence, *'1999 science fiction movies' and 'Keanu Reeves'*, and to lightly weight the evidence about the phones. Watson correctly answered, *"What is The Matrix?"* After supervised machine learning, Watson's performance was nearing the performance of human *Jeopardy!* champions.[57]

3.4.2. IBM Watson's Path to Victory

In 2009, IBM invited *Jeopardy!'s* producers to audition Watson for the show. IBM built a stage and hired previous *Jeopardy!* winners to compete with Watson for the audition. Watson lost the first two games and won the third game. *Jeopardy!'s* producers were concerned about Watson's erratic behaviours. For example, Watson responded to the clue: *"In a policy begun in 2002 as a symbol of the war on terrorism, US navy ships fly the 18th century flag with this four word motto"*, with the incorrect answer: *"What is the September 11, 2001 attack?"* (Correct answer: *"Don't Tread on Me"*.) Watson also did not recognise Roman numerals, so Watson pronounced *'Peter I'* as *'Peter one'*.[58]

IBM put Watson through more training. Watson went through hundreds of practice *Jeopardy!* games against human contestants. Watson was performing exceptionally well on factual questions, but struggled with cultural context. It could not always infer how to interpret a category, like the 'Alphabet Soup' category example from above. Another issue was that

119

Watson was not benefiting from data generated during the game because Watson could not 'hear' the other contestants' answers. If the human contestant got an answer wrong, Watson would sometimes repeat the first contestant's incorrect response. If the human contestant got it correct, Watson was missing an opportunity to learn how to answer a question correctly within the category. IBM fixed this by inputting the contestants' answers textually. This and other tweaks improved Watson's performance. IBM called back the *Jeopardy!* producers and the second audition went well. Watson was deemed ready for prime time television.[59]

**Figure 3.12: IBM Watson correctly responding to
a *Jeopardy!* question**

Over the course of three days in February 2011, Watson competed against the reigning human *Jeopardy!* champions, Brad Rutter and Ken Jennings.[60] Figure 3.12 shows an example of a question Watson answered correctly. The category was 'Literary Characters APB' (APB stands for 'All Points Bulletin').[61] The clue presented to the contestants was: *"Wanted for a 12-year crime spree of eating King Hrothgar's warriors; officer Beowulf has been assigned the case."* Watson correctly answered: *"Who is Grendel?"*, with 97 percent confidence. Watson won the *Jeopardy!* game, earning $1 million dollars. This bellwether event signaled that the age of cognitive computing was upon us.

3.4.3. IBM Watson after *Jeopardy!* – A Focus on Healthcare

From 2011, IBM sought to commercialise Watson. Often done through partnerships with its customers, some of Watson's most visible adopters are in healthcare and include WellPoint, MD Anderson Cancer Centre, Memorial Sloan Kettering, the Cleveland Clinic, and Baylor College of Medicine. Healthcare is an apt domain for Watson's main capabilities of analysing and extracting patterns from vast amounts of unstructured data. Consider first the data: There are over 50 million scientific papers (with a new one being published every 30 seconds),[62] 200,000 active clinical trials, 21,000 drug components, 22,000 genes, and hundreds of thousands of proteins. Given that the average medical researcher only manages to read 250 to 300 articles per year, researchers and physicians cannot easily access all the relevant information they need without the help of technology.[63] Furthermore, healthcare is expensive. For example, the average cost to bring a new drug to market is $2.5 billion; researchers clearly need a cheaper, better and faster way to identify the causes of disease and find viable drugs and therapies.[64]

Each adopter of Watson in the healthcare industry expressed a vision for using Watson to transform healthcare research and services. *Below we highlight some of these Watson adopters, but since the stories are based on press announcements, the reports are often forward-looking and aspirational rather than what has actually occurred.*

WellPoint. WellPoint was acquired by Anthem in 2014 and, now called Anthem Inc., is part of the largest for-profit managed health care company in the US-based Blue Cross / Blue Shield Association.[65] Headquartered in Indianapolis, Indiana, Anthem earned over $79 billion in revenues in 2015.[66]

On September 12, 2011, when the company was still called WellPoint, it announced – jointly with IBM – intentions to develop and launch Watson-based solutions to *"help improve patient care through the delivery of up-to-date, evidence-based health care for millions of Americans."* The plan called for WellPoint to use Watson to help physicians identify the most likely diagnosis and treatment options in complex cases.[67] In February 2013, WellPoint and IBM posted a YouTube video called, 'Transforming Healthcare', which outlined the vision and future plans for Watson. The last screenshot on the video reads, *"Forward looking statements containing words such as 'expect(s)', 'feel(s)', 'believe(s)', 'will', 'may', anticipate(s)', 'intend', 'estimate', 'project', and similar expressions are not intended to guarantee results."*[68] As of January 2014, WellPoint was using Watson to help determine if a physician's requested treatment met with company guidelines and a patient's insurance policy. According to Elizabeth Bigham, a WellPoint vice president, Watson initially took a long time to 'learn' WellPoint's policies – a common theme for systems based on machine learning.[69]

In February 2016, Anthem and IBM partnered with Harvard Medical School and GenieMD to deliver an app that suggests treatments based on a patient's self-reported symptoms. The app directs patients to nearby medical treatment facilities like urgent care centres, or offers telemedicine options such as a call centre helpline.[70]

MD Anderson Cancer Centre. The University of Texas MD Anderson Cancer Centre, based in Houston Texas, is a cancer centre established by the National Cancer Act in 1971. It is affiliated with two major medical schools: The University of Texas Medical School and Baylor College of Medicine, both in Houston. As of 2016, MD Anderson Cancer Centre was ranked first for cancer care in a survey of the best hospitals by *US News & World Report.*[71]

In the autumn of 2012, MD Anderson launched its 'Moon Shots Program', which aimed:

"... to save more lives more quickly by cultivating powerful, efficient connections between vast new scientific knowledge and our efforts to improve patient care, protect those at risk and prevent cancer outright."[72]

The program targeted eight cancers: acute myeloid leukemia and myelodysplastic syndromes; chronic lymphocytic leukemia; lung cancer; melanoma; prostate cancer; triple-negative breast cancer and high-grade serous ovarian cancer.[73] MD Anderson partnered with IBM, PwC, and AT&T to create evidence-based care that could be widely accessed using SMAC technologies (social, media, analytics, and cloud). Watson would be the engine that analyses massive amounts of clinical and patient data. MD Anderson raised over $200 million dollars for the program.[74]

Announced on October 2013, MD Anderson and the IBM Watson group launched the MD Anderson Oncology Expert Advisor as part of the 'Moon Shots Program'. The system is designed to help physicians improve cancer patient care by comparing patients, therapies, and outcomes. For example, the Expert Advisor helps physicians hypothesise which patient attributes might account for different responses to therapies.[75] However, according to an article in *The Wall Street Journal* in January 2014 – based on an interview with Manoj Saxena, the executive overseeing Watson – the IBM Watson project was *"in a ditch"*.[76] After the initial stumbles, Anderson and IBM officials said *"... the project is back on track. Lynda Chin, MD Anderson's Chairwoman of Genomic Medicine, says the leukemia-treatment adviser could be used later this year. It might be two more years before Watson could handle other types of cancer."*[77] One reason it takes so long to progress was that IBM developers and Anderson's physicians were not co-located, and both had trouble understanding each other's knowledge domains. IBM had its Chief Technology Officer meet with the lead physician at Anderson once a week and developers met several times a week with physicians to improve Watson's results.

As of January 2016, Chin told a *Financial Times* reporter, *"I am still convinced that the capability can be developed to what we thought... The way Amazon did for retail and shopping, it will change what care delivery looks like."*[78] However, in February 2017, MD Anderson announced that the Watson project was actually put on hold in 2016. An Audit conducted by the University of Texas revealed that results were far short of expected – even after spending $62 million on the project, of which $39 million went to IBM and $21 million to PwC. The audit report claimed Chin went around 'normal procedures' by bypassing the IT department and setting fees just under review thresholds.[79] In March 2017, MD Anderson President, Ronald DePinho – husband of Chin – resigned.[80]

Memorial Sloan Kettering. Memorial Sloan Kettering Cancer Centre (MSKCC) is a cancer treatment and research institution founded in 1884 and based in New York City. According to the US News & World Report, MSKCC is the second best cancer facility in the US for 2015-2016.[81] The centre treats more than 130,000 patients each year.

To help physicians keep up with current medical research, MSKCC partnered with IBM in March 2012 to build a decision support tool that aimed to help physicians diagnose and treat cancer.[82] This deal initially cost $15 million.[83] A team of physicians and analysts 'trained' IBM Watson for more than a year by inputting clinical research and clinical practices.[84] Two years later, the application was still under development: *"The tool – currently in development – is designed to help oncologists anywhere make the best treatment decisions for their individual patients. It learns to prompt physicians if missing information is needed to determine an initial set of treatment options. The goal is to display several choices for the physician with various degrees of confidence and to provide supporting evidence from guidelines, published research, and Memorial Sloan Kettering's breadth of knowledge."*[85]

In April 2016, IBM announced an iPad version of the oncology diagnosis application, trained by the top oncologists from MSKCC. The statement read: *"This is significant for patients who live in areas without world-class medical services, like lower-income countries or rural America."*[86]

Cleveland Clinic. Cleveland Clinic is a US nonprofit academic medical centre that integrates clinical and hospital care with research and education. Founded in 1921, Cleveland Clinic has produced breakthroughs such as coronary artery bypass surgery and the first face transplant.[87]

In 2012, the Cleveland Clinic and IBM entered into a six-year relationship where each donates time and resources to build Watson applications. By 2014, two prototypes had been built: an electronic medical record for physicians to access information faster; and a tool that medical students could use to help them solve complex scenarios.[88] The prototypes were demonstrated at the 2014 Cleveland Clinic Medical Innovation Summit. The first demo tasked Watson with analysing all of a patient's clinical notes – in the electronic medical record – to create a list of health issues, prescribed medications, lab test results, previous doctor's appointments and other information to help a physician come up with a potential diagnosis.[89]

The second demonstration involved training medical students. Medical students do not get grades, but rather they develop learning portfolios; Watson helps students with problem-based learning sessions. Watson independently reviews a patient's information to generate hypotheses as to what might be wrong with the patient and students compare their answers with Watson's answers. As of April 2014, the prototype was being used by medical students and resident staff, but was not yet released as a product.[90] As of 2014, Watson was considered as competent as a third-year medical student.[91]

In October 2014, Cleveland Clinic announced that it would use IBM's Watson Genomics Analytics *"... to advance the use of personalised medicine based on the patient's genetic makeup."*[92] A year later, IBM acquired Explorys, an innovation spinoff company from Cleveland Clinic in 2009. Explorys has a large clinical data sets on more than 50 million people. In December 2016, the partners extended their contractual relationship for five more years.[93]

Baylor College of Medicine. Baylor College of Medicine, located in Houston, Texas, is a medical university. Established in 1900, the medical school matriculates around 185 students each year.[94]

In 2013, Baylor College of Medicine and analytics experts at IBM research aimed to use Watson to enhance insight into cancer kinases so that potentially effective kinase[95] inhibitors could be developed for disease therapy. First, Baylor tested Watson using older data to see if it could predict particular types of kinases that were already known. Watson identified nine from the old data, prior to 2003, and Baylor research verified that seven had, indeed, been discovered. This gave Baylor a level of confidence in Watson's predictive analytics and it then let Watson have access to all the data up through 2013. Watson suggested an additional set of kinases and ranked the probability that each could do what researchers were looking for (i.e. that the kinases could phosphorylate the P53 protein). Baylor researchers took the top ranked suggestions and verified, in the lab, that Watson had discovered two new kinases with the desired properties.[96] This Watson experimentation served as a 'proof-of-principle' that Watson could help researchers mine medical literature and *"formulate hypotheses that promise the greatest reward when pursuing new scientific studies."*[97]

In December 2015, IBM announced that Baylor and IBM built 'KnIT' – the Knowledge Integration Toolkit – that read over 300,000 scientific publications in six months and extracted correlations between publications to identify relevant studies for busy doctors.[98]

3.4.4. Unbundling IBM Watson

Beyond these prominent IBM Watson healthcare adopters, IBM struggled to successfully commercialise Watson to scale.[99] As of October 2014, IBM

Watson was generating less than $100 million a year in revenues. Some customers were struggling to get results. For example, Citigroup, one of the 'Big Four' banks in the US, announced that it entered into an agreement with IBM in March 2012. Citi aimed to use Watson to process vast amounts of financial, economic, product and client data to enhance customer service.[100] In February 2015, an article in *The Financial Times* reported *"a far-reaching partnership with Citibank to explore using Watson across a wide range of the bank's activities, quickly came to nothing."*[101]

IBM has since restructured the Watson commercial unit, expanded and uncoupled Watson's capabilities, rebranded services, and engaged in multiple partnerships to train Watson in specific knowledge domains.[102] As of January 2016, forty parts of Watson are sold as separate capabilities available through Application Programming Interfaces (APIs).[103] – see Table 3.1 for examples. John Kelly, a senior VP for IBM, told a *Financial Times* reporter that although IBM does not disclose IBM Watson revenues, these grew quickly after IBM Watson moved from selling a single system to selling IBM Watson as components.[104]

As of September 2016, IBM has collected its various healthcare applications under the IBM Watson Health umbrella. Applications aim to help researchers accelerate discovery; physicians to increase health care; hospital administrators to improve efficiency; public health officials to find smarter vaccines; nutritionists to customise diets; personal trainers to customise fitness programs; care managers to improve patient outcomes; and payers to control healthcare costs.[105]

Unbundling allowed other organisations to adopt Watson for smaller applications that could shorten development time and reduce costs. LifeLearn is an example of a successful Watson implementation that uses an API. Deakin University, discussed in Chapter 5, is an example of a rapid launch.

Watson Curator	Increase the efficiency in assessing and gathering more relevant across multiple sources Intuitive, guided selection and review process for curation that matter experts to create higher quality information collections[106]
Watson Explorer	A technology platform that accesses and analyses structured and content. Explorer presents data, analytics and cognitive insights in a view. It gives you the information you're looking for while uncovering patterns and relationships.[107]
Watson Analytics	A data analysis solution in the cloud, Watson Analytics guides data and predictive analytics with automatic visualiations and enables effortless dashboard creation[108]
Watson Discovery	Designed to assist researchers draw conclusions from vast bodies of data.[109]
Watson Paths	A visualisation tool to give a sense of how Watson reached a conclusion.[110]

Table 3.1: Sample Watson products in 2016

LifeLearn. LifeLearn is a Canadian company that helps veterinarians keep up to date with medical and surgical knowledge through eLearning technologies.[111] It is based in Guelph, in the Ontario Provence. In 2014, LifeLearn used its own proprietary software and development team to create an application called LifeLearn Sofie™. LifeLearn connected the application to Watson through a standard API, and then started the comprehensive process of feeding information into Watson.[112] LifeLearn Sofie processes natural language. Veterinarians simply ask Sofie a question and within a few seconds, the application scans through hundreds of thousands of pages of medical resources, *"to return relevant, objective, and evidence-based treatment options tailored to that specific patient. Sofie will integrate seamlessly within the practice to empower veterinarians and enrich their bond with clients and patients."[113]*

In a press release, dated 1st September 2016, IBM stated the benefits of Sofie, *"LifeLearn is helping veterinarians become faster and more effective at diagnosing and treating animals by providing focused, accurate information at the point of care. The solution makes it easier for veterinarians to keep up with the latest medical advances and apply them in a clinical setting without having to spend hours outside the office doing research."[114]*

3.5. IPsoft's Amelia

"IPsoft is working with clients to establish tomorrow's digital labor models which drive better outcomes. Entire industries are rebooting. Those who redefine their businesses to embrace AI early will lead the market." **Chetan Dube, President & CEO, IPsoft, Inc.**

IPsoft is a software company founded by Chetan Dube in New York City in 1998. It's initial software platform, IPcenter, automates IT infrastructure operations. As of 2016, IPsoft had a delivery centre in Bangalore and offices in the United Kingdom, the Netherlands, Germany, Sweden, Singapore, Japan, Australia, Canada, Switzerland and Austria.

IPsoft launched its virtual cognitive agent, Amelia, in 2014. Where does Amelia fit into the overall 'virtual assistant' market? According to Edwin van Bommel, Chief Cognitive Officer for IPsoft, virtual assistant technologies target three markets: (1) Virtual Personal Assistants (VPAs) for consumers such as Apple's Siri or Amazon's Alexa; (2) Cognitive Virtual Agents (CVAs) that represent a company while assisting customers; and (3) CVAs that assist employees. As of 2017, VPAs are primarily task-oriented programs designed to execute commands. Edwin van Bommel explained how Amelia serves the latter two markets:

"Amelia is much closer to how real call centre agents converse with a customer. Her conversation adapts based on the customer's emotions. She is conversational AND she can execute processes. So, unlike some chatbots, she will not just answer questions – she can do things like onboard new customers and open up new

accounts. These features also apply to the employee assistant applications. Amelia can converse with employees, sense their emotions, learn from then, and help them do their work."

Amelia is not only the name of the software, but also the name of the avatar that serves as the software's user interface (see Figure 3.13). The avatar was named after the pioneering aviator, Amelia Earhart. IPsoft's Amelia aims to automate customer service interactions, just like a human agent would do, but with higher speed, efficiency and consistency. Amelia can read 300 pages in 30 seconds and manage thousands of conversations simultaneously.[115]

The software is designed to follow processes, thus ensuring consistent and compliant services. The software adapts its conversations in real-time based on the human's emotions by continually assessing the levels of three emotional states: arousal, dominance, and pleasure. If Amelia cannot answer a question, the software escalates the query to a human and stays in the conversation to learn how it was handled by the human.[116]

**Figure 3.13: Interface screens for IPsoft's 'Amelia' -
desktop and mobile versions**

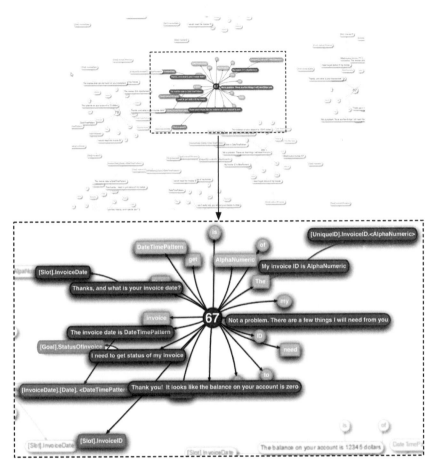

**Figure 3.14: Screenshot of Amelia's
episodic memory capability[117]**

Amelia uses inference-based processing to interpret a human's semantic
and emotional intent. Amelia's development environment captures four
ontologies: a neural ontology (i.e. formal naming and definitions of types,
properties, and interrelationships); episodic memory (previous conversations);
a process ontology; and an emotional state ontology. The episodic memory
capability captures high quality call centre conversations to use for training
and reference during live calls (see Figure 3.14).

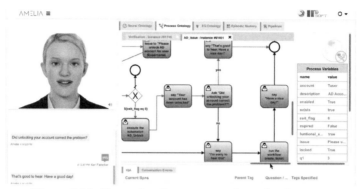

Figure 3.15: Example of process ontology development capability for Amelia

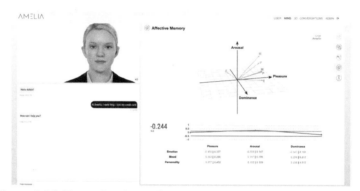

Figure 3.16: Example of Amelia's emotional responsiveness capability (Noting and responding to a 'happy' customer profile)

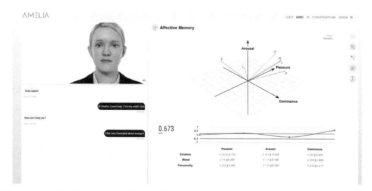

Figure 3.17: Example of Amelia's emotional responsiveness capability (Noting and responding to an 'unhappy' customer profile)

The episodic memory bank is paired with process maps (see Figure 3.15) to ensure a consistent and compliant execution of service. If Amelia cannot address an issue, the software escalates the conversation to a human colleague. The software remains in the conversation, adds the expert human's dialog to its memory, automatically adapts existing process maps, and requests the human to approve the adaptation. Thus, Amelia can be said to continue 'learning' by monitoring and interacting with human experts. The emotional state ontology assesses the level of arousal, dominance, and pleasure. The software adapts the avatar's facial expression, body language, and language based on the customer's emotional profile. Amelia can be trained to propose additional products or services to happy customers (see Figure 3.16) or to offer consolatory responses or offers (such as a discount) to unhappy customers (see Figure 3.17).

3.6. Expert System's Cogito

"There is a longstanding urban legend that, to be a good programmer, you must also be a good mathematician. After many years as a programmer and having hired many talented programmers in my career, I don't believe it's true. If we want the computer to understand what is written in a text or dialogue, in a natural way, then we have to go beyond the logic of the calculation."
Marco Varone, President and CTO, Expert System.

Stefano Spaggiari and two colleagues founded Expert System in Modena Italy in 1989. The company develops and sells RPA and cognitive automation software. Today, Expert System employs about 230 people, most of whom work in Italy, as that is where its major research and development centre is located.[118] Expert System also has offices in the US, Canada, France, Germany, Spain, and the UK. Its customers come from a broad range of industries, and include Chevron, GlaxoSmithKiine, ING Direct, Intesa SanPaolo, Microsoft, Raytheon, Sage, Vodafone, and Zurich Insurance – to name but a few.[119]

Expert System developed and patented its line of products called 'Cogito' (Latin for 'I think')[120] – a set of technologies that provide text analytics and cognitive computing capabilities. Under the Cogito banner, Expert System offers: Cogito Discover; Cogito Intelligence Platform; Cogito Answers; Analysts' Workspace; Cogito Studio; Biopharma Navigator; and Cogito API.[121] Enterprise companies and government agencies uses Cogito technology to make sense of their information and improve their decision making in strategic activities such as knowledge management (enterprise search[122], text analytics[123] etc.), cognitive automation[124] and intelligence.

We focus on Cogito Discover as an example. Discover automatically classifies and categorises content to support the automation of repetitive, information-intensive manual processes as well as the identification and extraction of relevant entities, concepts, relationships and any other data present in text (see Figure. 3.18). Cogito Discover has extraction, tagging, and classification features such as:

Meaning and context-based content analysis: Context, relationships and meaning are extracted using four forms of analysis (morphological, grammatical, logical and semantic).

Semantic tagging: Cogito Discover automatically generates a metadata map for more effective retrieval in search.

Customisable entity identification and extraction: Cogito Discover identifies any entity in content, including: people; places; locations; organisations; URLs; email addresses; phone numbers; dates; values; currency; percentages; and domain-specific entities.

Automatic document classification: Cogito Discover identifies and correctly associates content to the relevant classes and nodes. It identifies a document's main topics and assigns the document to one or more categories according to the reference taxonomy.

Customisable taxonomy creation: Cogito Discover supports the customisation of the category tree according to specific needs, even with large taxonomies of thousands of categories.

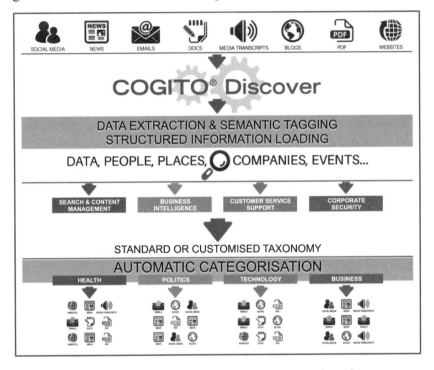

Figure 3.18: Expert System's 'Cogito Discover' product

3.7. Conclusion

Today's cognitive automation tools are indeed remarkable. Their core capabilities – reading natural language and images, evaluating evidence with machine learning algorithms, and quickly processing vast amounts of data – can be applied to many tasks involving unstructured data and inference-based processes. Watson's 2011 *Jeopardy!* win was certainly a striking testimony as to what machines are capable of doing. Since *Jeopardy!*, healthcare organisations have taken the lead at putting Watson to work on what Horst Rittel might have called 'wicked problems,' – that is: *"...problems which are difficult to solve because of complex interdependencies and incomplete, contradictory, and changing data and requirements. "*[125]

While celebrating CA's technical prowess, it is important for the public to realise that CA tools do not think or understand – they manipulate symbols based on algorithms. In his *Wall Street Journal* commentary, titled *Watson Doesn't Know it Won on Jeopardy!*, Philosopher John Searle wrote:

> *"The bottom line can be put in the form of a four-word sentence: Symbols are not meanings. Of course, Watson is much faster than me. But speed doesn't add understanding ...Literally speaking, there is no such thing as computer understanding. There is only simulation. "*[126]

A further caveat comes from a 1967 editorial by C. West Churchman, when he warned Operations Researchers (OR) about the morality of over-selling what OR solutions can do. He argued that OR solutions can take the 'growl' out of a wicked problem, but that OR solutions do not solve or 'tame' wicked problems.[127]

Having gained insight into cognitive automation tools and some major players and developments in the marketplace, we now examine, in detail, four cases of actual cognitive tool deployment. How are the tools developed and deployed in real workplaces, with what outcomes, and with what lessons learned? The next four chapters cover cognitive automation applied in diverse fields –education, professional services, banking and insurance – and for a variety of purposes.

Citations

1. Ginni Rometty's keynote address at the 2016 IBM 'World of Watson' conference.

2. Searle, J. (2011), 'Watson Doesn't Know It Won on *Jeopardy!*'. *The Wall Street Journal*, Feb 23, 2011. http://www.wsj.com/articles/SB1000142405274 87034073045761543131269876744.

3. Inference-based algorithms include both supervised and unsupervised machine learning algorithms where computers are programed to perform tasks competently based on prior examples, not just based on logic rules. (Lacity, M., and Willcocks, L. (2016), 'A New Approach to Automating Services'. *Sloan Management Review*, Vol. 57, 1, pp. 41-49).

4. Hadoop is a programming framework that distributes data across multiple machines for faster processing and replicates it multiple times to prevent failures. Hadoop-enabled queries can get answers in seconds compared to an hour or more in a pre-Hadoop world.

5. Google's TPU units were used in the AlphaGo program that beat Lee Se-dol in the game *Go* in 2016.

6. Mitchell, T. (1997). *Machine Learning*, (McGraw Hill), p. 2.

7. Many supervised machine learning algorithms use decision trees and Bayesian statistics, where the probability of a hypothesis being true is updated as more data is introduced.

8. In actuality, there are many other types of machine learning algorithms; Wikipedia lists nearly 200 common algorithms: https://en.wikipedia.org/wiki/Outline_of_machine_learning.

9. Unsupervised learning algorithms commonly use cluster analysis, anomaly detection, principle components analysis or generative topographic maps.

10. http://www.androidauthority.com/what-is-machine-learning-621659/.

11. McCulloch, W. and Pitt, W. (1943), 'A logical calculus of the ideas immanent in nervous activity'. *The Bulletin of Mathematical Biophysics*, Vol 5, pp. 115-133.

12. There are other configurations besides one-way structures, but this serves as an illustration of a common deep learning structure.

13. Source: https://en.wikipedia.org/wiki/Feedforward_neural_network#/media/File:Feed_forward_neural_net.gif.

14. http://neuralnetworksanddeeplearning.com/chap5.html.

15. http://www.androidauthority.com/what-is-machine-learning-621659/.

16. http://www.tei-c.org/Activities/Workgroups/CE/letter-a.jpg.

17. http://pippin.gimp.org/image_processing/images/sample_grid_a_square.png,

18. http://www.androidauthority.com/what-is-machine-learning-621659/.

19. http://www.androidauthority.com/what-is-machine-learning-621659/.

20. *Joseph Weizenbaum Writes ELIZA: A Pioneering Experiment in Artificial Intelligence Programming.* http://www.historyofinformation.com/expanded.php?id=4600.

21. http://afflictor.com/2014/01/10/extremely-short-exposures-to-a-relatively-simple-computer-program-could-induce-powerful-delusional-thinking-in-quite-normal-people/.

22. http://www.venturewerks.com/blog-siriprimer.html.

23. Presentation by Matt Tomlinson, Digital Workforce Summit, 31st May 2017, NYC.

24. Willcocks, L. and Lacity, M. (2016), *Service Automation: Robots and the Future of Work*, (SB Publishing, UK). www.sbpublishing.org.

25. Estimate calculated as follows: 32 hours per day time 7 days a week (since trains run daily) equals 224 hours per week of work. Assuming an FTE works 35 hours per week, the weekly FTE effort is 6.4 FTEs. After automation, the task was done in 4 hours per day, or 28 hours per week, or 0.8 FTEs; The total FTE savings are nearly 6 per week.

26. Reiter, E. and Dale, R. (2000), *Building natural language generation systems*, (Cambridge University Press, UK). http://assets.cambridge.org/052162/0368/sample/0521620368WSN01.pdf.

27. Puerto, S. (2012), *Automatic Speech-to-Text Alignment for Audio Indexing*. OpenSpires, University of Oxford, https://blogs.it.ox.ac.uk/openspires/2012/05/30/automatic-speech-to-text-alignment-for-audio-indexing/.

28. Quote from, Ng., A, (2016), 'What Artificial Intelligence Can and Can't Do Right Now'. *Harvard Business Review*, 9th November. https://hbr.org/2016/11/what-artificial-intelligence-can-and-cant-do-right-now.

29. Ginni Rometty has been CEO of IBM since 2011.

30. http://www.cvisiontech.com/library/ocr/accurate-ocr/ocr-accuracy-rates.html

31. https://futurism.com/apple-is-using-ai-to-unlock-previously-unusable-dark-data/

32. https://dupress.deloitte.com/dup-us-en/focus/tech-trends/2017/dark-data-analysing-unstructured-data.html

33. 'Showdown'. *The Economist*. Retrieved 19th November 2016.

34. *IBM Watson Hard At Work: New Breakthroughs Transform Quality Care for Patients*. Press release February 8, 2013. https://www-03.ibm.com/press/us/en/pressrelease/40335.wss

35. Voss, P. (2016), *Why Machine Learning Won't Cut It*. https://medium.com/@petervoss/why-machine-learning-wont-cut-it-f523dd2b20e3

36. Nick Bostrom, *SuperIntelligence: The future of humanity*. Digital Workforce Summit presentation, 31st May 2017.

37. Saxena, S. (2015), AI masters 49 Atari 2600 games without instructions. https://arstechnica.com/science/2015/02/ai-masters-49-atari-2600-games-without-instructions/.

38. Voss, P. (2016), *Why Machine Learning Won't Cut It*. https://medium.com/@ petervoss/why-machine-learning-wont-cut-it-f523dd2b20e3.

39. The 'singularity' is an idea that an AI will become more intelligent than all human intelligence combined.

40. Moore's Law has come to be interpreted as saying that computing power doubles every 18 months to 2 years. Originally it was an observation that the number of transistors in a dense integrated circuit seemed to double approximately every two years, and likely to do so for the foreseeable future.

41. Metcalfe's Law states that the value of a telecommunications network is proportional to the square of the number of connected users of the system.

42. Bostrom, N., *SuperIntelligence: Paths, Dangers, and Strategies*.

43. Epstein, R. (2016), *The Empty Brain*. Aeon Essay. https://aeon.co/essays/your-brain-does-not-process-information-and-it-is-not-a-computer.

44. Epstein, R. (2016), *The Empty Brain*. Aeon Essay. https://aeon.co/essays/your-brain-does-not-process-information-and-it-is-not-a-computer.

45. https://en.wikipedia.org/wiki/Dartmouth_workshop.

46. John von Neumann (1958), *The Computer and the Brain*.

47. http://aiimpacts.org/funding-of-ai-research/

48. Hern, A., 'Give robots 'personhood' status, EU committee argues'. *The Guardian*, January 12, 2017. https://www.theguardian.com/technology/2017/jan/12/give-robots-personhood-status-eu-committee-argues.

49. The Flashcrash was a trillion dollar stock market crash caused by high-frequency sell algorithms.

50. http://www.ibm.com/watson/what-is-watson.html.

51. https://en.wikipedia.org/wiki/IBM.

52. Newborn, M (1997), *Kasparov versus Deep Blue: Computer Chess Comes of Age*, (Springer, New York).

53. For a compete archive of every *Jeopardy!* question, see http://www.j-archive.com/; for game 851 see http://www.j-archive.com/showgame.php?game_id=4566.

54. https://en.wikipedia.org/wiki/Watson_(computer).

55. NOVA documentary, *Smartest Machine on Earth*, Aired 2nd May 2012 on PBS. http://www.pbs.org/wgbh/nova/tech/smartest-machine-on-earth.html.

56. https://en.wikipedia.org/wiki/Watson_(computer).

57. NOVA documentary, *Smartest Machine on Earth*, Aired 2nd May 2012 on PBS. http://www.pbs.org/wgbh/nova/tech/smartest-machine-on-earth.html.

58. NOVA documentary, *Smartest Machine on Earth*, Aired 2nd May 2012 on PBS. http://www.pbs.org/wgbh/nova/tech/smartest-machine-on-earth.html.

59. NOVA documentary, *Smartest Machine on Earth*, Aired 2nd May 2012 on PBS. http://www.pbs.org/wgbh/nova/tech/smartest-machine-on-earth.html.

60. NOVA documentary, *Smartest Machine on Earth*, Aired 2nd May 2012 on PBS. http://www.pbs.org/wgbh/nova/tech/smartest-machine-on-earth.html.

61. APB stands for 'All Points Bulletin', a message that alerts law enforcement agents about a suspect or a person of interest on the loose.

62. Picton, G. (2014), Study shows promise in automated reasoning, hypothesis generation over complete medical literature, https://www.bcm.edu/news/research/automated-reasoning-hypothesis-generation.

63. Chen, T., Argentinis, E., and Weber, G. (2016), 'IBM Watson: How Cognitive Computing Can Be Applied to Big Data Challenges in Life Sciences Research'. *Clinical Therapeutics*, Vol. 38, 4, p. 688-701.

64. Chen, T., Argentinis, E., and Weber, G. (2016), 'IBM Watson: How Cognitive Computing Can Be Applied to Big Data Challenges in Life Sciences Research'. *Clinical Therapeutics*, Vol. 38, 4, p. 688-701.

65. Source: https://en.wikipedia.org/wiki/Anthem_Inc.

66. Anthem 2015 Annual Report http://www.corporate-ir.net/media_files/irol/13/130104/anthem-ar-15/financial-highlights.html.

67. *WellPoint and IBM Announce Agreement to Put Watson to Work in Health Care.* Press release, 12th September 2011 https://www-03.ibm.com/press/us/en/pressrelease/35402.wss.

68. *Wellpoint and Watson: Transforming Healthcare.* Video published 27th February, 2013, available on https://www.youtube.com/watch?v=n_7CrLV2Ldg.

69. Ante, S. (2014), 'IBM Struggles to Turn Watson Computer into Big Business'. *The Wall Street Journal*, 7th January. http://www.wsj.com/articles/SB10001424052702304887104579306881917668654.

70. Green, M. (2016), *Harvard, IBM Watson, Anthem Blue Cross & GenieMD forge patient app partnership.* Becker's Healthcare, http://www.beckershospitalreview.com/healthcare-information-technology/harvard-ibm-watson-anthem-blue-cross-geniemd-forge-patient-app-partnership.html.

71. https://en.wikipedia.org/wiki/University_of_Texas_MD_Anderson_Cancer_Center.

72. *In year two, MD Anderson Moon Shots Program begins to spin off innovation.* MD Anderson News Release, 30ᵗʰ October 2014. https://www.mdanderson. org/newsroom/2014/10/in-year-two-md-anderson-moon-shots-program-begins-to-spin-off-in.html.

73. *MD Anderson Taps IBM Watson to Power 'Moon Shots' Mission.* MD Anderson News Release, 18ᵗʰ October 2013. https://www.mdanderson.org/newsroom/2013/10/md-anderson--ibm-watson-work-together-to-fight-cancer.html.

74. *In year two, MD Anderson Moon Shots Program begins to spin off innovation.* MD Anderson News Release, 30ᵗʰ October 2014. https://www.mdanderson. org/newsroom/2014/10/in-year-two-md-anderson-moon-shots-program-begins-to-spin-off-in.html.

75. *MD Anderson Taps IBM Watson to Power 'Moon Shots' Mission.* MD Anderson News Release, 18ᵗʰ October 2013. https://www.mdanderson.org/newsroom/2013/10/md-anderson--ibm-watson-work-together-to-fight-cancer.html.

76. Ante, S. (2014), 'IBM Struggles to Turn Watson Computer into Big Business'. *The Wall Street Journal,* 7ᵗʰ January. http://www.wsj.com/articles/SB10001424052702304488704579306881917668654.

77. Ante, S. (2014), 'IBM Struggles to Turn Watson Computer into Big Business'. *The Wall Street Journal,* 7ᵗʰ January. http://www.wsj.com/articles/SB10001424052702304488704579306881917668654.

78. Waters, R. (2016), 'Artificial intelligence: Can Watson save IBM?', *Financial Times*, 5ᵗʰ January 2016. http://www.ft.com/cms/s/2/dced8150-b300-11e5-8358-9a82b43f6b2f.html#axzz4JOiOCNyz.

79. Herper, M. (2017), 'MD Anderson Benches IBM Watson In Setback For Artificial Intelligence In Medicine'. *Forbes.* https://www.forbes.com/sites/matthewherper/2017/02/19/md-anderson-benches-ibm-watson-in-setback-for-artificial-intelligence-in-medicine/#3cb66bf93774.

80. https://www.houstonpublicmedia.org/articles/news/2017/03/08/191009/md-anderson-president-depinho-announces-resignation/.

81. https://en.wikipedia.org/wiki/Memorial_Sloan_Kettering_Cancer_Center.

82. Jinks, B (2012), 'IBM Watson to Help Memorial Sloan-Kettering With Cancer'. *Bloomberg Technology*, 21ˢᵗ March. Available at http://www.bloomberg.com/news/articles/2012-03-22/ibm-s-watson-to-help-memorial-sloan-kettering-with-cancer-care.

83. op. cit., Ante, S. (2014).

84. *Watson Oncology,* available at https://www.mskcc.org/about/innovative-collaborations/watson-oncology.

85. *Memorial Sloan Kettering Trains IBM Watson to Help Doctors Make Better Cancer Treatment Choices.* 11th April 2014. https://www.mskcc.org/blog/msk-trains-ibm-watson-help-doctors-make-better-treatment-choices.

86. Lorenzetti, L. (2016), 'Here's How IBM Watson is Transforming the Health Care Industry'. *Fortune,* http://fortune.com/ibm-watson-health-business-strategy/.

87. https://en.wikipedia.org/wiki/Cleveland_Clinic.

88. Townsend, A. (2014), *Cleveland Clinic-IBM Watson collaboration highlighted at Medical Innovation Summit.* 29th October 2014. http://www.cleveland.com/healthfit/index.ssf/2014/10/cleveland_clinic-ibm_watson_collaboration_highlighted_at_medical_innovation_summit.html.

89. Confidential Interview with Cleveland Clinic manager.

90. Confidential Interview with Cleveland Clinic manager.

91. Townsend, A. (2014), *Cleveland Clinic-IBM Watson collaboration highlighted at Medical Innovation Summit.* 29th October 2014. http://www.cleveland.com/healthfit/index.ssf/2014/10/cleveland_clinic-ibm_watson_collaboration_highlighted_at_medical_innovation_summit.html.

92. Gaudin, S. (2014), 'Cleveland Clinic uses IBM's Watson in the cloud to fight cancer'. *ComputerworldUK,* 29th October 2014. http://www.computerworlduk.com/news/it-vendors/cleveland-clinic-uses-ibms-watson-in-the-cloud-to-fight-cancer-3583302/.

93. IBM Press release, *Cleveland Clinic, IBM Continue Their Collaboration to Establish Model for Cognitive Population Health Management and Data-Driven Personalized Healthcare.* 22nd December 2016. http://www-03.ibm.com/press/us/en/pressrelease/51290.wss.

94. https://en.wikipedia.org/wiki/Baylor_College_of_Medicine.

95. Specifically, Watson was tasked with finding kinases that might phosphorylate the P53 protein.

96. Chen, T., Argentinis, E., and Weber, G. (2016), 'BM Watson: How Cognitive Computing Can Be Applied to Big Data Challenges in Life Sciences Research', *Clinical Therapeutics,* Vol. 38, 4, p. 688-701.

97. Picton, G. (2014), *Study shows promise in automated reasoning, hypothesis generation over complete medical literature.* https://www.bcm.edu/news/research/automated-reasoning-hypothesis-generation.

98. IBM Press release, 8th December 2015. http://www 03.ibm.com/software/ businesscasestudies/sa/en/corp?synkey=F713551X77664U56.

99. Ante, S. (2014), 'IBM Struggles to Turn Watson Computer into Big Business', *The Wall Street Journal,* 7th January. http://www.wsj.com/articles/SB1000142 4052702304887104579306881917668654.

100. *Citi and IBM Enter Exploratory Agreement on Use of Watson Technologies.* Citigroup Inc. news release, 5th March 2012, http://www.citigroup.com/citi/ news/2012/120305a.htm.

101. Waters, R. (2016), 'Artificial intelligence: Can Watson save IBM?'. *Financial Times*, 5th January 2016 http://www.ft.com/cms/s/2/dced8150-b300-11e5-8358-9a82b43f6b2f.html#axzz4JOiOCNyz.

102. Ante, S. (2014), 'IBM Struggles to Turn Watson Computer into Big Business', *The Wall Street Journal,* 7th January. http://www.wsj.com/articles/SB1000142 4052702304887104579306881917668654.

103. Waters, R. (2016), 'Artificial intelligence: Can Watson save IBM?'. *Financial Times*, 5th January 2016 http://www.ft.com/cms/s/2/dced8150-b300-11e5-8358-9a82b43f6b2f.html#axzz4JOiOCNyz.

104. Waters, R. (2016), 'Artificial intelligence: Can Watson save IBM?'. *Financial Times*, 5th January 2016 http://www.ft.com/cms/s/2/dced8150-b300-11e5-8358-9a82b43f6b2f.html#axzz4JOiOCNyz.

105. see https://www.ibm.com/watson/health/.

106. http://www-03.ibm.com/software/products/en/watson-curator.

107. http://www.ibm.com/watson/explorer.html.

108. https://watson.analytics.ibmcloud.com/product.

109. Crosman, P. (2014), 'IBM Announces $1 Billion Investment, 2 New Bank Clients for Watson'. *American Banker*, 9th January 2014. http://www. americanbanker.com/issues/179_7/ibm-announces-1-billion-investment-2-new-bank-clients-for-watson-1064783-1.html.

110. Waters, R. (2016), 'Artificial intelligence: Can Watson save IBM?'. *Financial Times*, 5th January 2016 http://www.ft.com/cms/s/2/dced8150-b300-11e5-8358-9a82b43f6b2f.html#axzz4JOiOCNyz.

111. http://www.lifelearn.com/about/.

112. Miller, N. (2015), 'LifeLearn taps into the power of IBM Watson to revolutionize veterinary medicine'. *Insights Magazine*, 19th February 2015. http://insightsmagazineonline.com/Assets/2015/February/Sofie-LifeLearn-Watson-CS#.V82of_krIdU.

113. *IBM and LifeLearn Tap the Power of Watson to Transform the Veterinary Industry.* 6th October 2014. http://www.lifelearn.com/2014/10/06/ibm-watson-lifelearn-sofie/.

114. https://www-03.ibm.com/software/businesscasestudies/us/en/corp?synkey=U246252I34447Z11.

115. http://www.ipsoft.com/amelia/.

116. Flinders, K. (2016), 'SEB is using AI software from IPsoft for customer service after a successful internal project'. *Computer Weekly.* http://www.computerweekly.com/news/450400413/Swedish-bank-uses-Amelia-the-robot-for-customer-services.

117. Baer, D. (2016), 'This 'virtual employee' is proof that the robot takeover is upon us'. *Business Insider.* http://www.businessinsider.com/ipsoft-amelia-profile-2016-4.

118. Company Overview of Expert System available at https://www.bloomberg.com/research/stocks/private/snapshot.asp?privcapId=33803738.

119. Expert System Customers http://www.expertsystem.com/customers/.

120. *Cogito: Human Intelligence for Cognitive Computing.* http://www.expertsystem.com/products/cogito-cognitive-technology/.

121. http://www.expertsystem.com/products/.

122. Gartner *Magic Quadrant for Insight Engines*, 30th March 2017. https://www.gartner.com/doc/3660018/magic-quadrant-insight-engines .

123. Forrester, *The Forrester Wave™: Big Data Text Analytics Platforms, Q2 2016*, May 2016 https://www.forrester.com/report/The+Forrester+Wave+Big+Data+Text+Analytics+Platforms+Q2+2016/-/E-RES122667.

124. Forrester, *Artificial Intelligence Can Finally Unleash Your Business Applications' Creativity. Five Things You Can Do With Cognitive Computing*, February 2015. https://www.forrester.com/report/Artificial+Intelligence+Can+Finally+Unleash+Your+Business+Applications+Creativity/-/E-RES115729.

125. Churchman credits Rittel with the term 'wicked problems' which Rittel used during a seminar. Churchman, C. W. (1967). 'Wicked Problems'. *Management Science.* Vol. 14 (4), 141-142.

126. Searle, J. (2011), 'Watson Doesn't Know It Won on *'Jeopardy!'*'. *The Wall Street Journal*, 23rd February 2011 http://www.wsj.com/articles/SB10001424052748703407304576154313126987674.

127. Churchman (1967) op. cit.

Chapter 4

Reimagining Professional Services with Cognitive Technologies at KPMG

By Mary Lacity

> *"Whereas RPA disrupts operating models, cognitive will disrupt business models."*

Todd Lohr, Principal, US Transformation Enablement Leader, KPMG

4.1. Introduction

In this chapter, we examine how KPMG, the global professional services firm, is deploying cognitive automation technologies to reimagine professional services. While prior research[1] has been able to study a number of early-adopters of RPA and BPM (Business Process Management) technologies, there are few visible adopters of cognitive technologies, beyond the widely covered IBM Watson applications in healthcare (e.g. Cleveland Clinic, Memorial Sloane Kettering, and WellPoint). The initial enthusiasm of Watson's *Jeopardy!* win in 2011 (see previous chapter) signaled a new age of machine learning, yet few organisations outside of healthcare have shared in detail their implementation journeys, which makes non-healthcare 'big idea' exemplars so valuable. In this report, we examine how KPMG is deploying cognitive technologies, most notably IBM Watson, to reimagine professional services. We explain how KPMG assessed cognitive tools, why it selected the tools it did, how it experimented with the technology, the status of its current deployments, and what has been learned so far. As of December 2016, KPMG's cognitive capabilities included a tracking service of well over 100 cognitive technologies, development of many IBM Watson use cases (of which three are discussed in detail in this report), and use cases in other CA products, most notably Microsoft's Cortana Intelligence Suite. KPMG continues to explore how new technologies, including Blockchain, will further advance the delivery of professional services.

4.2. KPMG - The Business Context for Cognitive Automation

To put the cognitive technology journey into context, we need to explain KPMG's business background. KPMG is a multinational cooperative of national, professional services firms with headquarters in Amstelveen, The Netherlands. It is considered to be one of the 'Big Four' professional services firms, along with PricewaterhouseCoopers (PwC), Deloitte, and Ernst & Young (EY).[2] Each national KPMG firm is an independent legal entity and is a member of the KPMG International Cooperative. In 2016, KPMG earned global revenues of $25.42 billion and employed nearly 189,000 people worldwide. John B. Veihmeyer, based in New York City, is the Global Chairman of KPMG International.[3] KPMG's motto is 'Passion. Purpose. Perspective.'[4]

Focusing on its main service lines, the KPMG network of member firms offers audit, tax, and advisory services (see Figure 4.1). According to the figures posted in 2014,[5] audit represented 42 percent of the network's global revenues, followed by advisory with 37 percent and tax with 21 percent. The service lines are supported by a number of groups, including Innovation and Enterprise Solutions (I&ES) – the program owner for exploring cognitive innovations.

146

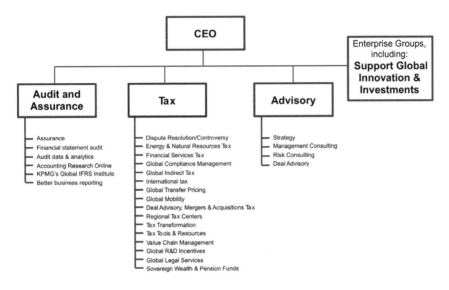

Figure 4.1: KPMG's major service lines

What made KPMG's leadership team recognise that cognitive automation was not only imminent, but something it needed to embrace? Well, KPMG began tracking cognitive technologies that were in various stages of development and deployment in the market. Some tools were quite impressive, but the maturity of IBM Watson in the healthcare sector gave KPMG's leaders the most confidence in the potential of cognitive technologies to transform the professional services industry. Both healthcare and professional services require advanced expertise and both industries are highly risk-aware and highly regulated. KPMG visited the key players at Watson's signature adopters – WellPoint and Memorial Sloan-Kettering (see Chapter 3). KPMG had enough preliminary data to envision how cognitive technologies could redesign professional services.

4.2.1. A Vision for the Future of Work

"We are at an inflection point in the way that humans relate to technology. This will be as impactful to labour as mechanical enablement was to workers in the Industrial Revolution. We

may see history record this exciting window of change as the 'Cognitive Revolution'." **Steve Hill, Global Head, Innovation and Investments, KPMG**[6]

A 2016 white paper summarises KPMG's views on how cognitive technologies will transform work (see Figure 4.2). KPMG asserts that cognitive technologies can accelerate the time required to make an employee proficient, augment decisions with machine generated insights, and scale expertise across the enterprise. As will be illustrated through the use cases described in this report, KPMG has shown that this vision is achievable.

A different kind of leverage model	
Cognitive automation is poised to remove constraints on people, time and capital throughout the enterprise:	
Casual expert → Skilled Expert	**Accelerate** time to employee proficiency
Inexperieced employee → Seasoned Veteran	
Speed and responsiveness	
Value through new insights	**Augment** decisions in the moment
Reduced risk	
Consistency of output	
Pursuit of adjacencies	**Scale** expertise within the enterprise
Revenue growth - without the proportional growth in headcount	

Figure 4.2: KPMG's vision for cognitive automation
(Source: Swaminathan (2016))[7]

KPMG had a clear vision for how cognitive automation technologies will affect its workforce. Like all the 'Big Four' professional service firms, KPMG relies heavily on their highly educated and highly certified workforces. ***KPMG aims to apply cognitive technologies to liberate skilled workforce*** *from routine tasks to more fully use their qualifications and critical thinking skills.* KPMG recruits thousands of employees each year, often people with advanced professional degrees and certifications. In the tax service line, for example, employees hold professional qualifications like Certified Public Accountants (CPAs) and many have passed their US State's bar exams. Such professionals expect their careers to be filled with challenging work that use their expertise, judgment, problem-solving, and decision-making skills. The reality in most organisations is that highly skilled professionals still spend too much time focused on mundane tasks. Auditors often search manually through reams of financial information to hunt down the anomaly that may give pause to the appropriateness of a company's assertion; lawyers spend too much time researching case law precedents and regulatory actions instead of advising courses of action. The mundane work, however, does not lend itself to RPA because audit, tax, and advisory work largely deal with vast amounts of unstructured data. Furthermore, outcomes are often multi-faceted and probabilistic rather than deterministic. For example, there could be multiple ways a client could comply with a regulation. So how might cognitive technologies help professionals do their jobs better? According to Cliff Justice, Partner, US Leader, Cognitive Automation and Digital Labour: *"Cognitive is a net positive for people to innovate and to allow people to invent new things."*

Cognitive technologies could increase profitability by taking out costs for many services, but cost reduction is not KPMG's major aim. KPMG recognised that a liberated workforce would yield a number of business benefits, most notably better services for clients and a distinct competitive advantage to being an early adopter. Todd Lohr, Principal, US Transformation Enablement Leader at KPMG, summarised the advantage as follows: *"Both within our internal services and for the services we provide to customers, automation is going to change the landscape of services and change the labour model."*

By 2015, KPMG leaders had enough compelling arguments and evidence to move forward with exploring cognitive technologies. The head of I&ES charged his group with figuring out how cognitive technologies could be infused in the overall digitisation of KPMG's core business lines, thus launching KPMG's cognitive journey.

4.3. KPMG's Cognitive Journey

The cognitive project was approved to go through I&ES's standard, three-phased innovation process (see Figure 4.3 for an overview of KPMG's innovation process).

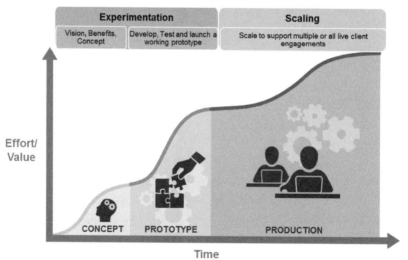

KPMG's holistic innovation execution approach

Balancing speed and risk while assisting clients execute their vision for transformation through cognitive automation

Figure 4.3: Conceptual voerview of KPMG's innovation process
(Source: KPMG, reprinted with permission)

Here's how the process typically works: During the first phase, KPMG experiments with an innovation to assess its technical capabilities and suitability for the specific context of KPMG. Vinodh Swaminathan, Managing Director, Innovation & Enterprise Solutions at KPMG, explained the reasoning for this phase: *"There's only so much we can rely on other people's experiences. We needed to experience cognitive for ourselves. We wanted our own fact base that is relevant to us."* The results of the experimental phase are reviewed to determine whether the innovation should proceed to the next phase. If approved, KPMG develops a prototype that applies the technology to a specific business service. Business sponsors are engaged; the prototype is tested using engagement data. Based on results, the business case is revised and reviewed for approval. If approved, KPMG develops and scales the application so that it will be ready for enterprise deployment. Once in the prototype phase, the business service sponsor owns every innovation, with I&ES employees serving as internal consultants and technicians.

KPMG initially selected two use cases that could demonstrate the value of cognitive, namely, business development and risk assessment of asset backed securities. An additional use case in audit was subsequently added. The company chose small projects that could serve as proxies for the type of work KPMG actually does at scale. Vinodh Swaminathan, Managing Director, Innovation & Enterprise Solutions at KPMG explained the logic: *"We wanted a contained environment where we could test this technology and concept in a relatively risk free setting."* KPMG aims to 'buy and configure' solutions rather than 'build and train' them. Internally, KPMG was tracking over 100 cognitive products, and realised early on that the business development case would likely be a 'buy and configure' project and the risk assessment case would likely be a 'build and train'. Next are the stories of the use cases.

4.3.1. Business Development Use Case

Business development was the first use case. At KPMG, an account manager is in charge of the client relationship. He or she coordinates the day-to-day account management activities and delivers on current obligations. The account manager also supports business development, such as identifying and proposing new services that will be valuable to the client.[8] Business development is challenging because of the data deluge. On the front end, the account manager has to keep track of the client's current challenges and opportunities, vis-à-vis the client's competitors and emerging trends, to identify new service opportunities. Then, the account manager needs to develop a compelling proposal that should draw on the experience from across KPMG. With 189,000 people working in member firms around the world - over 250 services in the service catalog, and thousands of client case studies of prior proposals - it's impossible for an individual account manager to know all what KPMG knows. For example, how does an account manager in Louisville, Kentucky confidently determine that she has accessed the best resources from the KPMG global network of member firms to pitch an optimal solution to her current client? And how might cognitive automation help? KPMG first looked for existing solutions to answer this question.

KPMG initially evaluated four different cognitive solution providers for the business development use case: IBM, two of IBM's ecosystem partners that use Watson, and an analytics company. IBM's Watson-based capability was the most closely aligned to KPMG's preference to 'buy and configure' as an approach for this use. IBM had already tested a business development-specific application based on Watson, and IBM had already piloted its own application internally to help IBM's sales force become better students of their own clients.

KPMG bought and configured Watson to help KPMG client account managers with business development. Six client account managers were recruited to work with the innovation team. One of their roles was to assess the quality of Watson's output. Watson's 'sweet spot' is accessing vast volumes of structured and unstructured data from a variety of sources and using inference-based logic to suggest options. KPMG gave Watson access to four news sources so KPMG's account managers could better track their clients: Twitter, Google News, S&P and Dunn & Bradstreet. Watson was also fed client-specific priorities; notes from account managers' meetings; access to the clients' websites; access to KPMG's service catalog that explains each service offering; the method for deploying the service; and additional context on when to suggest a particular service to clients. For one account manager, Watson suggested 10 service opportunities. The account manager was quite amazed – he had six of these on his radar but he never thought of the other four opportunities. He sold two of the four opportunities to his client. According to Cliff Justice, Partner, US Leader, Cognitive Automation and Digital Labour: *"Those account managers were pretty excited about the initial results."*

The prototype worked technically, but deployment was stalled by issues with some of the third-party content providers. Their revenue models charge for the number of *humans* who have access to their data. That model is easy to price and monitor. In a cognitive world, many content providers struggle with a pricing model. If a customer only needs Watson to read the data, process it, and retain it, what does this mean for their revenue model? It took months for the parties to work out an equitable arrangement. Ensuring the protection of data was another issue that delayed the launch; KPMG had to make sure that they had client consent related to the use of their data.

By end of 2016, KPMG had resolved the major issues and were scaling the use case and recruiting account teams across the organisation. KPMG planned to deploy this capability in a phased manner, keeping in mind that as a 'learning system', the application will continue to grow in expertise with exposure to more real-world situations. KPMG planned to add functionality after deployment, such as possibly extending Watson's natural language generation capabilities to actually build service proposals. Cliff Justice, for example, envisioned that in the future, businesses might move to completely digital business proposals and engagements for very small projects:

"So if you're a client, you might get an alert from your KPMG app that says, "you have this problem in this part of your business, would you like a proposal from KPMG to address it?" The client hits a button to request a proposal. If Watson's confidence score is high enough, Watson can send it through. If the confidence score is low, Watson can send it to the partner to review and sign off on it. It's a new way of engaging."

4.3.2. Risk Assessment Use Case

The second use case was assessing risk associated with financial investment instruments (e.g. securities) – a service provided by Advisory. KPMG knew this would be a bespoke solution because no other cognitive providers had developed an application for this particular context.

So what is this context? Investment banks hire KPMG to serve as an independent third party to make sure the bank followed procedures to create and offer new investment grade financial instruments. Only when KPMG is confident that the bank followed agreed upon procedures to create and offer the financial instrument, will KPMG sign the official 'comfort letter'. A comfort letter is one of many artifacts used by banks to demonstrate compliance.

The process works as follows: A bank hires KPMG to examine if the bank has followed all the agreed upon procedures that are associated with that particular financial instrument. The bank hands over all of the documents tied to the financial instrument. Each financial instrument is typically attached to a certain class of asset – e.g. residential property loans, commercial property loans, commercial loans, student loans, consumer loans and credit, etc. The underlying asset contains many supporting documents – for example, imagine all the documents a bank associates with a residential mortgage or commercial mortgage: promissory notes; environmental reports and surveys; tax returns; property photos; personal financial statement; and capital improvements summaries. All of this includes both structured and unstructured data. In the real world, sometimes these assets have changed ownership several times before becoming a part of the bank's portfolio of holdings. Collectively such documents hold a lot of information and insight into whether or not the bank followed due procedure and process to create the financial instrument. Using all of this data, KPMG builds its own independent assessment of risk. Vinodh Swaminathan, Managing Director, Innovation & Enterprise Solutions at KPMG, explained: *"In this particular service, it requires us to look at every single asset that is packaged as part of the financial instrument."* Once KPMG independently builds their assessment, the team evaluates the bank's compliance. KPMG informs the bank of any discrepancies the bank needs to fix. The bank and KPMG go through iterations of this process until KPMG can officially sign the 'comfort letter', attesting that the bank followed all of the procedures agreed upon to create the financial instrument properly.

For this use case, KPMG once again selected IBM Watson. The vision was that Watson would liberate the human experts from reading through documents so they could focus more of their time on gaining insights and doing analyses. Watson would be in charge of extracting risk related information from the documents to build KPMG's version of the truth. The human experts would be in charge of training Watson, doing the comparative analysis, suggesting changes, and ultimately approving the comfort letter.

During the prototype phase, KPMG trained Watson using historical data from one bank. The first task was to digitise all relevant documentation for Watson, such as using Optical Character Recognition (OCR) to scan paper documents. Watson was also fed a semantic ontology to define words and phrases used in the financial instrument context. Whenever Watson encountered a word or phrase that it could not confidently process, a human expert intervened. The human gave Watson the correct interpretation, thus training Watson and improving its accuracy over time. The results were promising according to Vinodh Swaminathan, Managing Director, Innovation & Enterprise Solutions at KPMG: *"Watson cranked through documents a lot faster."*

When scaling this use case, KPMG ran into a common front-end data problem that delayed the project by a few months. Although business strategists speak frequently about 'digital business', the reality is that many organisations still deal with scanned paper. Watson cannot easily read many PDF files of scanned documents. At KPMG, when Watson was making mistakes during training, one of the reasons was poor data quality. Once KPMG pre-processed the data, Watson's ability to read and identify potential risk factors improved.

For this use case, Watson showed promise. However, when KPMG calculated the hours saved if this application was scaled, the estimated ROI would not be large enough to justify the investment if Watson was deployed only on this one service. The use case did, however, enable KPMG to recognise that cognitive technologies could be applied to other services. Vinodh Swaminathan said: *"It opened our eyes to how we could completely transform the audit profession."* This prompted their most ambitious use case ...

4.3.3. Audit Use Case

The third, and most challenging, use case was auditing, a service provided by the Audit business line. Organisations hire KPMG to serve as an independent third party to give assurance over financial information used by investors and the capital markets. Only when KPMG has obtained sufficient audit evidence will KPMG sign the Report of Independent Registered Public Accounting Firm that accompanies the organisation's official filing of its financial statements.

Given the explosion of data and the digitisation of the business environment, KPMG determined that it was imperative that the firm evolve its tools and approach to allow for richer, more detailed audit evidence and provide its audit professionals with insights over processes, risks and controls to drive audit quality. Specifically, KPMG is embracing advanced technologies, including data and analytics, robotics and cognitive technology to manage processes, support planning and inform decision-making.

As a result of this, KPMG saw the potential for cognitive technologies to radically redesign the audit process. Once again, KPMG selected IBM Watson for the use case. According to a press announcement by KPMG and IBM:

> *"Cognitive technology helps allow for the possibility of a larger percentage of the data to be analysed [during an audit], providing KPMG professionals with the potential to obtain enhanced insights into a client's financial and business operations. At the same time, cognitive-enabled processes allow auditors to focus on higher value activities, including offering additional insights around risks and other related findings."*[9]

In the long term, instead of **statistical sampling**, a review of the **population** of documents could be possible.

KPMG focused the use case on auditing a financial instrument, thus piggybacking on the work of the previous use case. In a traditional audit, KPMG would audit a sample of commercial loans to assess the creditworthiness of individual loans. Depending on the size of the loan portfolio, a typical sample size would range from 40 to 150 loans. With Watson, all of the loan documents can potentially be read, and the Watson tool is trained to determine a 'confidence-based' loan grade, which is intended to be representative of the creditworthiness of the loan. This functionality can be expanded beyond the original sample size, and in some instances, can perform this activity for up to 100 percent of the population. Vinodh Swaminathan, Managing Director, Innovation & Enterprise Solutions at KPMG, explained how Watson was trained:

> *"The machine was trained using our subject matter professionals, including financial services auditors and credit risk professionals. It was also trained using historical data, which provides a treasure-trove of information."*

As of fourth quarter 2016, this use case was on track. Vinodh Swaminathan reported: *"We're well on our way to completion of this project and we are excited with the progress we have made to date."* Compared to the other use cases, no significant issues had delayed the project even though this use case required more sophisticated algorithms than the previous two. Several reasons account for this performance. First, KPMG was able to leverage its learning from the first two use cases, thus accelerating Watson's training process on this use case. Second, Watson has more data input options for this use case; for example, if the OCR quality for one document is too poor to read, Watson can extract the data from an alternative source. Vinodh Swaminathan concluded:

> *"It's been so successful that we have parts of our business now that are very keen to go to market. Although it doesn't provide the entire audit solution, they are comfortable selling just that piece of the capability."*

4.4. The Journey So Far and Future Use Cases

Within nine months of announcing its partnership with IBM, in March 2016, KPMG built a substantial internal cognitive capability. For the initial IBM Watson use cases, KPMG co-developed them with significant help from IBM technicians. Future use cases are expected to be developed using KPMG resources, with limited need for outside help. Use cases might include cognitive solutions for tax services; compliance services; regulatory risk consulting; due diligence; disclosures; contract analysis; contract compliance; call centres; contact centres; and customer care. As KPMG moves forward on its journey, the firm will also engage with, and seek input from, the Public Company Accounting Oversight Board (PCAOB).

So what's next? Although this report focused on KPMG's use of IBM Watson, it is vital to understand that the business strategy to transform professional services is leading KPMG. As such, KPMG does not have a Watson strategy or even a cognitive strategy – tools just enable the business strategy. Beyond cognitive technologies, KPMG is also looking to transform professional services with other emerging technologies, like Blockchain. We believe that Blockchain is to transactions, what the Internet is to information: it will likely decentralise, democratise, and disintermediate transactions.[10] How will the role of auditors be transformed where EVERY transaction in a Blockchain is public and verified over and over again? How will the role of lawyers be transformed when a Blockchain facilitates and executes smart contracts? There is already nearly $2 billion invested in Blockchain technologies[11], and KPMG is one such investor. Vinodh Swaminathan notes:

> *"KPMG is investing in Blockchain. If you look at life-cycle management, I would say it's probably where cognitive and digital labour was maybe 12 to 18 months ago, but that doesn't mean it's going to take 12 to 18 months to gestate. Technology cycles are getting faster. We're asking, "How does Blockchain innovate the professional services we provide?" We're already figuring out what Blockchain means for our business."*

4.5. Action Principles

As an early adopter of cognitive technologies, KPMG's case study offers a number of insights for other organisations considering similar technologies. The action principles derived from this case are listed below and discussed in detail in Chapter 8.

- Have a higher purpose
- Strategy drives CA investments
- Focus on the long-term value
- Use RPA as forward reconnaissance
- Manage as an innovation program
- Find the 'Lewis and Clark' program champions (see page 244)

- Look behind the provider's curtain
- Expect technical challenges as a first mover
- Find high impact CA use cases
- Don't underestimate the data challenge
- Find new data sources if 'dirty data' cannot be cleaned
- Compare CA training to human training
- Manage expectations up: Gain C-suite support without overselling
- Treat CA as lifelong learners
- Supervise all new CA learning
- Integrate service automation programs
- Prepare for a lot more effort than you think
- Plan for more work and jobs

Given KPMG's ambitions to reimagine professional services and its subsequent adoption of the widest ranging of all cognitive tools – IBM Watson – the action principles may not apply to organisations seeking more modest aims.

Citations

1. For a study of 13 early adopters of RPA tools, see Willcocks, L. and Lacity, M. (2016), *Service Automation: Robots and the Future of Work*, (SB Publishing, UK). Avaiulable from www.sbpublishing.org. Email info@sbpublishing.org.
2. https://en.wikipedia.org/wiki/Big_Four_accounting_firms.
3. https://en.wikipedia.org/wiki/KPMG.
4. 4https://home.kpmg.com/xx/en/home/about/international-annual-review-2015.html.
5. https://assets.kpmg.com/content/dam/kpmg/pdf/2014/12/kpmg-by-the-numbers-2014.pdf.
6. Quoted in Swaminathan, V. (2016), *Embracing the Cognitive Era.* KPMG White Paper.
7. Swaminathan, V. (2016), *Embracing the Cognitive Era.* KPMG White Paper.
8. Source: http://www.kpmg.com/id/en/careers/currentopenings/riskconsulting/pages/account-management-assistantmanagers.aspx.

9. *KPMG Announces Agreement With IBM Watson To Help Deliver Cognitive-Powered Insights.* March 8, 2016. http://www.prnewswire.com/news-releases/kpmg-announces-agreement-with-ibm-watson-to-help-deliver-cognitive-powered-insights-300231890.html.

10. See Lacity (2016) 'Technology Trends: Now, Soon, Later'. *Pulse Magazine,* Issue 26, p. 32-33.

11. https://www.cbinsights.com/reports/CB-Insights-BlockchainWebinar-March2016.pdf.

Chapter 5

Reimagining the University with Cognitive Technologies at Deakin

by Mary Lacity, Rens Scheepers, Leslie Willcocks and Andrew Craig

> *"Deakin University offers a personalised experience, enhanced by innovative digital engagement. We lead by creating opportunities to live and work in a connected, evolving world."*
>
> **Deakin University Website**[1]

> *"LIVE the Future essentially distills down to this: we don't care where a student is geographically, we care where they are academically and helping each student succeed during his or her entire journey."*
>
> **Professor Jane den Hollander AO, Vice Chancellor for Deakin University**

> *"Digital is the way we live."*
>
> **Professor Beverley Oliver, Deputy Vice-Chancellor (Education) for Deakin University**

5.1. Introduction

Nearly 40 Australian universities compete for national and international students in a country of 24 million people. In this chapter, we examine how one public university, Deakin University, competes for students by reimagining higher education through it's 'LIVE the Future' Vision. The vision is enabled by aggressive investments in digital technologies that enhance the student experience. Deakin University's adoption of IBM Watson is one such investment, and the focus of this chapter[1]. We focus on this particular investment because there are few visible adopters of cognitive automation (CA) technologies beyond the widely covered IBM Watson applications in healthcare. Potential adopters of IBM Watson and other CA technologies need realistic examples of the effort required to gain value from such investments.

Despite being located in what might seem to be 'distant' Australia, from a global perspective (see 'About Deakin' below), the university's innovativeness has brought it international attention. It had grown enrolments to 54,000 students by 2016. With its roots, in and reputation for, quality distance education, a third of its student body studies exclusively online. Deakin University's administrators think that online enrollments can increase substantially (to 100,000 or more) over the next ten years, provided the university delivers an exceptional student experience, significantly enabled by digital service.

This chapter first explains the university's vision and the role IBM Watson played within that larger picture. Then we describe the university's entire adoption journey from conception and deployment to future plans. We document the 'triple-win' value the investment yielded for the university, students, and staff. Finally, we list the key lessons on achieving that value, which will be fully explored in Chapter 8.

About Deakin: *Deakin University is a public university in the Australian state of Victoria. Established in 1974, in 2016 it had over 53,000 students[2] across its four physical campuses in Melbourne, Geelong, Warrnambool and Burwood.[3] The university calls its 'Cloud Campus' its fifth campus. About a third of its students study solely online.[4] Deakin prides itself on its overall student satisfaction score, which was rated the highest among Victoria's universities for six consecutive years. Deakin was also rated Victoria's top ranked university for students under 50 years of age for the past two years.[5]*

164

5.2. 'LIVE the Future'

Professor Jane den Hollander, the Vice-Chancellor, is credited as the architect of the 'LIVE the future' vision – a strategy that aims to put Deakin University at the edge of the digital frontier in higher education.[6] The Vice Chancellor, however, will be the first person to credit Deakin University's entire community for the plan. When she took the position in 2010, she was an outsider to Deakin, and engaged stakeholders to develop the new vision. She said: *"When I arrived, I knew we needed a new plan because the university was shutting down its distance learning. We assembled all the staff and invited everybody to answer the question: 'What should we do next?'"*

The university community settled on 'L-I-V-E the Future' – through Learning, Ideas, Value and Experience. Professor Beverley Oliver, Deputy Vice-Chancellor (Education), further explained:

> *"Underneath those words we have four large plans: student learning experience, research and development, community engagement and internationalisation. It's about giving people a brilliant education, wherever they're at physically, academically, philosophically and wherever they want to go in life."*

Focusing on the student experience part of the vision, the university creates effective and personalised digital experiences. Lucy Schulz, the Director of Cloud Campus, explained:

> *"The vision of the student journey program is to bring students to the centre of our thinking – in every area and on every level – so that students are enabled to be successful and feel supported throughout their time at Deakin."*[7]

Deakin University invests in technological innovations that enhance the student experience. William Confalonieri, Chief Digital Officer for Deakin

University, explained that technology investments are informed by the student culture, which he describes as 'the age of impatience' – students want digital technologies that are always on, always easy to use, and always fast.[8] Five megatrends inform the university's eStrategy: Place, Pace, Face, Space, and Trace. These correspond to mobility, flexibility, personalisation, collaboration, and information.[9] All of Deakin's technology investments, ranging from its learning management system to collaboration tools, are orchestrated under one seamless cloud-based hub called DeakinSync.[10] DeakinSync is the one-stop personalised dashboard that aggregates essential information for every student. When Deakin University decided to invest in IBM Watson, it was within the context of further enhancing the student experience and integrating the tool into the cloud-based hub.

5.3. Deakin University's IBM Watson Adoption Journey

As citizens of the world, many of Deakin University's administrators, staff and students were already familiar with IBM Watson from its televised championship on the game show, *Jeopardy!* For the purposes of the present chapter, it is worth recapping Watson's performance (see also Chapter 3). *Jeopardy!* is a US game show where humans compete to ask trivia questions after they are presented with convoluted clues. Clues contain innuendos, double entendres, metaphors, and puns. The game is extremely complex; it requires fast (under one second) processing of unstructured, culturally rich, natural language. IBM had to find a new way to program and subsequently developed its proprietary supervised machine learning algorithms. After four years in development, IBM Watson was tested live on television. Over the course of three days, in February 2011, Watson competed against the reigning human champions, Brad Rutter and Ken Jennings.[11] Watson won, earning $1 million dollars. This bellwether event signaled that the age of cognitive automation was upon us. For what other applications might Watson be used?

As we saw in Chapter 3, from 2011 to 2014, IBM Watson had primarily been deployed in healthcare. No university had bought the technology for any other application. In mid-2014, IBM personnel visited Deakin University's Vice Chancellor and Deputy Vice Chancellor to show them Watson. The administrators could immediately see the potential value, but they needed to learn more. They engaged IBM to do a cognitive value assessment. After that exercise, the administrators concluded there was enough potential value to pilot the new technology within a limited domain of responding to common asked questions using Watson's Engagement Advisor application.

5.3.1. Deakin University adopts Watson

In October 2014, Deakin University officially announced that it would adopt Watson. The aim was to provide students with a single source of accurate, current, and relevant information available on any device.[12] The university wanted Watson to improve the student experience by tailoring a student's queries to that particular student's own student profile. The Vice Chancellor summarised the vision as personalising the student experience by providing advice and information:

"Just in time, just for me, anytime, anywhere, on any device."[13]

IBM was the technical lead and Deakin University was the business lead. The university's IT department was also involved in various technical activities, such as linking Watson to Deakin's website. At that time in 2014, there were very few Watson experts in Australia, so IBM sent a team from the United States to launch the development.

5.3.2. Project Development

By December 2014, Deakin University and IBM had agreed to a plan, with three releases targeted for February, June, and September 2015. The first release would provide answers to commonly asked questions by incoming students, with access provided through its cloud-based hub, DeakinSync.

The second release would expand Watson's range of question categories, with the aspiration to make Watson a comprehensive destination for student queries. The third release aimed to personalise and contextualise the answers. The first release was divided into three stages:

Release 1, stage 1: Collect Questions. The first stage required collecting students' questions. The Deakin University team gathered nearly 20,000 questions from staff and administrators in charge of recruiting, scheduling, counseling, advising, and orientation. The IBM team helped to categorise the questions by student 'intent', as many were essentially seeking the same information, even though they were worded quite differently. From the initial collection of questions, 2,000 questions were selected for its first release.

Release 1, stage 2: Find Correct Answers. The second stage of the first release required getting the correct answers to each of the 2,000 questions. The content could come from many sources: verbal answers from experts, written responses contained in emails and documents, or multi-media content posted on webpages. As many first time CA adopters often discover, sources were not always up to date or accurate. The university had to assign a single content owner responsible for each subject area and have them provide the correct answers. For Watson's first public release, all the answers were handwritten to ensure accuracy and appropriateness with the help of 100 content owners from across campus.

Release 1, stage 3: Ready Content for Watson Ingestion. Once the correct answers were identified, the third stage entailed 'content uplift', where answers were appropriately worded and structured for Watson ingestion. Watson was ready to be tested.

The university asked students to volunteer, during their break, to test and train Watson. Over 200 students volunteered and indicated if Watson's answers were correct, incomplete, or inaccurate. Their feedback was incorporated into the application to improve Watson's performance (see Figure 5.1).

Figure 5.1: Student volunteers help train Watson in preparation for launch
(Source: https://www.youtube.com/watch?v=MK9gakgPDoc)

5.3.3. Release 1: Launch

Deakin University took just four months to get Watson ready for launch in time for student orientation week. During orientation week, the Watson team focused on creating awareness of Watson with new students. They erected a booth at orientation and showed students what Watson was and how to use it. According to one student who worked at the booth: *"We were inundated by student interest."* [14] The Watson developers explained that Watson was still learning, and that the university needed each student's help to further train Watson. The university launched a marketing campaign with the slogan, *'I'm helping train Watson'* to engage students and staff (see Figure 5.2).

Students and staff were told: *"The more you use Watson, the better it will get at helping you"*.[15] This campaign served to temper users' expectations of Watson's initial performance. Besides the booth at orientation, students were made aware of Watson on Deakin's website (see Figure 5.3) and on the current student webpage portal (see Figure 5.4). Students access Watson through DeakinSync by signing on with their logon ID and password.

Although Watson is designed primarily for students, Deakin staff members were encouraged to use it for their own enquiries. Additionally, about 100 staff members became content owners, responsible for Watson's content going forward.

Figure 5.2: Recruiting new students to train Watson at Orientation Week
(Source: https://www.youtube.com/watch?v=MK9gakgPDoc)

5.3.4. Watson's Initial Performance

Watson answered over 55,000 questions during the first twelve months. The university anticipated that students would most frequently ask questions about educational processes, such as how to enroll in classes. In reality, students most frequently asked Watson for information about finding dates, finding food, and the location of course materials – in that order.[16] Common questions, however, do change over the course of a semester. For example, questions about finding classrooms are more frequently asked at the beginning of the semester; questions about exams are more frequently asked later.

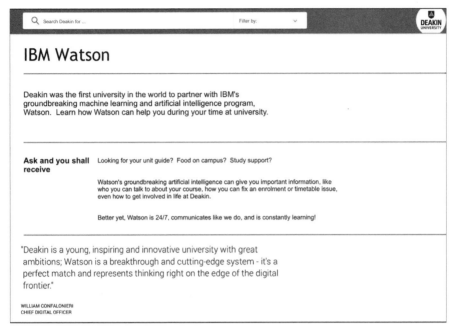

Figure 5.3: Deakin University's web portal explaining Watson to students
(Source: http://www.deakin.edu.au/life-at-deakin/why-study-at-deakin/ibm-waton)

Deakin University tracked Watson's response accuracy very closely – counting the number of direct questions Watson answered correctly or incorrectly, the options Watson generated appropriately or inappropriately, and the number of queries Watson indicated it did not know how to answer (see Figure 5.5). ***Watson performed quite well, correctly answering direct questions or offering appropriate options about 80 percent of the time.***

In addition to monitoring Watson's logs of actual conversations to assess performance, Deakin's Watson team members also looked at students' ratings of Watson's performance. After each conversation, Watson prompts the student to rate the quality of Watson's responses (see Figure 5.6). Based on a sample of 1,130 feedback ratings, students gave Watson 'good to excellent' ratings for 63 percent of the queries. This feedback was used to improve performance over time.

171

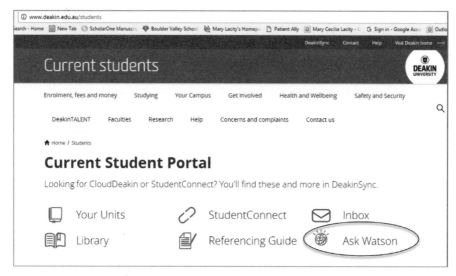

Figure 5.4: Student access to Watson through DeakinSync
(Source: http://www.deakin.edu.au/students)

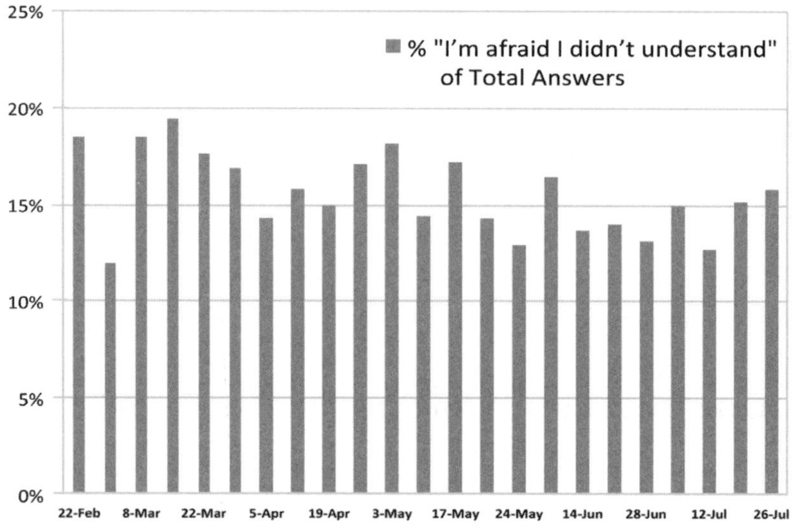

Figure 5.5: Percentage of questions Watson did not initially understand
Source: Deakin University presentation, March 2015

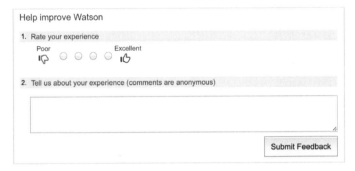

Figure 5.6: User feedback form for Watson

5.3.5. Releases 2 and 3: Expanded Capabilities

Deakin University continued to expand Watson's capabilities through its second and third releases. By November 2015, Watson was connected to Deakin's website and online handbook to find more answers; was further programmed to personalise information based on campus and student type (domestic vs. international); and started to share its confidence ratings for its answers with students.[17] As of 2017, Watson can guide students through common processes like submitting assignments, paying for parking, and re-enrolling in study.[18] Watson has been trained to answer 6,000 questions (see Figures 5.7(a) - 5.7(d) for sample conversations with Watson). Having concluded the IBM Watson adoption journey up to 2017, we discuss next the value generated from the investment. In addition, we outline subsequent developments, such as Deakin Genie, that emanated from the learning gained during the Watson project.

5.4. Case Discussion: Achieving the 'Triple-win'

Deakin's adoption of cognitive automation delivered value to three major stakeholders: the university as an institution, the students, and the staff (see Figure 5.8). Deakin University is not alone in achieving such results. Across all our cognitive automation cases, we have called the realisation of multiple sources of value the **'triple-win'** of service automation.[23]

173

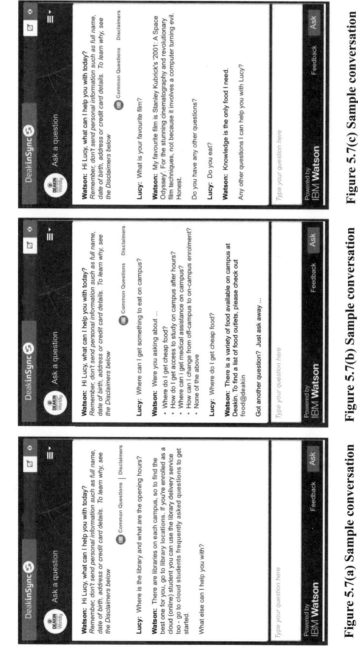

Figure 5.7(a) Sample conversation with Watson[19]

Figure 5.7(b) Sample conversation with Watson[20]

Figure 5.7(c) Sample conversation with Watson[21]

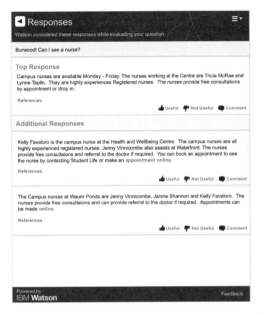

Figure 5.7(d) Sample conversation with Watson[22]

We note also that, as a fourth stakeholder, IBM's Watson team received value in terms of learning about developing and implementing their tools in specific contexts as was the case here with tertiary education.

5.4.1. Institutional value

"What were the outcomes? The main value was reputation and profile building for the university. It was worth the investment."
Professor Beverley Oliver, Deputy Vice-Chancellor (Education) for Deakin University

Deakin University was the first university adopter of IBM's Watson for student services, which gave the university worldwide media attention (see Figure 5.9). Deakin's Watson application won prestigious awards - for example, 1st place for the global 'Wharton-QS Re-imagining Education Stars' award within the ICT Support and Services category in 2015.[24]

INSTITUTIONAL VALUE	STUDENT VALUE	STAFF VALUE
♠ Improved competitive positioning	♠ Round the clock service delivery	♠ Learned new skills
♠ Raised brand awareness	♠ Faster access to critical human assistance without divulging personal details to another human being	♠ Focus on more critical tasks
♠ Increased personal attention at scale to support aggressive growth strategy		♠ Help deal with demand volatility
♠ Better content governance	♠ Learned new skills	♠ Raised awareness of the potential of cognitive service automation in teaching and research
♠ Created a single point of truth	♠ Increased response accuracy	
♠ Established a repository of questions students actually ask as input to business intelligence	♠ Multi-channel delivery	♠ Perceived investment as university commitment to growth

Figure 5.8: The 'triple-win' from cognitive automation at Deakin University

Requests for interviews, site visits, and speaking engagements came pouring in from across the globe. For instance, Deakin's Vice-Chancellor spoke at the 2015 IBM World of Watson as a keynote speaker.[25] The media attention, awards, and public events delivered institutional value in terms of improved competitive positioning and raising brand awareness.

Deakin University also gained value from its Watson investment in terms of progressing towards its goal of 'personal attention at scale'. University administrators aspire to double or even triple enrollments over the next decade, but scalability cannot cannibalise its rich student journeys. The administrators see Watson as enhancing the student experience while at the same time improving scalability.

Deakin University reported an unexpected source of value from its Watson investment: better content governance. In the process of curating content for Watson, Deakin University discovered that many of its data sources reported outdated or inaccurate content. So, for example, many sources reported

Figure 5.9: Sample media coverage of Deakin University's Watson adoption[26]
(Source: Deakin University presentation, 22nd April 2015)

conflicting library operating hours. The university remedied this by identifying content owners responsible for 'a single point of the truth'. Now, the content owners post the correct data on their own webpages and any other departments that want to include that content within their own domain webpages must point to the original source rather than copy and paste content. So, for example, the library is the sole content owner for library hours and other sources should point to the library's webpage rather than copy the content. Professor Jane den Hollander, Vice Chancellor for Deakin University, explained the value of a single point of truth: *"You go to Deakin, you ask a question, and it's always answered."* Deakin also experienced another benefit from establishing a repository of questions students actually asked: better business intelligence.

To present a balanced view on institutional value, we also report that Deakin University's investment did not produce measurable operational efficiencies or returns-on-investment (ROI) in the short-term. Indeed, Gartner reported on Deakin University's ROI in 2016:

> *"The university does not yet have hard return on investment (ROI) metrics for the Watson deployment. Attributing ROI budget benefits in terms of reputation and student satisfaction will likely remain hard to quantify. Part of the reason for this is the difficulty of attributing benefits to individual IT systems such as Watson."*[27]

This lack of measurable ROI was a common finding across our other CA adopters. In Chapter 8 'Action Principles', we answer the question: How does an organisation calculate a return on investment when members of staff are not laid off as a consequence of automation?

5.4.2. Student Value

> *"Watson revolutionises the student experience and engagement and transforms the way students get advice and answers to questions about their study and life at Deakin."*[28]

Deakin University reported that IBM Watson yielded multiple sources of student value, including round the clock service delivery, faster access to critical human assistance, enhanced skills, increased response accuracy, and multi-channel delivery.

Deakin University aimed to use cognitive automation to provide round the clock service availability and delivery. Prior to Watson, students were contacting the university's offices at any time of the day or night and on weekends to ask questions, but most offices closed at 4:00pm local time and only operated on weekdays. Students were forced to leave voice messages or send emails when the offices were closed. If a student left a message after hours on a Friday, it could take three days for the student to receive a response. Professor Jane den Hollander, the Vice Chancellor, explained: *"Our counsellors would come in the morning and immediately start dealing with 73 voicemail messages."* As Deakin University increasingly expanded its online programs to students around the globe, 24-hour service availability became critical. The Vice Chancellor continued: *"As our students started to come from everywhere, we knew our big vulnerability at the digital frontier was that we couldn't service them at 24/7. Watson is always up and running, making services available to students at anytime."*

Watson also provides fast access to critical human assistance. Student depression is a concern on every university campus. Deakin University has professional counselling services available for any student. Its website states:

> *"If there's something bothering you, however big or small, help is at hand. Our counsellors are registered psychologists and social workers. They have extensive experience working with students with mental health issues, ranging from adjustmet stress to common mental illnesses like anxiety and depression. The service is free and confidential."*[29]

Students do not always have the courage to contact the counselling office directly, but some students have confided their despair to Watson. Watson is programmed to point students to critical human assistance and it proactively alerts the counselling staff that a student needs help. Professor Jane den Hollander, the Vice Chancellor, explained:

> *"We've stopped more than a couple of people from spiraling down into depression through urgent intervention. Students know that when we are concerned for them, we have someone, confidentially, contact them."*

Hundreds of students were involved in the training and testing of Watson to ensure Watson understood the student voice. Professor Jane den Hollander, Vice Chancellor for Deakin University, explained:

"I wanted students involved because I thought "Who's going to be clever with this technology? It will be the students." So we got the students engaged and they thought the technology was cool. They loved the idea of training a machine. They understood quickly that the more they interacted with the machine, the better the machine performed. There were some very smart students who led all that."

Student engagement proved very valuable, not only in enabling the first release to be delivered on time, but it gave students the opportunity to learn new skills while developing a new leading-edge digital technology.[30]

The students recruited for Watson's content curation, testing, and training, learned valuable new skills about the technology. Additionally, their involvement also helped to hone more general skills; Deakin University has eight specific learning outcomes for all students, regardless of major. These are:

1. Digital literacy
2. Communication skills
3. Critical thinking
4. Problem solving
5. Discipline-specific knowledge
6. Self-management
7. Teamwork
8. Global citizenship

The university believes these skills are highly valued by employers and prepare students to be work-ready. The students involved in the Watson project had to work on a team to quickly solve problems so as to meet a tough deadline of just four months! They also had to help disseminate knowledge to the entire student body.

Students also gained value from the university's better content governance and single point of truth: they now get **more accurate responses** to their questions. Prior to Watson, phone contact and email enquiries were the main channels for students' questions. Watson opened **another channel for service delivery**.

5.4.3. Staff Value

Watson objective: *"Free up time for student service staff to enable them to respond and attend to more critical and complex issues."*[31]

Given that automation technologies can threaten human jobs, one might naturally assume that the staff would feel threatened by the technology. Deakin University initially faced a small amount of apprehension that was quickly overcome when the university told them the purpose of Watson was to help them, not eliminate them. Professor Beverley Oliver, Deputy Vice-Chancellor (Education), explained: *"We told the narrative very carefully when we introduced Watson, because we didn't want people to worry: 'Am I going to lose my job?'"* The university was very careful about messaging the purpose of Watson as an alternative channel and not as staff replacement.

Some value to staff members was evident. The staff members who serve as content owners learned new skills in curating content for Watson ingestion and ongoing upkeep. Watson also freed up staff for higher-value student support, which was a main objective from the start. Watson also helped to deal with demand volatility, as students' service needs are not uniform over a semester. As of 2017, Watson was answering about 3,000 queries per week – questions the staff did not have to answer. We note, however, that as enrolments increased, all channels experienced increased volumes, so while the staff was answering fewer common questions, they were no less busy.

The Watson project also made staff aware of the potential of cognitive automation in teaching and research in addition to student services. And certainly, the staff perceived the investment as evidence of the university's commitments to growth and quality.

181

In addition to Deakin University delivering value to the institution, students, and staff, the university also enacted a number of principles that serve as lessons for other organisations. These are listed in 5.6. below.

5.5. What's Next for Cognitive?

Deakin's Chief Digital Officer, William Confalonieri, explained the next phase vision for cognitive technology usage:

> *"The future of education is personalised, but to do that at scale will only be possible with technology…I'm not suggesting that the human element will be replaced, but the balance will change. I see a completely different education. We are taking the opportunity to define what is possible with this technology."[32]*

Deakin University was also considering the possibility of using Watson as a teaching assistant, much like Georgia Tech has done.[33] Georgia Tech deployed Watson as a teaching assistant for a large section of a course on Artificial Intelligence (AI). The professor, Dr. Ashok Goel, did not inform his class that 'Jill Watson' was an AI until the end of the semester. Most students were surprised to learn that Jill was not human.[34] Professor Beverley Oliver, Deputy Vice-Chancellor (Education) for Deakin University offered another potential Watson application: *"If MOOCs[35] can deliver course content to scale, perhaps cognitive virtual agents like Watson could engage students and perform student assessment to scale."* Deakin University will continue to reimagine higher education.

5.6. Action Principles

As an early adopter of cognitive technologies, Deakin University's case study offers a number of insights for other organisations considering similar technologies. The action principles derived from this case are listed below (and discussed in detail in Chapter 8):

182

- Strategy drives CA investments
- Consider competitors' reactions
- Focus on the long-term value
- Find the 'Lewis and Clark' program champions (see page 244)
- Put in place a strong in-house team
- Negotiate the optimal level of client-provider transparency
- Expect technical challenges as a first mover
- Find high impact CA use cases
- Don't under estimate the data challenge
- Fix discoveries about process flaws before implementing CA
- Manage expectations up: Gain C-suite support without overselling
- Manage expectations down: Envision, communicate and deliver value to employees
- Manage expectations out: Be transparent with customers
- Treat CA as lifelong learners
- Invite customers to try CA, but keep other channels open
- Supervise all new CA learning
- Keep subject matter experts continually engaged in curation[36]
- Integrate service automation programs
- Continually innovate because today's 'cool' is tomorrow's 'yawn'
- Prepare for a lot more effort than you think
- Plan for more work and jobs than many predict

Citations

1. http://www.deakin.edu.au/about-deakin.

2. http://www.deakin.edu.au/about-deakin.

3. https://en.wikipedia.org/wiki/Deakin_University.

4. Deakin University Vice Chancellor Professor Jane den Hollander's speech at IBM 'World of Watson'. https://www.youtube.com/watch?v=BQU7Ko63E5k.

5. Student satisfaction scores are measured by Australian Graduate Survey http://www.deakin.edu.au/.

6. https://en.wikipedia.org/wiki/Jane_den_Hollander.

7. Lucy Schulz, *Kicking goals with Watson.* Presentation at ATEM Student Services Centres conference, 29th May 2015.

8. William Confalonieri, *Creating effective and personalized digital experiences.* Presentation for the Connect Show, Melbourne, 22nd April, 2015.

9. William Confalonieri, *Creating effective and personalized digital experiences.* Presentation for the Connect Show, Melbourne, 22nd April, 2015.

10. William Confalonieri, *Creating effective and personalized digital experiences.* Presentation for the Connect Show, Melbourne, 22nd April, 2015.

11. NOVA documentary, *Smartest Machine on Earth.* Aired 2nd May 2012 on PBS. http://www.pbs.org/wgbh/nova/tech/smartest-machine-on-earth.html.

12. Adhikari, S., 'ANZ, Deakin University set to harness Watson'. *The Australian,* Oct 8, 2014. http://www.theaustralian.com.au/business/latest/anz-deakin-university-set-to-harness-watson/news-story/3b35da14a4571bb30406afab0cd f7a45.

13. Deakin University Vice Chancellor Professor Jane den Hollander's speech at IBM 'World of Watson'. https://www.youtube.com/watch?v=BQU7Ko63E5k.

14. Watson @ Deakin University. Video posted 18th March 2015. https://www.youtube.com/watch?v=MK9gakgPDoc.

15. Watson @ Deakin University. Video posted 18th March 2015. https://www.youtube.com/watch?v=MK9gakgPDoc.

16. Adhikari, S., 'ANZ, Deakin University set to harness Watson'. *The Australian,* Oct 8, 2014. http://www.theaustralian.com.au/business/latest/anz-deakin-university-set-to-harness-watson/news-story/3b35da14a4571bb30406afab0cd f7a45.

17. *IBM Watson helps Deakin drive digital frontier.* Press release 25th November 2015. http://deakinprime.com/news-and-publications/news/ibm-watson-helps-deakin-drive-the-digital-frontier.

18. http://www.deakin.edu.au/life-at-deakin/why-study-at-deakin/ibm-watson

19. Lucy Schulz, *Kicking goals with Watson*. Presentation at ATEM Student Services Centres conference, 29th May 2015.

20. Lucy Schulz, *Kicking goals with Watson*. Presentation at ATEM Student Services Centres conference, 29th May 2015.

21. Lucy Schulz, *Kicking goals with Watson*. Presentation at ATEM Student Services Centres conference, 29th May 2015.

22. Lucy Schulz, *Kicking goals with Watson*. Presentation at ATEM Student Services Centres conference, 29th May 2015.

23. See for Example: Lacity, M., Willcocks, L. and Craig, A. (2017), *Service Automation: Cognitive Virtual Agents at SEB Bank*. The LSE Outsourcing Unit Working Research Paper Series.

24. Deakin University Vice Chancellor at IBM 'World of Watson'. http://application.reimagine-education.com/the-winners/2015.

25. https://www.youtube.com/watch?v=BQU7Ko63E5k.

26. William Confalonieri, *Creating effective and personalized digital experiences*. Presentation for the Connect Show, Melbourne, 22nd April 2015.

27. Ingelbrecht, N., and Lowendahl, J. (2016), *Deakin University Uses Smart Machines to Innovate Student Engagement*. Gartner Report G00300625.

28. Watson@Deakin - Reimagine Education Award Announcement, 2015. http://application.reimagine-education.com/the-winners-individual/2015/72/6e06cbde6c4067bc9b8edc6d624c222f/Deakin+University.

29. http://www.deakin.edu.au/life-at-deakin/support-services/counselling.

30. Watson@Deakin - Reimagine Education Award Announcement, 2015. http://application.reimagine-education.com/the-winners-individual/2015/72/6e06cbde6c4067bc9b8edc6d624c222f/Deakin+University.

31. Watson@Deakin - Reimagine Education Award Announcement, 2015. http://application.reimagine-education.com/the-winners-individual/2015/72/6e06cbde6c4067bc9b8edc6d624c222f/Deakin+University.

32. Adhikari, S., 'ANZ, Deakin University set to harness Watson'. *The Australian*, Oct 8, 2014. http://www.theaustralian.com.au/business/latest/anz-deakin-university-set-to-harness-watson/news-story/3b35da14a4571bb30406afab0cdf7a45.

33. Trounson, A. (2015), 'Answers are elementary to Deakin's Watson Computer'. *The Australian*, 25th November 2015. http://www.theaustralian.com.au/higher-education/answers-are-elementary-to-deakins-watson-computer/news-story/9fc95931f3576f2f2a01d8f376ec69c4.

34. *A teaching assistant named Jill Watson.* Professor Ashok Goel's Tedtalk at https://www.youtube.com/watch?v=WbCguICyfTA.

35. MOOC in an acronym for Massive Open Online Courses.

36. Data 'curation' is a broad term used to indicate processes and activities related to the organisation and integration of data collected from various sources, annotation of the data, and publication and presentation of the data such that the value of the data is maintained over time, and the data remains available for reuse and preservation.

Chapter 6

Cognitive Virtual Agents at SEB

by Mary Lacity, Leslie Willcocks and Andrew Craig

> *"Somewhat as a surprise, the people most motivated by having Amelia in both cases – the internal and the external services – are the service desk personnel. That's what we found."*
>
> **Nicolas Moch, Head of Information, Strategy & Architecture**

> *"It's still a very early technology. It's not a magic wand. I advise not viewing cognitive tools as the ultimate cost cutting tool because, while it can help do that, the real value is the way it changes the way you operate."*
>
> **Nicolas Moch, Head of Information, Strategy & Architecture**

6.1. Introduction

In this chapter, we examine how IPsoft's cognitive virtual agent (CVA), called 'Amelia', is being deployed at SEB, a leading Nordic corporate bank. CVAs like Amelia are software platforms designed to perform like a human service agent using natural language interactions (see Chapter 3 - 3.5: 'About IPsoft Amelia'). As a CVA, Amelia has attributes of both Cognitive Automation (CA) and Robotic Process Automation (RPA) tools as we define them.[1] Like other CA technologies, Amelia automates tasks using ***inference-based*** processes to interpret ***unstructured*** (and structured) data, but unlike other CA tools, Amelia does not produce a set of likely results. Instead, Amelia is a deterministic platform that executes enterprise processes according to instructions, much like RPA tools do.

In this case study, we describe SEB's successful implementation of IPsoft's Amelia. SEB's installation was Amelia's first Swedish speaking engagement. The bank first deployed the software for internal services on the IT service desk. As of August 2016, SEB deployed Amelia to help with two internal IT service desk functions: Identity Access Management and Knowledge Management. These represented 15 percent of the call volume at the time (see Table 6.1). Following the success of that implementation, in December 2016 SEB launched the software as an additional channel to service external customers. By May 2017, SEB was surprised to discover that the CVA was attracting a new customer base. SEB describes the initiative as a learning project, conducted live, with active customers. Together, SEB and its customers will help shape the future of digital services.

Customers	Live Deployment Date	Services	Channel	Initial Results
Internal Customers	August 2016	Identity Access Management and Knowledge Management (IT Service Desk)	Web and mobile app	• Software executed 50% of calls without human intervention – representing 15% of call volumes • Services were delivered up to five times faster • Services were more consistent
External Customers	December 2016	Customer queries	Web app	• The additional channel attracted a new customer base • CVA successfully handled about 90 percent of the 300 conversations per day

Table 6.1: SEB's cognitive virtual agent adoption at a glance

Organisations still considering the adoption of virtual agents can learn valuable insights from SEB. A major lesson for future organisational adopters: If you just think of CVAs as a staff reduction tool, you will miss the competitive advantage and transformative potential of the technology. SEB, and other early adopters of automation technologies that we have studied, gained a 'triple-win' from automation: a win for customers, a win for employees, and a win for shareholders.

To put the adoption journey and nine practices into context, we next explain SEB's business background.

6.2. SEB - The Business Context

> *"SEB's long-term vision reflects a future in which customer orientation and digitisation increase in importance. In this environment, the bank's ambition is to be the undisputed leading Nordic corporate and institutional bank, and the top universal bank in Sweden and the Baltic countries. SEB will focus on providing a leading customer experience, investing in digital interfaces and automated processes, and on being the most attractive employer."*
> **SEB 2015 Annual Report**[2]

SEB is a Nordic financial group that provides banking and financial services in Sweden, Estonia, Latvia, Lithuania, Denmark, Norway, Finland, and Germany. Headquartered in Stockholm, in 2016 it had over 13,500 employees and generated revenues of over 44 SEK billion (approximately €4.6 billion euros). Annika Falkengren served as President and CEO from 2005 to 2016; Johan Torgeby became CEO in 2017. As of 2016, SEB served 2,300 large corporations, 700 financial institutions, 267,000 corporate home bank customers and 1.4 million private home bank customers.[3]

The organisational structure is aligned with these customer segments, comprising the Large Corporations and Financial Institutions division, the Corporate and Private Customer division, and the Baltic division (see Figure 6.1). Life & Investment Management was formed in 2015 to provide life insurance and fund management services to it three customer divisions. The Business Support and Group Staff Division, headed, since 2011, by Martin Johansson, support the customer-facing divisions.

Across the organisation, SEB aims to be the leader in digitally-enabled financial services:

> *"SEB's focus will be on customer journeys using digital solutions and support in order to create a leading customer experience in all segments. This includes offering personalised advice and transforming the first line of service to digital solutions and portals so that customers can choose where and in what manner they want to be served."* **SEB 2015 Annual Report**[4]

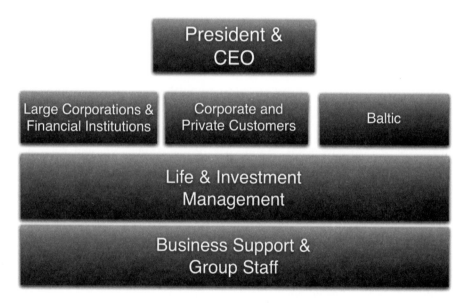

Figure 6.1: SEB's organisational structure

Some of the key players leading the digital strategy agenda include the Chief Strategy Officer, the Chief Digital Officer, the Group CIO and Head of IT Services. The bank has been doing proof-of-concepts and developing use cases with a number of advanced cognitive tools across all their customer divisions. This case study focuses on one such tool – their adoption of IPsoft's cognitive virtual agent.

6.3. SEB's Cognitive Virtual Agent Journey

Digital innovations are driving transformation in both front and back offices at SEB, as exemplified by SEB's journey to adopt cognitive virtual agents. SEB first adopted the technology for internal services (back office) and then adopted it for external services (front office). SEB chose to first deploy IPsoft's Amelia for its internal IT service desk in 2016. The selection of this particular platform was a natural progression, as SEB had previously adopted IPsoft's IPcenter in 2014. IPcenter is an ITIL[5], Six Sigma[6], and COBIT[7]-compatible product that helps automate and govern IT service delivery.[8]

6.3.1. IPsoft Amelia selection

When SEB adopted IPcenter, it was aware that IPsoft was developing a cognitive virtual agent, and continued to track IPsoft's progress on bringing Amelia to market. Beyond Amelia, SEB was also tracking other cognitive tools to see which tools would provide SEB customers with the fastest, best and most innovative services. Cognitive tools would also transform the workforce, as described by Nicolas Moch, Head of Information, Strategy & Architecture at SEB: *"We knew we were going to have virtual assistants and robots as part of our workforce in the next few years. We wanted to learn quite fast by being an early innovator."*

After assessing many cognitive automation tools[9], SEB decided to select Amelia as its first virtual cognitive agent. Amelia could be integrated with IPcenter, allowing Amelia to execute tasks rather than simply initiate a service desk ticket"[10], thus enabling end-to-end process automation. Nicolas Moch said: *"When we scanned the market, we didn't find really anything that is comparable to Amelia that could be quick to get something to the market and to meet our goal to learn quickly."*

The Amelia project was co-sponsored by the Group CIO (Nicholas Moch) and the Head of IT Services (Anders Collin). SEB decided to install the Amelia software on SEB's internal servers rather than deploy as a cloud service because of compliance and legal concerns with cloud delivery. According to Edwin van Bommel, Chief Cognitive Officer for IPsoft, SEB's choice is typical of most customers in the banking, insurance and financial services and asset management sectors: *"These customers prefer to keep their data on premises."*

To train SEB employees how to use Amelia, some of IPsoft's top Amelia developers from New York came to Sweden to conduct onsite workshops. SEB employees learned to configure Amelia by specifying neural, process, and emotional ontologies (see Chapter 3: About IPsoft's Amelia). Initially, three SEB employees were trained. In addition, IPsoft also has implementation partners like Deloitte, Accenture, NTT Data and others to help customers learn and implement Amelia.

6.3.2. Use case selection

For the first live deployment, SEB wanted to try Amelia out on internal services. Mikael Andersson, transformation lead at SEB, explained that SEB wanted to become accustomed to the platform before offering it as a service option to external customers: *"We decided pretty quickly to try it out in our IT service desk."* [11] The IT service desk provides SEB employees with all sorts of services, ranging from routine to complex. During the workshops, employees identified about 80 services as candidates for Amelia. The list was narrowed down to four services based on volume of calls: password resets; unlocking active directory accounts; unlocking mortgage applications for home loans; and pointing employees to the right IT service solution. SEB describes these first three use cases as 'Identity Management' services, and the last use case as 'Knowledge Management'. Two such services are described next, in more detail. These four use cases account for about 15 percent of the total call volume.

Identity Management example: Password reset. Using data gathered from the IPcenter, SEB could quite clearly detect, for example, a high number of calls on Mondays from employees who forgot their passwords. Employees can reset their passwords from their own computers, but in order to do that, employees need their passwords to log in! Given the high call volume, some employees were waiting up to 30 minutes for their calls to be answered, generating many lost hours of productivity across the bank. This was a perfect test case for Amelia – the process was simple enough: configure Amelia to prompt employees for correct information, verify information against systems of record, and then execute the password reset without human intervention. Nicolas Moch, Head of Information, Strategy & Architecture, explained:

> *"This was a simple use case that was not too complicated for Amelia. We wanted to be able to connect Amelia to actually do something, not just start a conversation and pass the call to a human. For us, the real value is about driving automatic process execution."*

Knowledge Management example: Finding the right IT service. Many employees call the IT service desk simply to find out how to access services. Typical questions include:

"How do I order remote access?" [12]
"Where is the form to request a new computer?"
"How do I access to this software?"

6.3.3. Streamline and standardise business processes

SEB documented and reviewed its existing processes in preparation for training Amelia. As the team went through drawing the processes on a whiteboard, they discovered legacy steps that no longer served a business purpose, but were still being executed by the human service agents *"because we have always done it this way."* SEB was forced to confront its own bad processes. While this could be alarming, it had an overall positive impact on the business. Nicolas Moch, Head of Information, Strategy & Architecture, said: *"There is no way of lying, there is no way of getting around and finding shortcuts. You have to expose the process as it is."*[13]   During development, SEB streamlined and standardised processes to ensure faster, more consistent services. Thus, a traditional process improvement method, combined with automation, delivered the ultimate business benefits.

6.3.4. Amelia deployed for internal services

The Amelia pilot rolled out on August 29, 2016. SEB alerted employees that Amelia was now a service option through its IT service desk phone system. When employees called the IT service desk, the automated phone system told employees they could go to the Amelia website or could use the Amelia mobile app loaded on all corporate mobile phones to execute certain IT service requests, e.g. password resets, unlocking accounts, or finding IT services. SEB employees engage Amelia by using natural language chat (i.e. text, *not* voice). In addition, the software collected the employees' feedback. Within three weeks, Amelia handled 4,000 conversations with over 700 SEB employees.[14] Amelia resolved about 50 percent of the calls without human intervention.

6.3.5. Amelia granted green light for external services

The four internal use cases were deemed successful. According to one source:

> *"Huge benefits have been derived from the IT service desk pilot. The company had not had a text-based chat channel for the IT service desk before Amelia arrived, and its primary channel was phone support."*[15]

SEB had always intended to deploy Amelia for customer-facing services, but the bank wanted to master the technology with internal services first. According to one press announcement: *"The decision to place Amelia in the front office builds on the successful first phase deployment of Amelia in an internal IT Service Desk supporting SEB's 15,000 strong workforce.*[16]

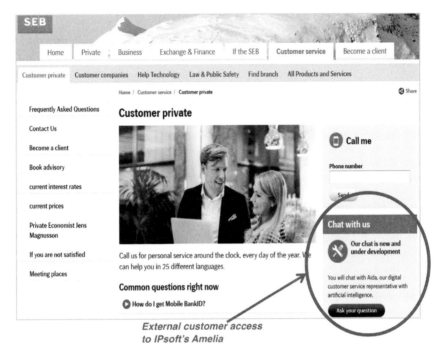

Figure 6.2: SEB customer website with option to chat with IPsoft's Amelia (called Aida)
(Please note: Page was translated from Swedish to English using Google Translate)

SEB selected its first external use case by applying the same criteria: which are the most common and the simplest requests to complete? Three external service requests met these criteria: providing information on how to become a customer, ordering an electronic ID, and explaining how to do cross-border payments. Concerning the first service request, SEB's service line (called the 'phone bank' internally) quite commonly received calls from potential customers asking, *"How can I become a customer of SEB?"* In Sweden, bank customers need to verify their identity in person before they are allowed to open accounts, so Amelia cannot complete this transaction end-to-end. But the software informs customers of all the steps in the process for becoming a customer of different types of services (bank account customer, mortgage customer, etc.). Amelia can perform the step of ordering an electronic ID without any issues. For the third service, Amelia explains to customers all the steps needed for cross-border payments. Amelia's knowledge base was also loaded with many other types of data, including the human experts to contact directly when the software escalates calls.

Amelia was named 'Aida' for these external customer-facing services. Aida was deployed as an alternative channel on the web-based application (see Figure 6.2). The Bank was very transparent that Aida was a virtual cognitive assistant (see Figure 6.3) and is not yet available on the customer mobile application. Figure 6.4 shows a sample conversation with Aida.

**Figure 6.3: Customer interface with SEB's implementation of
IPsoft's Amelia (called Aida)**
(Please note: Page was translated from Swedish to English using Google Translate)

Figure 6.4: Sample conversation with Aida and a customer

(Please note: Page was translated from Swedish to English using Google Translate)

Note that SEB did not spend time or money on market research to assess their customers' potential interest in Aida – SEB viewed this as a live experiment. The bank wanted to learn how customers reacted to the software, how Aida affected their behaviours, and how well Aida helped them. Mikael Andersson, SEB Transformation Lead-Amelia Exploration, said: *"We will see which customer base this appeals to, but our hopes are that it will grow. What should help is the fact that the trial is in Sweden, because people here are*

197

pretty fast at adapting to change."[17] One month after the launch, the customer feedback had been positive, but suggested a need to be more human-like in the conversational space.

By May 2017, Aida was competent at helping customers with mobile bank ID; accounts, cards; SEB products and services; banking terms; booking a meeting with a banker; and providing branch office information. Aida was successfully completing about 90 percent of the 300 conversations she was handling a day. Among the successfully executed conversations are the 30 percent of conversations for which Aida is instructed to escalate the conversation to a human agent. For SEB, the CVA is not about removing human contact, but about finding the best way to service a client.

6.3.6. Building an Enterprise Competency

> *"Amelia's performance to date has inspired SEB to continue the journey of exploring Amelia.*"[18]

SEB plans to scale and expand its cognitive capabilities across the enterprise. SEB set up its own cognitive **Centre of Excellence** (CoE) to build an in-house talent pool of individuals who develop and operate automations based on cognitive technologies. The Group IT division focuses on strategy and the IT delivery division focuses on operations. They jointly manage the CoE, which reports to the Business Board.

By 2017, SEB had trained about 15 employees from both IT and client business lines to staff the CoE. For the Amelia application, CoE employees supervise Amelia's learning, monitor performance and identify new opportunities for applying the technology to transform customer journeys.[19] Why were these individuals selected? While a basic understanding of how computers are programmed was deemed a necessary prerequisite skill, SEB did not find that any specific knowledge about cognitive technology was required. Rather, SEB recruited employees based on their interest in the project. According to

Nicolas Moch, Head of Information, Strategy & Architecture at SEB: *"I don't think you need special knowledge. Fascination, an interest in the technology, and a willingness to learn are the best criteria."*

Edwin van Bommel, Chief Cognitive Officer for IPsoft, also talked about the new jobs and skills organisations need in a CoE to sustain, improve, and integrate all the organisation's AI solutions:

> *"People like AI trainers and subject matter experts are needed for day-to-day execution at one level, but at a higher level, organisations need cognitive capabilities that capture intelligence about your operations, further improve and further automate processes."*

6.4. Case Discussion: Achieving the 'Triple-win'

Our research on SEB and on other early adopters of automation technologies has found that best practice organisations gain a 'triple-win' from automation: a win for customers, a win for employees, and a win for shareholders (see Figure 6.5).

CUSTOMER VALUE	EMPLOYEE VALUE	SHAREHOLDER VALUE
♠ Faster service resolution	♠ More interesting work	♠ Competitive advantage
♠ Improved service consistency	♠ Learn new skills	♠ Increased scalability
♠ Round the clock availability	♠ Increased employee satisfaction	♠ Increased agility
♠ Multi-channel delivery		♠ Operational efficiencies
		♠ High long-term ROI
		♠ Increased compliance

Figure 6.5: The `triple-win' from cognitive automation at SEB

199

6.4.1. Customer Value

"Customer service is a key differentiator. By making Amelia available to respond to queries, we enhance our customers' flexibility of receiving individualised support at a time that suits them and without any delays in response," **Rasmus Järborg, SEB's Chief Strategy Officer[20]**

SEB reported multiple customer benefits from the CVA applications, including faster service resolution, improved service consistency, round the clock availability, and multi-channel delivery.

Faster service resolution. SEB aimed to use cognitive virtual agents to speed service delivery, and the internal use cases produced measurable results within a few weeks. Before Amelia, a typical Monday-morning service resolution time for password resets was 20 minutes – most of which was time employees waited on hold before interacting with a human service desk agent. After Amelia, the typical resolution time was three to four minutes. Thus, services were delivered five times faster!

Improved service consistency. When humans are trained to perform a service, variability will inevitably result. While the human factor can enhance a service, it also leads to the possibility of misinformation or lack of compliance with standards. SEB found that some service desk teams within the organisation were indeed using an old process to reset passwords, and using old security questions that employees had forgotten.

SEB found that service consistency improved because of Amelia. 'She' executes exactly as instructed each and every time. Training Amelia also proved to be faster and cheaper than training the equivalent number of humans because the information only needed to be given once.[21]

Round the clock service delivery. The Amelia software is always up and running, thus making services available 24 hours a day. Mikael Andersson,

SEB Transformation Lead-Amelia Exploration, said: *"Opening this up to users gave them Amelia as first-level support on their terms, 24 hours a day."*[22] In most companies, 24-hour service using human labour requires painful overnight shift work or offshoring to different time zones around the world.

Multi-channel service delivery. Phone contact was the main channel for external customer service, although the bank is also active on various social media platforms. Amelia opened another channel for service delivery. Initially, Amelia was deployed on the web application, but SEB will likely open up additional channels. Mikael Andersson, SEB Transformation Lead-Amelia Exploration, said:

> *"We will use a kind of alpha/beta method, with our main website initially giving access to Amelia interactions. We will then expand its reach, for example to our mobile app and other channels where we interact with customers."*[23]

6.4.2. Employee Value

> *"Amelia is handling the repetitive services that are boring, allowing service desk personnel to solve more interesting problems, together, with a client."* **Nicolas Moch, Head of Information, Strategy & Architecture at SEB**

Given that SEB was able to reduce the number of staff manning the IT service desk as a consequence of automation, one might naturally assume that the staff would feel threatened by the technology. At SEB, the bank initially faced a small amount of apprehension that was quickly overcome when the employees saw a demonstration of the tool. Rather than feel threated by automation, the employees on the IT service desk welcomed Amelia to the team. Nicolas Moch, Head of Information, Strategy & Architecture at SEB, explained:

"Somewhat as a surprise, the people most motivated by having Amelia in both cases – the internal and the external services – are the service desk personnel. That's what we found."

At SEB, the service desk employees are typically young people, often students, who use this experience to learn about servicing customers and dealing with an array of problems. Nicolas Moch, Head of Information, Strategy & Architecture at SEB described the typical service desk employee:

"Our service staff members are dynamic people who want to learn from a forward-looking organisation. They are not afraid of losing their jobs because they quickly want to move to other customer care positions."

The value to employees was clearly evident. Amelia **freed up staff for higher-value customer service work** – a main objective from the start. Mikael Andersson, SEB Transformation Lead- Amelia Exploration, said:

"Our main aim at the moment is to use this technology to improve our services and customer support, because we think using it will enable staff in customer support to focus on value-added work by removing mundane processes." [24]

Eliminating the tedious tasks **increased the service desk staff's job satisfaction.** Additionally, for the small number of service desk staff who moved into the Centre of Excellence, the real value to them was **learning new skills.**

6.4.3. Shareholder value

"The biggest strategic benefits are the increased flexibility, the fact that you can easily scale services up and down, and you can teach new things to a virtual agent much more easily than you can teach it to many employees. Your workforce will focus more on customer

care. So cognitive tools are not about getting rid of people, but about creating agility." **Nicolas Moch, Head of Information, Strategy & Architecture at SEB**

By employing Amelia, SEB is accelerating progress towards its innovation goal to differentiate its services from others in the market, leading to **competitive advantage.** The bank was surprised that the CVA attracted new customers who did not want to access bank services using traditional channels. Nicholas Moch said: *"People love Aida. We reached a new group of customers we didn't have before - who didn't want to call or go visit a branch office. Now they had a channel they could use to become a customer."*

The bank, as well as other adopters of cognitive automation adopters we have studied, uniformly reported that service automation delivers shareholder value in terms of **long-term returns on investment.** In the short term, there are minor **operational efficiencies**, but the real financial impact comes later, when deployments are **scaled,** and when the benefits of **agility** accrue. To this list, Edwin van Bommel, Chief Cognitive Officer for IPsoft, added **increased compliance** as a common benefit:

> *"Amelia increases compliance directly by following processes consistently. But we also have customers who increase compliance indirectly by having Amelia 'whisper' to a human agent to find out if they are authorised to pursue a certain client or enact a certain request. If the human is authorised, Amelia helps them execute the process. If the human is unauthorised, Amelia directs him or her to the person authorised to help the customer."*

While competitive advantage, scalability, and agility are the main contributors to shareholder value, SEB also reported short-term efficiency gains. For example, SEB was able to reduce the number of employees on the internal service desk by five to ten percent. These cost savings, however, have not yet generated an overall positive return on investment. SEB projected only long-term substantial financial benefits. Nicolas Moch, explained:

> *"It's still a very early technology. It's not a magic wand. I advise not viewing cognitive tools as the ultimate cost cutting tool because, while it can help do that, the real value is the way it changes the way you operate."*

6.5. Action Principles

As an early adopter of cognitive technologies, SEB's case study offers a number of insights for other organisations considering similar technologies. The action principles derived from this case are listed below and discussed in detail in Chapter 8.

- Strategy drives CA investments
- Focus on the long-term value
- Manage as a learning project
- Find the 'Lewis and Clark' program champions (see page 244)
- Expect technical challenges as a first mover
- Find high impact CA use cases
- Don't under estimate the data challenge
- Fix discoveries about process flaws before implementing CA
- Compare CA training to human training
- Manage expectations up: Gain C-suite support without overselling
- Manage expectations down: Envision, communicate and deliver value to employees
- Manage expectations out: Be transparent with customers
- Treat CA as lifelong learners
- Invite customers to try CA, but keep other channels open
- Supervise all new CA learning
- Decide optimal time to escalate to humans
- Prepare for a lot more work than you think

Citations

1. We define cognitive automation as: 'tools designed to automate or augment tasks using inference-based processes to interpret unstructured (and structured) data, resulting in a set of likely results as opposed to a single result, i.e. a probabilistic outcome.' We define robotic process automation as: 'tools designed to automate tasks using rules to process structured data, resulting in a single correct answer, i.e. a deterministic outcome.' See: Lacity, M., and Willcocks, L. (2016), 'A New Approach to Automating Services'. *Sloan Management Review*, Vol. 57, 1, pp. 41-49.

2. SEB 2015 Annual Report http://sebgroup.com/siteassets/about_seb1/who_we_are/ar15_strategy_en.pdf.

3. Ibid.

4. SEB 2015 Annual Report http://sebgroup.com/siteassets/about_seb1/who_we_are/ar15_strategy_en.pdf.

5. ITIL (Information Technology Infrastructure Library) is a best practice framework for managing IT services that are aligned with business needs. The ITIL framework covers best practices for IT service strategy; service design; service transition; service operations; and continual service improvement.

6. 'Six Sigma' is a method that uses historical data and statistical analysis to eliminate defects from manufacturing or service processes. Achieving six sigma means that a process has only 3.4 defects per million opportunities.

7. COBIT (Control Objectives for Information and Related Technologies) is a best practice framework for ensuring proper controls in IT service delivery. COBIT was created by international professional association, ISACA, in 1996 to help the financial audit community assess and manage controls in IT-related environments (source: Wikipedia).

8. IPcenter includes over 40 integrated applications that consolidates IT governance, enforces process adherence, and automatically aims to fix IT incidents without human intervention. For example, IPcenter automatically fixed 56 percent of IT service incidents without human intervention for one large client. See: IPcenter General Overview. https://www.youtube.com/watch?v=-NxjH6aAb0c, posted 5th October 2015.

9. Examples of other cognitive virtual assistants include: Apple's Siri; Google's Google Home; Google Now (and later Google Assistant); Amazon Alexa; Amazon's Evi; Microsoft's Cortana; the open source Lucida; Braina for Microsoft Windows; Samsung's S Voice; LG G3's Voice Mate; BlackBerry's Assistant; SILVIA; HTC's Hidi; IBM's Watson; Facebook's M (app); and One Voice Technologies (IVAN).

10. IPsoft case study: *Amelia in Action: IT Service Desk Agent for SEB Bank.*

11. Flinders, K. (2016), 'How a Swedish bank prepared robot Amelia to provide customer services'. *ComputerWeekly*, 8th-14th November.

12. IPsoft case study: *Amelia in Action: IT Service Desk Agent for SEB Bank.*

13. Pioneers Panel, http://www.ipsoft.com/wp-content/uploads/2016/12/Pioneers_Panel.pdf.

14. IPsoft case study: *Amelia in Action: IT Service Desk Agent for SEB Bank.*

15. Flinders, K. (2016), 'How a Swedish bank prepared robot Amelia to provide customer services'. *ComputerWeekly*, 8th-14th November.

16. 'IPsoft's Cognitive Agent Amelia Takes on Pioneering Role in Banking with SEB'. *BusinessWire*. Oct 6, 2016. http://www.businesswire.com/news/home/20161005006546/en/IPsoft's-Cognitive-Agent-Amelia-Takes-Pioneering-Role.

17. Flinders, K. (2016), 'How a Swedish bank prepared robot Amelia to provide customer services'. *ComputerWeekly*, 8th-14th November.

18. IPsoft case study: *Amelia in Action: IT Service Desk Agent for SEB Bank.*

19. 'IPsoft's Cognitive Agent Amelia Takes on Pioneering Role in Banking with SEB'. *BusinessWire*. Oct 6, 2016. http://www.businesswire.com/news/home/20161005006546/en/IPsoft's-Cognitive-Agent-Amelia-Takes-Pioneering-Role.

20. 'IPsoft's Cognitive Agent Amelia Takes on Pioneering Role in Banking with SEB'. *BusinessWire*. Oct 6, 2016. http://www.businesswire.com/news/home/20161005006546/en/IPsoft's-Cognitive-Agent-Amelia-Takes-Pioneering-Role.

21. Pioneers Panel, http://www.ipsoft.com/wp-content/uploads/2016/12/Pioneers_Panel.pdf.

22. Flinders, K. (2016), 'How a Swedish bank prepared robot Amelia to provide customer services'. *ComputerWeekly*, 8th-14th November.

23. Flinders, K. (2016), 'How a Swedish bank prepared robot Amelia to provide customer services'. *ComputerWeekly*, 8th-14th November.

24. Flinders, K. (2016), 'How a Swedish bank prepared robot Amelia to provide customer services'. *ComputerWeekly*, 8th-14th November.

Chapter 7

Cognitive Automation at Zurich Insurance[1]

By Leslie Willcocks and Gero Gunkel

> *"You would assume that people are very hostile to automation. Obviously it's a change for people, but overall, our people preferred the notion of being decision-makers and negotiators. It basically takes away all the tasks that they're not very keen to do and focuses on exactly what we've actually trained them to do."*
>
> **Richard Wood, Senior Transformation Manager,**
> **Zurich Insurance**

> *"We can use the technology across our organisation because many business operations in the insurance world are nothing more than a huge information processing factory, but few of the data that we process are structured numbers; that's why – especially for the insurance industry, but also most other industries – natural language processing and natural language understanding are becoming high priority."*
>
> **Gero Gunkel, Cognitive Automation Program Manager at**
> **Zurich Insurance**

7.1. Introduction

Reading the headlines and multiple reports, one would think that by mid-2017, most organisations had already automated most of their repetitive, routine activities and processes, and were now well into automating knowledge work – reasoning; natural language processing; probabilistic decision-making;

judgment; prediction; understanding context; converting unstructured data into information; and answering *"why?"* questions. But this is far from the case. Given this context, it becomes valuable to study, empirically, actual implementations – not least because, in the cognitive automation space especially, we are very short of independently researched cases that can provide valuable lessons to those just starting their journeys, or still waiting on the sidelines.

At Zurich Insurance, Blue Prism RPA software has been already applied to several insurance processes.[2] These processes exhibited the typical attributes for successful RPA deployment – namely structured data; manual (screen-based) and repetitive rules-based activities; high volumes; and mature, stabilised processes that required definitive outcomes. Zurich Insurance's further venture was to build an understanding and capability in cognitive automation in order to improve customer service and process productivity. This arose from an early 2015 Technology and Operations review that identified automation of knowledge work as a key trend in the insurance industry. Subsequently, Zurich Insurance sought partly to see how far cognitive automation could complement and enhance RPA usage, but more importantly, to build learning and a platform for future automation tools and their application for strategic business purpose.

In this chapter, we focus on Zurich Insurance's application of cognitive automation to an injury claims process, taking this through from the prototype to full implementation. We then identify the lessons and what we call 'Action Principles' that emerge from the case. These will be detailed further in Chapter 8.

7.2. Zurich Insurance: The Business Context

Founded in 1872, Zurich Insurance Group Ltd is a leading multi-line insurer, with headquarters in Zürich, Switzerland. By 2017, the group was the world's

78th largest public company, employing about 54,000 people and serving customers in more than 210 countries and territories.[3] Its capital position in 2016 was solid and stable. It had a strong balance sheet with low investment risk and a strong customer franchise and brand, but recognised it had clear opportunities to improve, including the need to improve underwriting performance, and become more efficient[4]. It aimed to raise its return on equity to above 12 percent[5]. It sought to manage exposures and use reinsurance to reduce earnings volatility.[6] These overall targets had implications for the use of technologies and the pursuit of automation, as we shall see.

On revenues of over US $67 billion, Zurich had a $US 10.3 billion cost base in 2015, delivered more than $300 million of expense savings that year, and was looking to deliver $1.5 billion savings by 2019.The centre (10-15 percent) and group operations (35-45 percent) were expected to deliver a substantial share of these savings.[7] From 2016 it was looking to invest some $800 million into the business.[8]

How does this translate into actions? Zurich Insurance recognised the need to: become more customer focused organisation; strengthen digital capabilities across the value chain; simplify products and processes; provide customer self-service for retail and commercial customers; invest in state-of-the-art technology (e.g. consolidate 70 data centres to eight by 2019, and 140 network providers to one); upgrade end-user services (500 plus applications to be decommissioned); invest in technical skills of people; consolidate/replace systems & tools for underwriting policies, billing and claims; develop faster processing and better use of data; and upgrade the flexibility, quality and value of shared services (while reducing costs by $150-$180 million per annum).[9] Continued standardisation of operations and the IT backbone would enable process improvements in the middle and front offices.[10]

Automation figured highly in most of these forward plans and actions. Thus, in underwriting, Zurich Insurance had already adopted automation of straight-through flow underwriting and cognitive computing in Germany, UK and Switzerland, and would be rolling this out in Spain and Italy by 2018. Predictive analytics were being used to improve risk retention decisions in crop insurance. In claims, robotics were being used in production in three countries, and this was set to be rolled out for all core markets by 2019. Likewise straight-through claims processing (or 'one-and-done') was being increased from 20 percent to 40 percent of all claims by 2019. Meanwhile predictive analytics in four countries would be rolled out globally by 2019, to reduce claims costs and shorten time to close. Enhanced automation of claims processes would also improve the customer experience, as well as functional effectiveness[11]. This case study looks at a particular example of this – improving injury claims efficiency and efficacy through cognitive automation.

7.3. Zurich Insurance's Cognitive Automation Journey

"Moving from testing to production is a different conversation altogether." **Gero Gunkel, Zurich Insurance**

7.3.1. Outcomes

We chart the beginnings rather than the end of a bigger and longer cognitive automation journey. But, in the context of the strategic plans detailed above, it is useful to take stock of the results by June 2017. Zurich Insurance initiated a successful prototype that demonstrated the power of the technology, leading to subsequent full-scale deployment and additional implementations across the whole insurance value chain. The initial tool deployment yielded significant benefits in that:

1. Time taken to analyse a medical report was cut from 58 minutes, with a human claims handler, to a matter of seconds with a cognitive tool

2. 39,000 hours per annum of freed up capacity was achieved

3. The tool will yield US $5 million run rate savings per year

Did the application yield multiple business benefits – what we call 'the triple-win' – for customers, shareholders and employees? The business benefits are obvious from the above. But what about customers? According to one senior executive:

> *"A key benefit is faster processing because this leads to faster service and happier customers, especially when it involves a personal injury claim. It's also about speed, standardisation, and getting better data analytics because it starts as unstructured data – these tools provide a structure. So you can actually do data analytics that you couldn't do before."*

Turning to employees, they continued to be integral to the process, doing much the same job after automation, except they did not have to read the medical reports or re-key information between systems. Instead, they could focus on the two thirds of the work that was more interesting, while also being freed up to get back, much more quickly, to Zurich claimants and customers. As Richard Wood, Senior Transformation Manager Zurich Insurance UK, said:

> *"You would assume that people are very hostile to automation and obviously it's a change for people. But overall, our people preferred the notion of being decision-makers and negotiators. It basically takes away all the tasks that they're not very keen to do and focuses on exactly what we've actually trained them to do, which is to settle the claim."*

Furthermore, replicating our finding in earlier cases,[12] the claims processing unit had come under a lot of pressure from a rising numbers of claims; cognitive automation provided a great deal of relief to these employees. CA also allowed one person to continue to deal with each claim all the way through, allowing that person to do all the assessments for evaluation, determine liability and possible fraud, and do the negotiation at the end. Cognitive automation also allowed the employee more time per case – to speak to the customer, or carry out further investigations. Customers, as well as employees, benefited from these practices.

7.3.2. Starting with Cognitive Automation – April 2015

Key technology trends were explored as part of the revision of Zurich's Technology & Operations strategy through late 2014 and early 2015 (see Figure 7.1). One of those trends was the 'Automation of Knowledge work' – given the advances in computing power and the exponential growth of data. Zurich wanted to test how mature intelligent automation systems were and, therefore, decided to run a portfolio of prototypes to test these solutions. The team made responsible was a joint task force with representation from the Group's business innovation and development team, and the UK Claims team. Zurich already had robotic process automation software operating in several processes, this being initiated and managed by local business units with their own project managers, reflecting Zurich's structure as a more federated organisation.

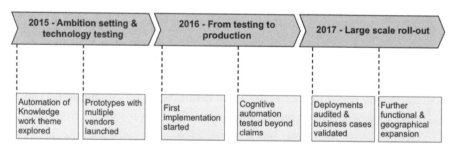

Figure 7.1: The cognitive automation journey at Zurich Insurance

Use Case. The Zurich Insurance project team points to several initial challenges emerging by April 2015. A key issue was to identify the right technology vendor, given that the whole industry was still in its infancy, making it very difficult to get suitable references or other external proof points from suppliers. At the same time, the process selection was also a key challenge because a very complex process would have increased the risk of a project failure, leading potentially to a situation where Zurich would have concluded that the technology was not yet ready for deployment in a real world business environment just because the wrong process was chosen. On the other hand, a too simple process would have not really proved the maturity of the technology, raising a *"so what?"* question. At the same time, Zurich Insurance recognised that internal engagement for technology exploration might change over time. It was, therefore, important to assess the maturity of the technology quickly to keep up momentum, given the limited change absorption capacity – there being, as we have seen, so many other organisational priorities.

Vendor selection. Cognitive automation started very much as an experimentation project (see Figure 7.1). Through mid-2015, multiple supplier prototyping was conducted to compare different vendors, using a 'champion vs. challenger' approach.[13] Looking for a fair and comprehensive comparison in an immature vendor market, the prototype design was inspired by randomised control trials in medical research. Each vendor obtained roughly the same amount of training data, the same problem statement, the same implementation timeline and the same time with the subject matter experts. Performance differences could, thus, be fully linked to the tool performance and the capabilities of each vendor. The results were very encouraging, and a winner – a specialised NLP technology provider – emerged.

Process selection. For the first prototype Zurich carefully selected a claims valuation process for personal injury claims. Here, to decide on compensation value for pain and suffering, claims handlers review medical reports that are submitted by claimants. The process step took about 58 minutes for a claims handler. The process was selected for two reasons: firstly, it is a representative insurance process/activity; and secondly, it is quite a complex and demanding activity with claims handlers requiring significant training to perform this task effectively. According to Richard Wood the thinking here was: *"If we can automate the evaluation of medical reports, it proves we can automate a* *significant part of today's processes and activities across the whole insurance value chain."* It was time to test CA with a live process.

7.3.3. Deploying Cognitive Automation: The Insurance Claims Process

Having chosen a preferred vendor and cognitive automation tool, Zurich's Business Innovation and Development team confirmed a suitable process, and split the project into two phases. There was the completed fast prototyping phase, focusing on the most difficult elements of the medical report evaluation process to prove the power of the technology. When the prototype met the success criteria established, then a second, full-scale implementation phase was started, supported by a larger investment of funds and resources likely to yield a significant return.

The chosen process was the key one of insurance claims:

> *"The payment of legitimate claims represents the delivery of the promise at the heart of the insurance contract."* **UK Airmic Best Practice Claims Guide**

Zurich Insurance operates the claims process through the UK Ministry of Justice (MOJ). The Ministry is a neutral player providing the platform for Zurich and other insurers to engage with the counterparty for fast flow personal injury claims worth less than 25,000 pounds sterling. The platform was introduced to accelerate the speed of claims handling and to reduce the number of cases that go to court. The rationale was that a faster claims process also reduces the claims handling costs for both sides. The medium to long-term benefit from this is that the premiums for young drivers stop rising, or even decline. By way of background, clearly both insurers and brokers want satisfied clients. For this a smooth claims process is vital. What makes a satisfactory claims process? According to Stuart Dymond, Zurich's Commercial Property Claims Manager, the fundamentals are:

- Notify loss as soon as possible
- Include as many details as possible
- Provide a policyholder contact name with decision-making powers
- Stay involved
- Help the policyholder understand the process and insurance terms

The first notification should include: policy number, date of loss, risk address and circumstances of loss, including cause to the extent that it is known. Zurich's objective is to receive, record and move a claim forward within two working days of receipt – earlier if possible. Moving the claim forward means much more than opening a claims diary. It frequently involves: asking for more details, appointing a specialist such as a loss adjuster, or indicating that the loss is not covered under the policy. The handler will track all the steps through the claims system. Zurich's philosophy, which it aims to apply to every claim, is the rule of three: take ownership of the claim; move it forward; satisfy the customer. Stuart Dymond comments:

> *"It is helpful if the broker is involved during the life cycle of the claim. We both want to keep the client as happy as possible. When there are complications on claims it's always 'good to talk' and we like to pick up the 'phone and discuss issues by taking ownership, moving the claim forward to ultimately satisfy our customers."*[14]

Zurich ran the chosen claims process through the UK Ministry of Justice. The claims process is shown in Figure 7.2.

Here's an illustrative example: A person is harmed by a car driven by a Zurich customer. The person gets a claims solicitor to submit a claim to Zurich via the MOJ portal. If Zurich accepts the claim and liability, then it moves to the claims valuation stage. Typically this would involve a medical doctor writing a 10 to 40 page report – looking at medical history, pain experienced, impact on social and work life, prognosis, recovery time (see screenshot in

Figure 7.3). The claims solicitor sends the report to Zurich, together with a settlement offer. Typically a negotiation process follows. The cognitive automation tool is focused on the steps of reading the medical report and determining the appropriate compensation amount. This has three steps – inputting the medical report, pricing, and output.

The claims process

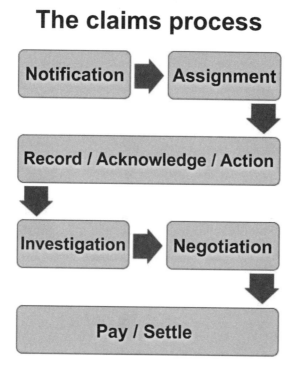

Figure 7.2: The insurance claims process
(Source: www.insider.Zurich.co.uk)

Before cognitive automation, this took about an hour per claimant. The claims handler would read the medical report – this took up most of the time – after which, the officer would transpose this unstructured information into some kind of structure for the pricing. Here the handler would click on Zurich's pricing support tool and avatar to aid the compensation process, and apply this to the injured human body part. By clicking on this avatar, each of the injuries – for example to the neck, the thorax, and the right shoulder – are linked to an international ICD medical code. Each medical code selected calculates a certain compensation value based on previous settlements, whilst taking also other factors for the claims compensation into account. All the injuries and treatments get priced and then a total compensation range is compared against the claim. This supports the handler in valuing, negotiating and settling the claim.

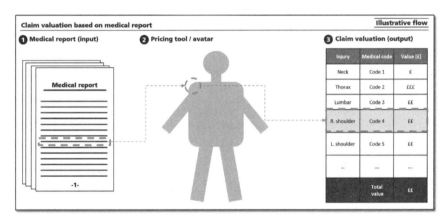

Figure 7.3: Illustrative and simplified process flow – valuation of a single injury
(Source: Zurich Insurance, with permission)

Time and motion studies highlighted that reading the report was time consuming and that a combination of robotic process automation and cognitive automation software could greatly enhance execution:

> *"The key here is the use of multiple intelligent automation technologies working together to solve a complex business process. Our cognitive tool is used to understand and extract injury details, prognosis and key data from a medical report and supporting documentation. It is then passed to our RPA tool which interacts with other tools and techniques to value the injury."* **Adam Briggs, Claims Automation Manager UK.**

The results are shown in Figure 7.4. The impressive outcome is the reduction in report reading time from around one hour to a matter of seconds, but note also how standardised decision-making through automation reduces exceptions and inaccuracies, and the high level of availability of the automation tools compared to human labour. One should also point out how employees are freed up to focus on the other process tasks that require more distinctively human attributes.

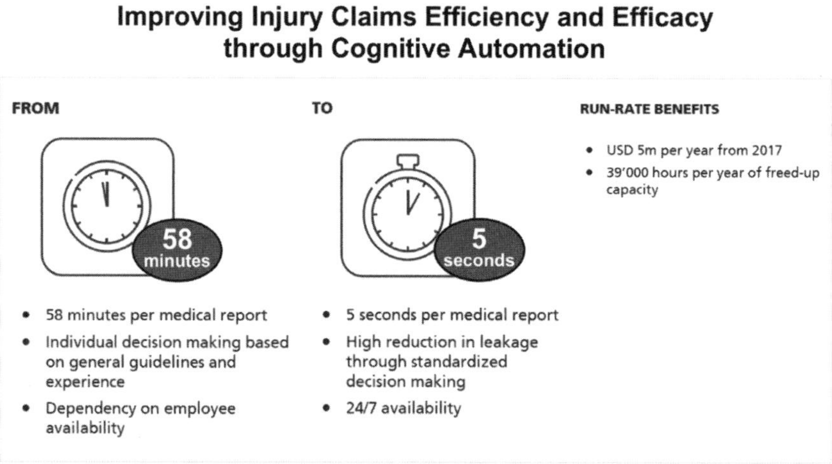

Improving Injury Claims Efficiency and Efficacy through Cognitive Automation

Figure 7.4: Improving the injury claims process

7.3.4. About Cognitive Automation and Tool Choice

On tools, Zurich Insurance sourced the robotic process automation and cognitive automation tools externally. Zurich was already using Blue Prism software and had built up internal knowledge on its deployment. On the cognitive tool, the Innovation and Business Development team recognised that it was impossible, with the resources available, to build a language tool for the application intended. Language is too complicated. Simple analytics were possible, but not a tool to read a 40 page medical report and gain the right meaning and understanding.

One interesting aspect is Zurich's choice of a semantic engine, rather than a tool that did a statistically based analysis such as keyword search or term frequency. The reason why is explained by a simple example. As a senior team member told us:

> *"Consider the difference between pain and discomfort in the back of the neck and pain and discomfort in the back and in the neck. You and I know they mean something completely different. Semantic analysis will tell you it's different but keyword analysis won't be able to tell you that."*

The tool emerged as powerful enough to give a huge efficiency gain without losing quality. The testing showed that a medical report that took a human an hour to read was taking the cognitive tool just a couple of seconds. A key success criterion was that the tool had to be at least as accurate as a human handler. Checking the outcomes – for example identifying a right shoulder and right foot injury – against the case handler notes demonstrated during testing that the information being produced was correct. Disagreements were investigated, an expert case handler adjudicated and, if necessary, the cognitive tool updated. Zurich Insurance also tested the precision of the cognitive tool, e.g. correct injury code chosen, and its recall, i.e. did it find everything it should have found? The cognitive tool emerged as at least as good as a human handler in assessing medical reports.

7.4. Developments to July 2017

After this very promising start, Zurich Insurance resolved to exploit further the potential uncovered with cognitive automation. Here we look at how Zurich Insurance moved cognitive further into the organisation, even though historically Zurich has been quite decentralised; how projects are launched and managed; and the in-house automation capability they have been building.

7.4.1. Moving Cognitive Automation Further into the Organisation

By July 2017, Zurich had several cognitive automation projects in production in multiple areas of the business. The innovation and business development group had built sufficient confidence in the technology to look for diverse processes that were text based to which to apply their cognitive tool capabilities. They have been seeking to apply it, for example, to contracts, and any other areas where they deal with a lot of documents, especially those requiring document understanding. But of course scaling cognitive automation tools entails some further challenges:

> *"Production is a different conversation. But when we started implementing some more projects, we began thinking – it's a general software for reading and understanding text. We're looking at artificial intelligence, a classifier for natural language. So why can't we go across the board? And that's when we actually started to take a more systematic approach and ask which other processes would be keen to automate or at least semi-automate. Which other pain parts do we have? And the whole thing moved in six months from a small prototype into a structured programme with a portfolio of projects."* **Gero Gunkel, Zurich Insurance**

At Zurich Insurance, a typical project was taking six to eight weeks to carry out the 'proof-of-concept' stage, and once a subset of work was tested and proved to work it was moved to the implementation stage. The cognitive automation project group had built up learning with every implementation, and so, by 2017, had developed data collection, testing and training strategies and a reference architecture. These knowledge and data assets helped to roll-out these technologies in a faster way with lower execution risk and costs.

Again, convincing stakeholders has proven easier than it was in the first implementation, because of the successful reference cases now available. The organisational learning and speedier stakeholder engagement have seen project time sometimes be cut by as much as a third, e.g. from six down to four months.

7.4.2. Building In-House Automation Capabilities

Zurich Insurance already had robotic process automation capabilities, though these were spread around an historically decentralised, if global, organisation. Nevertheless, in Zurich, sometimes project managers experienced with RPA were used on cognitive deployments, but equally, business units were free to nominate their own project managers. The cognitive automation group worked with them initially, either as member of the project team or advisor to support them in the launch of their cognitive automation journey. At Zurich, the plan was not to build a central pool of people on cognitive, but for business units and operations to do it themselves, because ultimately, as one respondent told us: *"it's something that the business has to drive itself."*

So what in-house capabilities has Zurich built? For the implementations so far they actually had used mostly external developers from the vendor, simply because Zurich employees would not know all the tools and algorithms so central to cognitive tool operations. Basically, vendor staff did the configuration of tools, while data scientists from Zurich audited this, learned, and selected the tasks they then wanted to pick up subsequently. Zurich managers believed that in order to move fast in the market, they could not really start with building in-house capability. Rather they started with an external assistance to quickly prove the technology, the business case, and the business application. They then put it into production, gained the first benefits and subsequently argued the case for more internal human and financial resources.

By mid-2017 the cognitive automation capability consisted of an enterprise data and analytics team. These were data scientists, some of them also with a very strong background in natural language processing, and many from other relevant technical areas. These would be the people used to do configurations in-house. The other major part of the cognitive automation capability was several people making up project management. These had skills gained from both the business and technical sides of the insurance business, some with data science backgrounds, some performing as project managers, and others as business requirement gatherers. Their overall role was to build and automate new processes together with the relevant tools vendors. This added up to a delivery capability that collaborated with external resources to initially deal with complex new technologies, gradually transitioning capability to the internal team over time. The expansion of the cognitive automation portfolio continued, looking more strongly also on complex processes and activities in underwriting for the retail and commercial customer segments as well as customer-facing operations to further improve the digital customer journey. For the continued enhancement of the technology, portfolio collaborations with leading engineering and technology universities were strengthened to resolve remaining obstacles to end-to-end automation through joint research.

CUSTOMER VALUE	**EMPLOYEE VALUE**	**SHAREHOLDER VALUE**
♠ Enhanced customer journeys	♠ More interesting work	♠ High first year ROIs
♠ Improved service quality	♠ Learned new skills	♠ Easier audits
♠ Remove pain points	♠ Increased employee satisfaction	♠ Better analytics
♠ Round the clock service delivery	♠ More attractive employment for data scientists	♠ Kick starts standardisation
♠ Improved service consistency		♠ Operational efficiencies
♠ Faster access to critical human assistance		♠ Increased accuracy
♠ New services online quickly		♠ Increased speed
		♠ Workforce flexibility
		♠ Competitive advantage

**Figure 7.5: The 'triple-win' from cognitive automation
at Zurich Insurance**

7.5. Case Discussion and Lessons

To begin the discussion let us revisit the subject of business benefits. Zurich Insurance's adoption of cognitive automation delivered value to three stakeholders (see Figure 7.5). Zurich is not alone in achieving such results. Across our cognitive automation cases, we have called such multi-value delivery of benefits the 'triple-win' of service automation.[15] Some of the CA benefits for Zurich shown in Figure 7.5 are still at an early stage, given that the company is still scaling its use of service automation tools generally. Nevertheless the 'wins' are emerging as real and valuable.

As a further point, the Zurich Insurance team stressed the gains to be had when dealing more effectively with data. Given the exponential data explosion organisations are facing – globally possibly a 50 percent increase in the amount of data to be processed every year – these also are highly valuable. Here are some examples of gains experienced by Zurich:

- Cognitive tools can process large documents within seconds.

- Automation tools also leverage large amounts of data for learning, leading to the tools learning and coming to make fewer errors than humans.

- The tools also make available large amounts of data that provide the opportunity to gain significantly better insights from unstructured data

- All case related information is centrally stored in digital control rooms allowing for quick and inexpensive audits.

7.5.1. Emerging Lessons

In this Zurich Insurance case, we identified rich lessons that also worked as Action Principles in the specific context we were studying. Many of these lessons emerged in the earlier case studies of KPMG, Deakin University and SEB. Let us look at the common lessons first:

223

Make business strategy drive technology investments. Zurich Insurance started looking at cognitive automation in the context of broader strategic business issues and decisions. The starting point of the discussion was not test a technology for its own sake, but to assess how new technologies can be used to support the achievement of key strategic priorities.

Be selective on the best work to automate by choosing high impact use cases. Potential adopters of cognitive technologies will want to know how to assess the suitability of the technologies to their existing services. Cognitive experts and early adopters report that *cognitive is most suitable for services that rely on vast amounts of unstructured data and expertise, have enough scale to justify the investment, and are strategic to the business.* Zurich Insurance's use case on personal injury claims processing was consistent with these criteria. This process uses a vast amount of unstructured data, requires skilled claims handlers, and offered great opportunities to improve the service and reduce the costs. It also wanted to select a process that was complicated enough to convince skeptics about the power of next generation automation technologies, but not so complicated that it exhibits a high risk of failure.

Manage as a learning project that is part of a broader innovation program. Zurich Insurance managers suggested:

> *"Always start with a quick prototype (6-8 weeks) in order to get stakeholder buy-in (proofing the case with your own data), proof the technology maturity and the viability of the use case."*

This lesson has also been common practice across our other cognitive automation case studies. Zurich practice fits with other lessons allied to prototyping, namely: manage cognitive automation initially as a learning project and as part of an innovation program; start with a high impact CA use case that can deliver a relatively quick win which will stir the imaginations of stakeholders.

Create a new process flow. Keep in mind that cognitive automation is often not about automating the existing process, but more about creating a new process flow that fits the machine. Hence, you need to move from a human-centric process flow to a machine-centric process flow. This means also that existing rules and guidelines sometimes need to be challenged and changed to fit into an environment where machines are taking over significant more tasks than previously thought possible.

Engage employees fully. Zurich Insurance endeavored to engage employees from the beginning and be absolutely honest about the objectives of a project. One of the objectives at Zurich Insurance was to increase process productivity, but not to reduce staff. To avoid any misunderstandings about the purpose of a project, it is important that senior managers – right from the beginning – are as equally clear about the objectives of the project as they are about what aims are NOT being pursued.

Integrate Service automation programs. Expect to increasingly use robotic process automation and cognitive automation tools in complementary ways (see also Chapter 2). Zurich's use of cognitive automation is particularly interesting for the way it builds on, complements and enhances RPA software deployment. One of the recognised limitations of RPA is that it needs structured data to work with. In the claims handling process, the RPA tool downloaded all case files and relevant information from external sources and inserted them into the cognitive tool.

The cognitive tool then conducts the task of a person having to think, read the text, understand it, put all the different evidence together and establish what is relevant. As a final step, the RPA tool takes this structured data and carries out the repetitive, high volume rules-based activities formerly carried out by the human handler, allowing the human to focus on tasks more suited to their experience, specialist knowledge, decision-making and negotiating abilities. Hence, the CA tool is embedded into a RPA process flow. More broadly, in the automation services market, we are increasingly seeing tools providers offering both RPA and CA capabilities, while some are also developing platforms that enable the use of different tools sets – both trends reflecting the direction of travel seen at Zurich Insurance.

Additionally, several distinctive lessons, that were sometimes present but less clear in the other three cases, emerged from the Zurich Insurance case experience. These were:

Don't look for a 'Swiss army knife'. We like this lesson, not least because of its Swiss connotations! A Swiss army knife is designed to deal with most small operational problems on, for example, an expedition or camping trip. At Zurich Insurance CA tools were being designed for very specific purposes and not generally applicable in the same way.

Test the provider's tool with a controlled experiment. Amongst the four cases, we found this practice distinctive to Zurich Insurance, although we have seen it before in the context of several RPA deployments.

It's a lot more work than you think – set realistic expectations. The media can be highly misleading about cognitive automation capabilities, and frequently underplays the amount of work it requires to get tools to perform proficiently.

There will be more work and jobs than many predict. Some studies have predicted considerable job losses arising from automation. We deal with this issue in detail in our final chapter, but, as we will discuss in more detail in Chapter 8, the Zurich Insurance experiences of automation are consistent with a more complex and nuanced picture.

In Chapter 8, we will look in detail at how these lessons can become Action Principles for other CA adopter organisations.

7.6. Summary

The potential, broader significance of the cognitive automation capability described in this chapter was summarised by Gero Gunkel at Zurich Insurance:

> *"We can use the technology across our organisation because many business operations in the insurance world are nothing more than a huge information processing factory, but little of the data that we process is structured numbers; roughly 80 percent of the data we process is unstructured, written text. The big shift now is that the cognitive classifiers achieve a text understanding level that is comparable to the human level. The impact of this is tremendous because computing didn't change our business model much. It could focus only on the 20 percent structured data. With cognitive and AI we will be impacting the 80 percent. With unstructured data, the amount of human intervention is so large that, just achieving a little bit of automation, you already get quite a big benefit. And that's why you see, especially for the insurance industry, but also most other industries, natural language processing and natural language understanding becoming high priority."*

7.7. Action Principles

As another early adopter of cognitive technologies, Zurich Insurance offers a number of insights for other organisations considering similar technologies. The action principles derived from this case are listed below and discussed in detail in Chapter 8:

- Strategy drives CA investments
- Use RPA as forward reconnaissance
- Manage as an innovation program
- Put in place a strong in-house team
- Don`t look for a 'Swiss army knife'
- Test the provider's tool with a controlled experiment

- Be selective on the best work to automate by choosing high impact use cases
- Manage expectations down: envision, communicate and deliver value to employees
- Create a new process flow
- Integrate service automation programs: expect to increasingly use robotic process automation and cognitive automation tools in complementary ways
- Prepare for a lot more work than you think
- Plan for more work and jobs than many predict

Citations

1. Disclaimer: This publication has been prepared in collaboration with Zurich Insurance Group Ltd and the opinions expressed therein are those of Zurich Insurance Group Ltd as of the date of writing and are subject to change without notice. This publication has been produced solely for informational purposes. All information contained in this publication have been compiled and obtained from sources believed to be reliable and credible but no representation or warranty, express or implied, is made by Zurich Insurance Group Ltd or any of its subsidiaries (the 'Group') as to their accuracy or completeness. This publication is not intended to be legal, underwriting, financial, investment or any other type of professional advice. The Group disclaims any and all liability whatsoever resulting from the use of or reliance upon this publication. Certain statements in this publication are forwardlooking statements, including, but not limited to, statements that are predictions of or indicate future events, trends, plans, developments or objectives. Undue reliance should not be placed on such statements because, by their nature, they are subject to known and unknown risks and uncertainties and can be affected by numerous unforeseeable factors. The subject matter of this publication is also not tied to any specific insurance product nor will it ensure coverage under any insurance policy. This publication may not be distributed or reproduced either in whole, or in part, without prior written permission of Zurich Insurance Group Ltd, Mythenquai 2, 8002 Zurich, Switzerland. Neither Zurich Insurance Group Ltd nor any of its subsidiaries accept liability for any loss arising from the use or distribution of this publication. This publication does not constitute an offer or an invitation for the sale or purchase of securities in any jurisdiction.

2. Case studies of RPA use can be found in Willcocks, L. and Lacity, M. (2016) *Service Automation, Robots, and The Future of Work*. (SB Publishing, UK). Available from www.sbpublishing.org. Email info@sbpublishing.org.

3. Information from the Zurich Insurance Investor Day presentation, 17th November 2016, London.

4. Information from the Zurich Insurance Investor Day presentation, 17th November 2016, London.

5. Information from the Zurich Insurance Investor Day presentation, 17th November 2016, London.

6. Information from the Zurich Insurance Investor Day presentation, 17th November 2016, London.

7. Business units (excluding operations) accounted for 59 percent of the cost base in 2015 and were mandated to reduce this by around USD 800 million over the next three years.

8. Information from the Zurich Insurance Investor Day presentation, 17th November 2016, London.

9. Information from the Zurich Insurance Investor Day presentation, 17th November 2016, London.

10. Information from the Zurich Insurance Investor Day presentation, 17th November 2016, London.

11. Information from the Zurich Insurance Investor Day presentation, 17th November 2016, London.

12. As examples only, see the nPower and Telefonica O2 cases in Willcocks and Lacity op. cit. (2016). We have found automation utilized very frequently in situations where a dramatic increase in work has occurred, typically over two to three years, or more.

13. This is normally called a 'champion vs challenger' approach but the immature market and lack of sitting CA vendor at Zurich led to an approach that set up criteria and parameters – the 'check' part – enabling comparison between vendors and Zurich's expectations.

14. www.insider.Zurich.co.uk accessed 25th June 2017.

15. See for Example: Lacity, M., Willcocks, L. and Craig, A. (2017), *Service Automation: Cognitive Virtual Agents at SEB Bank*. The LSE Outsourcing Unit Working Research Paper Series.

Chapter 8

Action Principles for Cognitive Automation

By Mary Lacity and Leslie Willcocks

"We don't disrupt for the fun of it – that would be reckless. We disrupt to solve a problem."

Professor Beverley Oliver, Deputy Vice-Chancellor for Education at Deakin University

"Cognitive is not for the faint of heart – it is really for people who understand how to implement and manage impactful innovation programs... Disciplined execution of an innovation approach can help accelerate time to value from cognitive investments."

Vinodh Swaminathan Managing Director, Innovation & Enterprise Solutions at KPMG

"Building a team of AI evangelists early on is crucial for fostering company-wide acceptance."

Tom De Carlo, Managing Director, Head of Client Services at UBS[1]

8.1. Introduction

In this chapter, we share the action principles gleaned from our Cognitive Automation (CA) case study research. We've organised the CA 'Action Principles' into the categories of: Strategy; Program Management; Tool Selection; CA Design & Build; Stakeholder Buy-in; CA Run; and Maturity (See Table 8.1). We also have a final category of 'General' action principles.

Category	Action Principle	KPMG	Deakin University	SEB Bank	Zurich Insurance
Strategy	1. Have a higher purpose*	✓			
	2. The dog wags the tail: Strategy drives CA investments	✓	✓	✓	✓
	3. Consider competitors' reactions*		✓		
	4. Focus on the long-term value*	✓	✓	✓	
	5. Use RPA as forward reconnaissance*	✓			✓
Program Management	6. Manage as an innovation program*	✓			✓
	7. Manage as a learning project*			✓	
	8. Find the 'Lewis and Clark' program champions*	✓	✓	✓	
	9. Put in place a strong in-house team			✓	✓
Tool Selection	10. Look behind the provider's curtain	✓			✓
	11. Don't look for a 'Swiss army knife'*				✓
	12. Test provider's tool with a controlled experiment				✓
	13. Negotiate the optimal level of client-provider transparency*		✓		
	14. Expect technical challenges as a first mover*	✓	✓	✓	
CA Design & Build	15. Find high impact CA use cases	✓	✓	✓	✓
	16. Don't under estimate the data challenge*	✓	✓	✓	
	17. Find new data sources if dirty data cannot be cleaned*	✓			
	18. Fix discoveries about process flaws before implementing CA		✓	✓	✓
	19. Compare CA training to human training*	✓		✓	
Stakeholder Buy-in	20. Manage expectations up: Gain C-suite support without overselling	✓	✓	✓	
	21. Manage expectations down: envision, communicate and deliver value to employees		✓	✓	✓
	22. Manage expectations out: Be transparent with customers		✓	✓	
CA Run	23. Treat CA as lifelong learners*	✓	✓	✓	
	24. Invite customers to try CA, but keep other channels open*		✓	✓	
	25. Supervise all new CA learning*	✓	✓	✓	
	26. Decide optimal time to escalate to humans*			✓	
	27. Keep subject matter experts continually engaged in curation*		✓		
Maturity	28. Move to a federated model to broadly infuse CA				✓
	29. Integrate service automation programs	✓	✓		✓
	30. Continually innovate because today's 'cool' is tomorrow's 'yawn'*		✓		✓
General	31. Prepare for a lot more effort than you think	✓	✓	✓	✓
	32. Plan for more work and jobs than many predict	✓	✓		✓

As a caveat, the absence of a '✓' does **not** mean that the organisational adopter did not enact or subscribe to the principle; it merely indicates the lesson did not arise during our conversations with research participants.

* 19 Action Principles emerge as unique to CA compared to RPA.

Table 8.1: Action principles for cognitive automation

These do not fit precisely into the automation life cycle, but nevertheless emerge strongly as shaping principles that need consideration. We identified 32 action principles based on the four case studies – at KPMG, Deakin University, SEB, and Zurich Insurance. We also draw on participants' experiences from our other research projects, and from public sources.

We aim to extract action principles that are distinctive to CA programs (and indicated by asterisks in Table 8.1) compared to RPA programs discussed in Chapter 2. Certainly the size of CA investments compared to RPA investments requires an escalated program management structure. The principles for designing, building, and running CA applications are also different from RPA applications. We identify 19 action principles unique to CA programs. We note, however, that 13 CA action principles are also common to RPA programs. These principles are so vital that they are revisited here. Common principles include: strategy leading investment decisions, getting stakeholder buy-in, and integrating CA with other automation tools.

Potential CA adopters will gain a strong sense as to the pervasiveness of a principle and its potential applicability to their own organisational contexts. We present considerable evidence for action principles mentioned across multiple organisational contexts. Such meaty action principles can be considered to be 'robust'. Other action principles have less evidence; they surfaced as unique within a case, but are quite interesting and worth considering as potentially applicable nonetheless. There is a huge learning curve to overcome, and our aim in this research is to help organisations accelerate the learning curve and avoid common mistakes that can stall or even derail innovation programs by sharing experiences from early adopters.

8.2. The Innovation Learning Curve

"It's really important to start the learning curve early on, to put the [CA] technology out there, to get feedback from colleagues at

first and eventually customers so you can really start delivering business value results." **Stefan Visser, Digital Cooperation Catalyst, VGZ**[2]

The innovation learning curve in Figure 8.1 depicts five phases of adoption and the action principle categories applicable to each. In Phase 1, the organisation needs strong program champions to get the strategy right, and to establish an effective program management structure. Five strategy and four program management action principles discussed in this chapter, help to launch the organisation on the right path. The biggest misstep is focusing **only** on short-term returns on investment, as innovations should produce multiple sources of value for shareholders, customers, and employees.

In Phase 2, organisations need to select the appropriate tool to enact the strategy, find high impact use cases, and begin developing the innovation. For CA innovations, there are unique considerations during this phase, particularly around data, processes, and subject matter expert engagement. Employees and customers affected by the innovation will need to be informed, assuaged, and brought on board. We have identified the following action principles to help: five 'Tool Selection', five 'CA Design and Build', and three 'Stakeholder Buy-in'.

In Phase 3, the innovations are deployed into production. For CA applications, organisations need to manage the run phase differently from other enterprise applications. Change management involves more customer feedback and continual subject matter expert engagement to continually curate content and to adjust algorithms for performance improvement. Five action principles are suggested for this phase.

By Phase 4, the adoption reaches maturity. The organisation has developed deep expertise with the innovation; has disseminated the innovation across the enterprise; and can integrate the technology with other innovations. For this stage, three action principles are suggested.

Eventually, innovations become institutionalised – that is, part of the fabric of the enterprise architecture. Phase 5 has not yet occurred among our case studies of cognitive automation, but eventually today's hot innovations become part of an organisation's standard enterprise architecture. New innovation adoption cycles are launched.

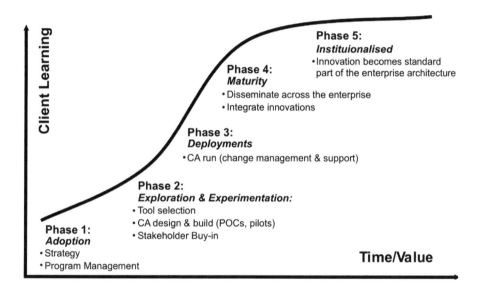

Figure 8.1: Action principles to accelerate learning

8.3. Strategy Action Principles

We have long argued that organisations should not develop a technology-specific strategy per se, but rather should identify how technologies like CA can contribute to the enterprise's long-term goals.[3] Successful organisational adopters imagined using CA for a higher purpose and as an enabler of a larger business strategy – often as part of a digital transformation strategy. Compared to RPA programs, organisations took a long-term view on value derived from CA investments and considered the reaction of competitors.

(1) Have a higher purpose

"Our use case with [IBM] is to reinforce confidence in the capital markets. How do we instill more integrity around capital markets globally?" **Todd Lohr, Principal, US Transformation Enablement Leader at KPMG**

Given the investment of time and resources required to implement many CA technologies, it is no surprise that some organisational adopters were driven by higher purposes than just generating shareholder value. For KPMG, the higher purpose remains as 'reinforcing confidence in capital markets'. This is a noble purpose in light of the 2008 global financial crisis – possibly the greatest economic disruption since the Great Depression of 1929. Many people stopped trusting financial institutions after they pushed people to take on more debt than they could service. Movements like 'Occupy Wall Street' railed against wealth inequality and the influence of large financial institutions on government policy. KPMG wants to help restore the integrity of the financial services industry, and their adoption of IBM Watson is one enabler of that greater purpose.

Organisation	Announcement Date	Vision/Purpose
WellPoint	September 2011	Improve patient care[4]
MD Anderson Cancer Center	February 2012	Recommend cancer treatments[5]
Memorial Sloan Kettering	March 2012	Advance the future of personalised cancer care[6]
Cleveland Clinic	October 2012	Uncover new patient treatment options and deliver personalised medicine[7]
LifeLearn	April 2014	Transform how veterinarians access and interpret unlimited amounts of structured and unstructured information[8]
Baylor College of Medicine	August 2014	'Proof-of-principle' to help researchers mine all public medical literature and formulate hypotheses that promise the greatest reward when pursuing new scientific studies[9]

Table 8.2: Prominent IBM Watson adopters in healthcare

Beyond our case studies, other early adopters of IBM Watson were primarily in healthcare. These organisations aimed to use Watson to dramatically 'improve patient healthcare', primarily by assisting physicians with the diagnosis and treatment of disease. WellPoint, MD Anderson Cancer Center, Memorial Sloan-Kettering, Cleveland Clinic, LifeLearn, and Baylor College of Medicine all mentioned a higher purpose in their adoption announcements (see Table 8.2). Not every organisation will have higher purposes, but such lofty missions were associated with the 'moon shot' programs.

(2) The dog wags the tail: Strategy drives CA investments

"We don't disrupt for the fun of it – that would be reckless. We disrupt to solve a problem." **Professor Beverley Oliver, Deputy Vice-Chancellor for Education at Deakin University.**

Across our cases, it is vital to understand that strategy was driving cognitive automation investments. Our four organisational adopters do not have a 'Watson Strategy' or an 'IPsoft Strategy' or, at Zurich Insurance, an 'Expert System Strategy'; rather they have a business strategy enabled by technology investments. This action principle was also evident in our study of other organisations that, using RPA, achieved the triple-win for shareholders, customers, and employees.[10]

While KPMG's purpose is to reinforce confidence in capital markets, its business strategy is to transform professional services. KPMG has a clear vision for how cognitive automation technologies will enable that strategy. As discussed in Chapter 4, KPMG aims to accelerate time to employee proficiency, augment decisions in the moment, and scale expertise within the enterprise. In short, KPMG wants to liberate their skilled workforce from routine tasks to more fully use their qualifications and critical thinking skills.

Deakin University has an international growth strategy focused on enhancing the student journey via its 'LIVE the Future' vision discussed in Chapter 5.

The vision is enabled by aggressive investments in digital technologies that enhance the student experience. Watson just happens to be one among many investments that enables the strategy.

SEB aims to be the leaders in digitally-enabled financial services by investing in digital solutions that enhance customer journeys (see Chapter 6). SEB wants to deliver a personalised service so that *"customers can choose where and in what manner they want to be served."*[11] The IPsoft Amelia investment directly supports this strategy by opening up alternative digital channels.

In Chapter 7 we saw that Zurich Insurance had started looking at cognitive automation in the context of broader strategic business issues and decisions. The starting point of the discussion was not test a technology for its own sake, but to assess how new technologies can be used to support the achievement of key strategic priorities.

(3) Consider competitors' reactions

Deakin University offered a unique insight among our cases thus far: it thought about how its CA adoption might be perverted by outsiders. Professor Beverley Oliver, Deputy Vice-Chancellor for Education, said:

> *"We were careful about the narrative. I did not want our competitors to twist what we doing and launch their own campaign: 'Come study here and talk to a real person because Deakin only lets you speak to a robot.'"*

Many organisations are skittish about advertising their automation capabilities. With the intense public focus on job creation, the optics of automation can be perceived as 'job killers'. In contrast to public opinion, investors generally react favourably to automation, just as they reacted favourably to offshoring and other practices that reduce costs. What's interesting about CA investments is that cost reduction was not an expected benefit – at least not in the short term, leading to the next practice:

(4) Focus on the long-term value

"The long term ROI will be very, very big. If we need to change something in delivery, we change it once in the software... compare that to trying to update 10,000 client representatives." **Nicolas Moch, Head of Information, Strategy & Architecture at SEB**

Most CA technologies require a significant financial investment, particularly when compared to RPA investments. People interviewed for this research indicated that proof-of-concepts for a Watson implementation cost between $500,000 and $1 million, and a full-blown deployment might cost over $20 million. As noted in Chapter 3, Watson comprises a number of technologies, and the full cost will depend on the parts of Watson used. IPsoft's Amelia costs around $500,000 according to interviewees. Expert System's software licenses vary between $60,000 and $300,000 per year, depending on the modules used, complexity of the business cases, and support services needed. In contrast, RPA software licenses cost around $10,000 to $15,000 per year. Unlike RPA adoptions that delivered double or triple digit ROIs within six months to a year,[12] CA adoptions did not generate positive one-year ROIs in our case studies. Instead, CA adopters are focusing on the long-term value based on business re-design, strategic enablement, competitive advantage, and brand reputation.

In KPMG's experience, value is realised along the journey at various milestones, if managed in a disciplined way. Vinodh Swaminathan, Managing Director, Innovation & Enterprise Solutions at KPMG said: *"It all comes down to the level of thought and diligence that goes into setting up the innovation journey and cognitive project."*

Gartner reported that Deakin University has an 'untested ROI' and wrote:

"The university does not yet have hard return on investment (ROI) metrics for the Watson deployment. Attributing ROI budget benefits in terms of reputation and student satisfaction will likely

remain hard to quantify. Part of the reason for this is the difficulty of attributing benefits to individual IT systems such as Watson." [13]

SEB reports that the short-term business case did not generate a positive ROI. However, in the long term, the ROI will be enormous (see quote above). Long-term ROI will happen because of increased scalability and increased agility. For example, when a new business rule is introduced, IPsoft's Amelia will be updated once, compared to retraining many human agents.

Measuring value is another challenge. How does an organisation calculate a return on investment when no staff is laid off as a consequence of automation? Deakin University was experimenting with financial measures, such as the cost per query. In our other research, 'hours given back to the business' was an emerging value metric.[14] These calculations are based on estimating the number of hours it would have taken if humans were still performing the tasks. In Deakin's case, that measure might be calculated by estimating how many hours it would take for humans to answer the 3,000 questions that Watson now answers per week.

(5) Use RPA as forward reconnaissance

This rather intriguingly worded lesson emerged from the KPMG case. Before many senior executives are willing to invest in expensive and time-consuming CA programs, they may need to see substantial results from the less expensive, and faster deployed, RPA automation projects. RPA can often generate enough savings to help fund the next investment in cognitive tools. Todd Lohr, Principal, US Transformation Enablement Leader at KPMG, explained that companies that have been successful with RPA programs, will have a higher rate of experimentation in cognitive. He said the RPA program heads could say to senior managers:

"We've done automation. We've built 290 bots. We've saved a ton of money. RPA just scratches the service on what automation can do. The transformative value is in the cognitive-type technologies.

We want to start experimenting with those – finding use cases and investing in that area. Are you supportive? They say 'Yes!' If they had asked for that 12 months ago before delivering tens of millions of dollars in savings [from RPA], they would have been denied."

Zurich Insurance, as we saw in Chapters 2 and 7, also adopted RPA first, and moved to cognitive automation as a complementary technology later.

8.4. Program Management Action Principles

How should CA programs be managed? Who should champion them? Unlike RPA programs that are typically managed as business projects within business operations, the scope, scale, and cost of CA technologies seems to suggest a different model. KPMG chose to manage IBM Watson as a centralised innovation program. Zurich Insurance used a central innovation and business development team, but otherwise had quite a decentralised organisation structure; it wanted to move to a more federated structure to support more local initiatives. SEB chose to manage IPsoft's Amelia as a live learning project. At Deakin, cognitive automation was a centralised project consistent with business and digital strategy – though exploratory in nature. As far as who should manage the programs, we discovered that CA programs didn't rely on a single powerful champion like many RPA programs; successful CA programs needed multiple powerful champions. And finally, having a strong team at all levels ensures that the champions' vision is actually executed.

(6) Manage as an innovation program

"We did not want to experiment with cognitive in one business unit, somewhere in a corner. When the entire firm gets behind something like this, it helps us to scale it very effectively." **Vinodh Swaminathan, Managing Director, Innovation & Enterprise Solutions at KPMG**

Innovation programs are centrally managed and report high up in the organisation. The benefit of this approach is an enterprise-wide innovation strategy that is consistent, coherent, and aligned with the broader business strategy.[15]

KPMG chose to house the IBM Watson program within its Innovation and Enterprise Solutions (I&ES) group. It wants the program to focus on disrupting the entire professional services business, not just one service silo. KPMG made a substantial investment in developing human resources that will build KPMG's long-term cognitive capability. For each use case, KPMG assigned about eight people to shadow the IBM technical teams so KPMG could learn how to harness Watson. And to date, over a thousand people at KPMG are trained across various disciplines in cognitive automation.

At Zurich Insurance, the Innovation and Business Development Group managed the CA program. This group did the initial tool assessment and tool selection. It did the first proof-of-concepts, built the first pilots, and launched the first application. As Zurich's cognitive capabilities matured, it moved to a more federated model to disseminate the technology broadly across the enterprise (see Action Principle 28).

For organisations that do not possess KPMG's and Zurich Insurance's level of resources, they can engage partners to help build cognitive capabilities. As Vinodh Swaminathan said:

> *"Our lesson on this topic is that cognitive is not for the faint of heart – it is really for people who understand how to implement and manage impactful innovation programs. If they don't have it, they should find a partner who can help. Disciplined execution of an innovation approach can help accelerate time to value from cognitive investments."*

(7) Manage as a learning project

"We view it as a learning project, where we learn together with the customers and the business." **Nicolas Moch, Head of Information, Strategy & Architecture at SEB**

For IPsoft's Amelia adoption at SEB, the bank treated it as a **learning project**, which it described as a 'hybrid project' (see Figure 8.2). A learning project has a substantial upfront investment like an R&D project, and has active participation from operations like a business project. A learning project has well-defined goals, but, unlike a business project, it does not specify well-defined measures of when financial benefits will occur. Unlike an R&D project, a learning project gets deployed into operations immediately. Thus, a learning project is a live exploratory experiment. Nicolas Moch, Head of Information, Strategy & Architecture at SEB, said: *"We need the latitude to switch directions as we learn together. If I am tied into a business case of delivering 50 FTE savings by year end, we'll miss the strategic value."*

BUSINESS PROJECTS	"LEARNING" PROJECTS	R&D PROJECTS
♠ Owned by business operations	♠ Co-owned, business and innovation group	♠ Owned by central innovation group
♠ Clear business case with concrete goals, measures and expected ROI	♠ Clear goals, no measures	♠ General goals, no measures
♠ Live deployments after testing	♠ Live experiments	♠ Controlled experiments

`Figure 8.2: Attributes of a 'learning' project

(8) Find the 'Lewis and Clark' program champions

"Building a team of AI evangelists early on is crucial for fostering company-wide acceptance." **Tom De Carlo, Managing Director, Head of Client Services at UBS**[16]

Project management research over several decades consistently identifies a project champion as a critical success factor for project success.[17] Normally, the project champion is the person within an organisation who takes on the burden of ensuring everyone involved is on board and behind the eventual success of the project.[18] In our first RPA case studies, we could certainly identify a single leader championing the RPA cause. In our CA case studies, however, this role did not fall upon one individual – it required a cadre of program champions with the vision and influence to lead something risky and pioneering.

The program champions need that single-minded focus that Meriwether Lewis and William Clark had when leading US President Thomas Jefferson's Corps of Discovery Expedition. Lewis and Clark's objective was to find a practical route across the western half of United States. They faced a perilous journey that took over two years to complete, lasting from May 1804 to September 1806. They succeeded despite near starvation, bitter winters, and brutal terrains. Their success was largely credited to Lewis and Clark's ability to build relationships within their own team as well as with over twenty Native American tribes.[19] Here are some examples of the 'Lewis and Clark' program champions from our own case studies:

At KPMG, the program champions include Steve Hill, Global Head of Innovation & Investments; Cliff Justice, Partner, US Leader, Cognitive Automation and Digital Labor; Vinodh Swaminathan, Managing Director, Innovation & Enterprise Solutions; and Todd Lohr, Principal, US Transformation Enablement Leader. These program champions prophesise the vision of cognitive technologies both internally and externally through white papers, presentations, demonstrations and interviews. Cliff Justice exemplifies KPMG's stance that *"cognitive technologies are the game-changer."*[20]

At SEB, the program champions included the Chief Strategy Officer, the

Chief Digital Officer, the Group CIO and Head of IT Services. However, Nicolas Moch, Head of Information, Strategy & Architecture, stands out as the primary evangelist – giving speeches online and in-person on at least two continents.

At Deakin University, we can certainly point to Jane den Hollander, the Vice Chancellor for Deakin University; Beverley Oliver, Deputy Vice-Chancellor; and William Confalonieri, Chief Digital Officer, as the program champions, but they preferred to credit the entire team, which leads to our next action principle ...

(9) Put in place a strong in-house team

It is critical to have dedicated team members in place at both operational and executive levels to ensure continuity throughout the different stages of CA projects of this magnitude. Having such team roles in place also reduces the risk of project delays, reinvention and scope creep. Certainly, this was a key to Deakin University's success. It had a team in place that supported all the stages of an organisation's cognitive service automation journey from start to end. The team incorporated:

1. Subject matter experts in the areas of student support and associated university policies.
2. Facilitators who could interact with students to develop the initial set of questions at the onset and augment these questions throughout the project duration.
3. In-house technical experts, with knowledge about the different Deakin systems as sources of information to address student questions.
4. A dedicated Watson Project manager who could orchestrate the overall journey from start to end internally, and work closely with IBM as external technology partner.
5. Program champions at executive level who supported the project execution, resourcing and overall direction, including its future innovation potential.

8.5. Tool Selection Action Principles

In 2016, KPMG was tracking 120 tools being sold as some form of cognitive automation. Because the space is relatively new to many clients, it is difficult to assess the actual capabilities and suitability of these tools. In our prior research, we identified RPA action principles to vet automation software, including the principles: 'match tool capabilities with strategic objectives'; 'consider overall value of tool capabilities, not just price'; and 'have IT help vet the software.'[21] These principles certainly apply to the selection of CA tools. In addition, five more principles arose from the CA adoption cases:

(10) Look behind the provider's curtain

> *"You can't expect a provider to just pick up and throw a few data scientists at it to build a cognitive solution in a year, based upon the disruption that they are claiming."* **Todd Lohr, Principal, US Transformation Enablement Leader at KPMG**

> *"Some of the tools out there are probably theoretically better [than what we do now] but they're not practically better because they can't work in a messy real life environment with missing data, small data sets and a lot of other problems."* **Adam Briggs, Zurich Insurance**

Given the proliferation of tools marketed as 'cognitive' or as 'artificial intelligence', clients must be aware of hype and 'automation washing'. The term 'automation washing' refers to the phenomenon of providers spending more resources on advertising and marketing – claiming to have new AI capabilities – than actually building new automation capabilities. Cliff Justice, a partner at KPMG said:

> *"Absolutely, we see evidence of 'washing'; we see real differences in capabilities across the tools and providers. This is a new market with emerging technologies. Some are more mature than others."*[22]

Some software providers are immature, have unproven track records, negative cash flows, and uncertain futures. Some have invested millions in infrastructure and only collect revenues from licensing fees – will they remain viable, particularly as more open sourced technologies become available? Organisations are advised to select a provider with a sound financial position and with stable customers who have been using the technology successfully. For KPMG, IBM was the right partner at the right point in their cognitive innovation journey. Todd Lohr said: *"At the end of the day, IBM has been doing this for 20 years, they've made the investment."* KPMG also uses Microsoft's cognitive tools, e.g. Cortana and Azure machine-learning studio.[23]

(11) Don`t look for a 'Swiss army knife'

Rather nicely, this principle actually emerged, strongly, from our Zurich Insurance case! No tool or technology is able to do everything and, thus, it is necessary to develop a portfolio of complementary technologies to enable end-to-end automation – e.g. one tool for extraction, one for categorisation, one for analytics. Competitive advantage is not derived from the selection of one technology or service vendor, but through the ability to identify and connect different technologies that maximise the full potential of automation technologies. When studying RPA tools, we identified that not all were the same, and sent out a caveat emptor ('Buyer Beware') message. This is even truer with CA tools since they are being developed to do so much more than RPA. They can be impressive on the task they have been designed for, but not for a range of tasks.[24] They also do not come close to being 'plug and play'.

(12) Test the provider's tool with a controlled experiment

> *"Some clients will run dual proofs-of-concept with different automation technologies – for example, robotic process automation and business process management tools – to find the most efficient solution for their requirement."* **Sarah Burnett, Vice President of Research at the Everest Group**

Among the four cases, Zurich Insurance was distinctive in its approach to choosing a CA tool. It decided to use a controlled experiment to assess multiple tools prior to selection. Zurich gave the tool providers the same challenge and provided each with identical datasets and time with Zurich's subject matter experts. This approach allowed them to pick the tool that best met their needs. It also won over senior stakeholders that might have favoured a different solution, as the whole selection process was transparent and minimised conflating factors as much as possible. This made sure that the assessment was considered as fair by all parties involved.

According to a Zurich manager, a 'champion vs. challenger' approach helped also to maximise the effort put in by the vendors to achieve the best possible result: *"The vendors knew that they needed to try hard to win this, given the heated competition."* Working with different vendors did not only help to identify the best technology fit, but also to measure the 'hidden costs' of an implementation, such as the change capacity needed for each vendor to deliver the project. In fact, the benefits of a champion vs. challenger project also extend beyond the proof-of-concept phase – the direct comparison includes not only tool performance, but also the total cost of ownership. This heads-up comparison on price and performance helps to identify the best value for money option for each use case.

We had seen this approach used before in the context of selecting RPA tools. Back in 2010, Telefónica O2 did what most companies do when they are considering the adoption of a new technology: they did a proof-of-concept. An interesting twist extended the proof-of-concept into a controlled experiment when Telefónica O2's IT department claimed that its Business Process Management (BPM) software could do everything that the RPA software could do. A controlled experiment allowed Telefónica O2 to directly compare RPA with another BPM. Functionally, the solutions were nearly identical, but RPA delivered better financial value for the types of processes Telefónica O2 aimed to automate. BPM would have likely emerged the victor if the automation required the re-coding of business logic or data access layers.[25]

(13) Negotiate the optimal level of client-provider transparency

"The challenge for us during the project was trying to get an understanding of what was going on inside the black box. We were not invited to [IBM's] technical meetings with the people who understood the machine learning algorithms...we kept asking them to let us in the tent." **Interviewee from Deakin University**

For our early CA adopters, clients worked closely with the tool provider to jointly develop applications. The clients needed the tool provider because they had a significant learning curve to climb regarding the technology. Clients wanted to learn everything they could about how the tool worked and expected full transparency into the provider's tool, algorithms and processes. The tool provider needed the client's deep domain expertise and wanted full access to client's proprietary data – particularly as they sought to introduce the tool to new industries. Neither party wanted to share too much. Initially, many clients and providers get frustrated, as evidenced by many of our prior case studies. Eventually, clients and providers negotiate an appropriate level of transparency in high-performing relationships.[26]

This typical scenario was also evident at Deakin University. Initially, members of the IT staff at the university wanted the provider to be fully transparent. The provider excluded Deakin's IT staff from their technical meetings. In the end, the parties negotiated the appropriate level of transparency on a 'need to know' basis. Deakin University learned enough about Watson's functional components and architecture to optimise Watson's performance and to provide ongoing support. The university understood that IBM needed to protect its intellectual property on machine learning algorithms and how the technology classifies natural language. IBM also gained valuable insights from a high level of transparency into Deakin's environment – certainly Deakin University informed some of Watson's product development directions. The same employee quoted above, explained that by the end of the process: *"We both definitely gained from working with each other."*

(14) Expect technical challenges as a first-mover

As noted in Chapter 5, Deakin University gained considerable gravitas from being the first university to adopt Watson for student services. The university gained a first-mover competitive advantage in terms of heightened brand awareness, globally, but it also brought the challenges of dealing with a young tool. IBM designed Watson to win the US game show *Jeopardy!* and thus did not initially design the architecture, nor its interfaces, for commercial usage. This meant that Deakin University's IT staff was working with some rudimentary tools and with unfriendly scripts and configuration files. Also, Watson was initially designed to load data; it was not designed for on-going curation. This meant that IBM was simultaneously improving the tool while developing the student query application. Such parallel developments are quite common experiences for first-mover adopters. Members of IBM Watson staff were also relatively unfamiliar with applying IBM Watson tools to the university education sector (unlike, for example, in the health sector). This meant that Deakin's in-house IT teams and project managers had to take more work than first envisaged. The good news for later Watson adopters is that Deakin University helped to pave the way for improvements from which other organisations will benefit.

A similar experience happened at SEB. The bank was the first organisation to implement IPsoft's Amelia in Swedish. Initially, some SEB staff members were quite frustrated with Amelia's poor Swedish language capabilities. According to one source, the software initially misinterpreted about 90 percent of dialog. However, SEB was able to quickly improve Amelia's Swedish language competency in text chat. Compared to teaching a human to learn a new language, this cognitive tool learns rapidly. Nicolas Moch, Head of Information, Strategy & Architecture at SEB said: *"Amelia's capacity to swiftly learn was an unexpected surprise."*

8.6. CA Design and Build Action Principles

Organisations have several risks to mitigate during CA launch to prevent initial projects from failing technically, financially and/or politically. Picking the right projects to automate/augment is paramount. In Chapter 2, we identified three RPA action principles to mitigate these risks that also apply to CA: 'Select 'wow' projects based on impact to customers and employees'; 'Redesign human work for automation'; and 'Consider Pareto's Principle' (the 80-20 rule). Five more action principles surfaced from CA adoptions:

(15) Find high impact use cases

> *"I challenge customers to pick use cases of significance, something that will deliver real business value in terms of reducing costs, increasing revenue, and improving compliance."* **Edwin van Bommel, Chief Cognitive Officer at IPsoft**

Potential adopters of cognitive technologies will want to know how to assess the suitability of the technologies to their existing services. Organisations should aim for use cases that will generate value for shareholders, customer and employees (see Figure 8.3).

To generate shareholder value, *cognitive experts and early adopters report that cognitive is most suitable for services that rely on vast amounts of unstructured data and expertise, have enough scale to justify the investment, and are strategic to the business.* Organisations also need to consider customer preferences. Certain customers in certain situations prefer to interact with a machine. Julia Aymonier, CIO for École Hôtelière de Lausanne, offered this example: *"I know, in certain hotels, people have asked questions of the concierge AI system, which they would not ask a human, that's for sure."*[27] Eliminate 'pain points' for customers by asking: *"Are there bottlenecks to delivering good customer service that could be alleviated with CA?"* Customer pain points should be resolved from initiation through to execution, thus delivering a frictionless, end-to-end service experience.

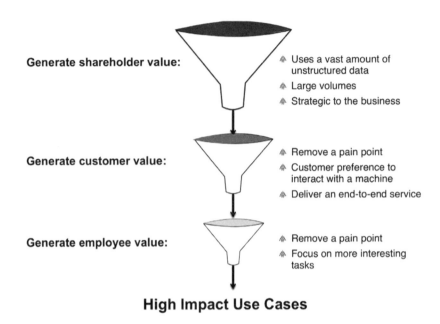

Generate shareholder value:
- Uses a vast amount of unstructured data
- Large volumes
- Strategic to the business

Generate customer value:
- Remove a pain point
- Customer preference to interact with a machine
- Deliver an end-to-end service

Generate employee value:
- Remove a pain point
- Focus on more interesting tasks

High Impact Use Cases

Figure 8.3: High impact use cases

As for employees on the front lines of customer service, what pain points can be eliminated for them? Are they spending too much time extracting natural language text from multiple sources before they can begin servicing the customer? Here's how our case study companies identified high impact use cases ...

For KPMG, selecting services across all service lines – advisory, audit, and tax – meet these criteria for cognitive adoption. For organisations in other industries, Todd Lohr, Principal, US Transformation Enablement Leader at KPMG predicted that cognitive technologies would be widely applied in organisations with large customer service centres:

"If your competitive differentiator is customer service, and if you have a huge call centre and spend large sums of money on maintaining and providing that centre, you should probably be

thinking seriously about what cognitive automation can do for your business on a very real way."

Todd Lohr also noted why scale matters:

"You're not going to see small companies investing in cognitive because they won't have the volume. It will be cheaper for them to put 10 employees on the task. You need the people that are putting thousands of employees on it."

Deakin University wanted to use Watson to provide students with a single source of accurate, current, and relevant information available on any device.[28] It also wanted Watson to improve the student experience by tailoring a student's queries to their own student profile. Deakin's use case of having Watson answer student queries meet the criteria of: vast amounts of unstructured data and expertise (e.g. students ask a lot of questions that knowledgeable staff need to answer); enough scale to justify the investment (e.g. Deakin was seeking to double or triple enrollment); and strategic to the business (e.g. student experience is Deakin's differentiating advantage). Certainly, some students preferred to express their anxiety to a machine rather than an advisor or counselor. Watson offers suggestions for assistance.

SEB's use case was consistent with these criteria. It also wanted use cases where Amelia could execute a simple end-to-end service and eliminate a pain point for their customers, thus getting high-impact and senior management attention. SEB's password reset use case illustrated this beautifully: it was a high volume service, it was a simple service, yet it was a painful service because people had long wait times before their problem was resolved. Amelia could actually complete the service without human intervention in the majority of cases, thus meeting all the criteria. Employees manning the help desk no longer had to perform rote tasks and instead could focus on more challenging calls.

Zurich Insurance also selected a high-impact use case – claims processing for personal injury claims. This process uses a vast amount of unstructured data; requires skilled claims examiners; was painful for customers; and offered great opportunities to improve the service and reduce the costs. The process was complicated enough to 'wow' its stakeholders, but not so complicated that it risked failure. The employees could focus on customer service and negotiations.

(16) Don't under-estimate the data challenge

As noted in Chapter 3, organisational adopters of CA tools have to deal with *difficult data* that is hard for a machine to read, such as fuzzy images, unexpected data types, or poorly-worded natural language text. Much of an organisation's data may be *dark data* that is un-locatable, untapped, or untagged. Organisations may have only a *dearth of good data* with which to train the tool. Finally, organisations have to clean up *dirty data* that is missing, incorrect, inconsistent or outdated (see Figure 8.4).

Organisations used a number of practices to establish a reliable 'ground-truth', all of which involved significant human intervention. When Deakin University discovered that data sources were not always up to date or accurate, the university assigned a single content owner responsible for each subject area and had them provide the correct answers to questions for Watson ingestion. KPMG pre-processed data before feeding it into their cognitive tools. SEB had to make sure Amelia only learned from 'good' agent conversations.

(17) Find new data sources if dirty data cannot be cleaned

What else can be done besides cleaning up existing data? Progressive companies, like KPMG and Standard Bank in South Africa[29], found alternative data sources. In KPMG's audit use case (described in Chapter 4), we saw that KPMG enabled Watson to extract a single, needed attribute from multiple data sources, thus accelerating the front-end data feed. Standard Bank in South Africa eliminated old data sources altogether. Its use case was a

The Data Challenge for CA Ingestion

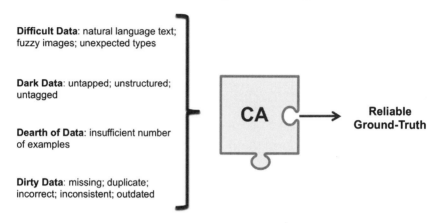

Difficult Data: natural language text; fuzzy images; unexpected types

Dark Data: untapped; unstructured; untagged

Dearth of Data: insufficient number of examples

Dirty Data: missing; duplicate; incorrect; inconsistent; outdated

CA

Reliable Ground-Truth

Figure 8.4: The 'Data Challenge'

customer application process to apply for a current account and overdraft. In the legacy world, the process required the customer to provide pay slips; three months of bank statements; identification such as a passport; and utility bills to confirm their income, identity, and residency. The OCR technology often had difficulty interpreting poor quality images, resulting in bank employees calling the customer to gather all the required data. The entire process took, on average, 22 days. Standard Bank re-imagined the entire process, beginning with using the newly available digital data services prompted by the South African government's Know Your Customer (KYC) regulations. Using these digital services – combined with credit checks to serve as a proxy for employment, and service automation technologies – the new system pulls the required data from the third-party databases, performs 19 verification checks, loads the data into the legacy systems, and passes the outcome back to the customer in just 5 minutes.[30]

(18) Fix discoveries about process flaws before implementing CA

"Clients need to be open to changing the user experience with cognitive technologies. While an online form with 32 questions, in

order to get a car quote, may work for that channel, clients need to think how an intelligent platform can transform and uplift the experience to a new level." **Edwin van Bommel, Chief Cognitive Officer at IPsoft**

Data is not the only challenge – processes might also be unnecessarily onerous, inconsistent or incorrect across an enterprise. Gary Hoberman, CEO and founder of Unqork and previously CIO of MetLife, was one of the earliest adopters of IPsoft's Amelia. He wanted to connect Amelia to a customer-facing website, to help deal with customers' questions about insurance products. The website escalated unanswered queries or requests to a call centre in India. To train Amelia, the team fed in 170 chat logs. Initially, the software performed poorly. Rather than abandon the technology, Hoberman investigated the problem:

> *"We didn't stop. Instead, we asked 'why?' We found that the call centre people were telling customers to clear the cache, or clear the browser, on their PCs as opposed to telling them: 'actually, this is not a product we offer'. So it was Amelia who was correct after all and we had to go back and re-train the people."*[31]

As discussed in Chapter 6, SEB discovered some bad processes while it was documenting existing processes in preparation for training Amelia. As the team went through drawing the processes on a whiteboard, they discovered legacy steps that no longer served a business purpose, but were still being executed by the human service agents, *"because we have always done it this way."* Deakin University's web publishing practices were ad hoc, with no standard process, leading to outdated information being posted on different webpages. Both SEB and Deakin streamlined and standardised processes to ensure faster, more consistent services before automation. Thus, traditional process improvement methods combined with cognitive automation helped to deliver benefits.

As discussed in Chapter 7, Zurich Insurance created a new process flow. It found that cognitive automation is often not about automating the existing process, but more about creating a new process flow that fits the machine. Hence, Zurich Insurance moved from a human-centric process flow to a machine-centric process flow.

(19) Compare CA training to human training

"People ask me why it takes Watson a few years to learn oncology, but I ask them how long does it take a human to learn it? The oncology leaders we are working with have spent decades learning what they know, so a few years for Watson seems reasonable."[32]
Mike Rhodin, head of IBM's Watson business unit

We have discussed data and process challenges, but there is also the training challenge to consider. Sophisticated CA technologies, like Watson, may take years to train because of the vast corpus of knowledge needed for many of the applications. Watson's corpus of knowledge in healthcare, for example, had, as of 2013: 1.5 million patient records, 600,000 pieces of medical evidence and two million pages of text from 42 medical journals and clinical trials in the area of oncology research.[33] Helping Watson interpret such a large amount of knowledge required thousands of hours of supervised machine learning (see Chapter 3 for an explanation of machine learning).

IBM Watson adopters often compare the time it takes to train Watson with the time it takes to train a human, arguing that Watson learns much faster than humans. Vinodh Swaminathan, Managing Director, Innovation & Enterprise Solutions at KPMG, explained that training Watson takes less time than training a human:

"Yes, training Watson is a long process because, even in machine terms, it is the equivalent of taking 16 years of education for a human, plus years of an apprenticeship, and compressing it in time; so it could take 18 months to train Watson instead of 18 years for a human – but it still takes 18 months."

At Deakin University, the university turned the immense amount of human supervision into an opportunity for students. The university recruited 200 student volunteers to test and further train Watson just prior to launch. Students indicated if Watson's answers were correct, incomplete, or inaccurate, and their feedback was incorporated into the application to improve Watson's performance.

As noted above, SEB devoted human labour to teach Amelia Swedish. The software became competent in the new language much quicker than a human could.

8.7. Stakeholder Buy-in Action Principles

As covered in Chapter 3, the media is awash in both hype and fear about cognitive automation's true capabilities, and it often underplays the amount of work required to get tools to perform proficiently (see also Action Principle 31). Therefore, any organisation that adopts CA technologies will have to set realistic expectations, overcoming both inflated expectations caused by splashy 'artificial intelligence' victories, as well overcoming deep cynicism caused by notorious defeats. The action principles, which also applied to RPA, are setting realistic expectations up the chain of command, down to employees, and out to customers.

(20) Manage up: Gain C-suite support without overselling

> *"To really transform businesses with this technology requires top executive attention and drive to make it happen. Whether companies are working with Amelia, Watson, or another platform, you need to get these projects out of digital labs and into the business."* **Edwin van Bommel, Chief Cognitive Officer at IPsoft**

The C-suite needs to understand that cognitive automation projects are investments in the future. Program champions are advised to get the C-suite excited about the innovation without promising immediate financial returns.

Program champions at KPMG, Deakin University, SEB and Zurich all reported that their leaders are highly supportive of their cognitive programs. Vinodh Swaminathan explained:

> *"Maybe KPMG is different, but every time I've gone to my leadership team and demonstrated Watson in action for different use cases, they're very excited about the possibilities. Our leadership team is focused on the legacy we are going to leave to our future employees. They know that the world is going to be different five to ten years from now, and it's our responsibility, as leaders, to make sure that the brand, the enterprise, and the firm successfully navigates this and places us in a great position to succeed in that new world."*

At SEB, Nicolas Moch, Head of Information, Strategy & Architecture, described SEB's CEO as: *"very driven to try new things"*,[34] but he was also clear that the bank needed to invest significant resources in training the software, building and deploying targeted use cases, and figuring out how these tools will ultimately transform service delivery on a larger scale. At Deakin University, the IBM Watson decision occurred at the upper-most level of the university, so the program champions were the top managers.

(21) Manage down: envision, communicate, and deliver value to employees

> *"The response is always positive when we introduce Amelia to the staff. As soon as Amelia is demonstrated, the room fills with positive energy."* **Nicolas Moch, Head of Information, Strategy & Architecture at SEB**

As with any automation technology, employees may feel threatened by cognitive automation. From our RPA and CA research[35], organisations are advised to envision, communicate, and deliver the following value to employees:

- Employees will perform fewer repetitive and boring tasks
- Employees will focus more on customer service, problem solving, creative, and complex tasks
- Employees will learn new skills
- Employees who embrace service automation will be recognised as innovators

Concerning the last bullet point, Rich Pierle, CIO of Becton Dickenson, gave cash awards to each agent who developed a new process for its Cognitive Virtual Agent.[36]

Returning to our cases, Chris Williver, Technical Project Manager for Deakin University, explained:

> *"The engagement with the university community was really important. The message was, 'Yes, let's be excited because it's an exciting technology', but we also distilled the message that Watson was never going to be perfect or even great from day one."*

The university's staff members understood that they were not going to be replaced; they were going to be an integral part of Watson's success in terms of content curation, management and training.

At SEB, the bank initially faced a 'prejudiced resistance,' from employees, which was overcome by demonstrating the practical advantages of adopting the new technology. SEB reported that the response to the technology had been uniformly positive. SEB found that many people working on its service desk were actually happy that Amelia was joining the team as they saw the potential for it to *"take away a lot of the repetitive tasks that most of the people working on service desk don't like doing."*[37]

At Zurich Insurance, the claims examiners embraced the CA tool because it took the dreariest task – reading medical reports to extract data – out of their work and allowed them to focus on higher valued tasks such as interacting with customers and negotiating settlements. They were also given more time to do these higher-valued tasks after the CA tool performed the previously time-consuming tasks, which relieved their job stress. Gero Gunkel, Program Manager of Innovation and Business Development at Zurich said:

> *"You would assume that people are going to be very hostile to automation, because, obviously, it's a change for them. But overall, our people liked the notion of being decision-makers and negotiators. It basically takes away all the tasks that they're not very keen to do and focuses on exactly what we've actually trained them to do – which is to settle the claim for a good price for us, that is still fair to the other side, and so we don't have to go to court to seek settlement."*

(22) Manage out: Be transparent with customers

Across our CA case studies, managing customer expectations was an important practice. Among the cases that had already deployed customer-facing CA applications, all were transparent about the fact that customers were interfacing with a piece of software. They set customer expectations about the tool's performance by saying the tool was still learning. Additionally, organisations quickly diverted customers to a human when conversations became unproductive (see Action Principles 24 and 26).

For Deakin University, the 'customers' are students. The university set realistic expectations by telling students that Watson was still learning and that the more they used it, the more its performance would improve. Setting such expectations prevented students from complaining too much about the 20 percent of queries that Watson, initially, did not answer.

As discussed in Chapter 6, at SEB, customers were invited to try Aida (SEB's rebranding of Amelia), but set expectations by writing *"Our chat is new and under development. Aida is our digital employee with artificial intelligence. She will help you with your questions and when she cannot answer, you will get the opportunity to continue to chat with a coworker from customer service."*

Once customers interacted with Aida, SEB invited them to provide feedback on the experience, with Likert Scale ratings and an open text box (see Figure 8.5). This is the epitome of a learning project (see Action Principle 7), as SEB collects the conversations and incorporates the customers' feedback.

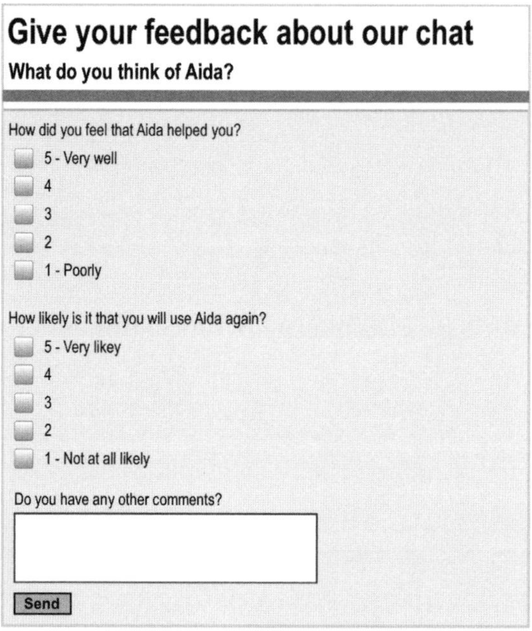

Give your feedback about our chat

What do you think of Aida?

How did you feel that Aida helped you?
- 5 - Very well
- 4
- 3
- 2
- 1 - Poorly

How likely is it that you will use Aida again?
- 5 - Very likey
- 4
- 3
- 2
- 1 - Not at all likely

Do you have any other comments?

Send

Figure 8.5: Customer feedback form for SEB's Amelia (called Aida)
(Please note: Page was translated from Swedish to English using Google Translate)

8.8. CA Run

CA applications in production require different management practices than those typically used for other types of enterprise software. Enterprise software is normally excessively tested and quality is assured before moving the software into production. Organisations need to think differently about when cognitive technologies projects are 'finished' and ready for production. Our case studies uncovered five action principles that are unique to CA applications:

(23) Treat cognitive technologies as lifelong learners

Like human learners, cognitive technologies are never 'finished', because they can continually improve performance over time as more data is entered and as more users provide feedback. Based on early CA adopters, one can infer the lesson to treat cognitive technology-based applications as lifelong learners.

At KPMG, the required level of cognitive accuracy depends on the use case. Some business services such as audit and risk assessment – much like healthcare – cannot afford false positives. Other uses cases, like the business development case discussed in Chapter 4, have more leeway; Watson is not expected to identify every single relevant opportunity and it's understandable if Watson initially suggests some unlikely services. Across all use cases, humans will continue to check and verify Watson's outputs and humans will continue to help Watson improve with time. Ultimately, the business sponsors of each service will set the thresholds of acceptable performance.

Deakin University actually made Watson's incompletion a selling point for its users by recruiting students to help train Watson. As explained in Chapter 5, it launched Watson with only 2000 question-answer pairs. During orientation week in 2016, the university explained that Watson was still learning and that the university needed each student's assistance to further train Watson. Students were given buttons with the slogan *'I'm helping train Watson'* to engage students and staff.[38] As of 2017, Watson can respond to 6,000 different questions and personalise responses based on student profile.

(24) Invite customers to try the automation, but keep other channels open

Because CA technologies produce probabilistic outcomes rather than deterministic outcomes, and because organisations can never predict how customers will actually interact with the technology, initial performance will not be perfect. At Deakin University, Watson correctly answered direct questions or offered appropriate options about 80 percent of the time. At SEB, IPsoft's Amelia initially handled 50 percent of text chat conversations without needing human intervention. So that customers do not get frustrated with the 20 to 50 percent of incomplete responses, it's best to keep alternative customer channels running in parallel with CA.

For both the internal and external services, SEB invited customers to try Aida (Amelia) but they also keep all other channels available. Mikael Anderson, SEB Transformation Lead – Amelia Exploration, expected there would be hurdles to overcome: *"because every customer is different and wants support in different ways. There is also a trust issue to overcome with customers, so the company will ease the technology in."*[39]

(25) Supervise all new learning

"One of the weaknesses is we can't train it fast enough to keep up with humans. So AI's great – but it's not as clever as a human." **Professor Jane den Hollander, Vice Chancellor for Deakin University**

Managers need to design a training program for machines, just as they would a human. The first decision is whether to select supervised or unsupervised machine learning (see Chapter 3 for details).[40] Many CA tools have unsupervised learning capabilities, but organisational adopters need to consider whether it is wise to enable such features. One only has to remember the unintended consequences of unleashing Microsoft's TayTweets to understand the issue.[41] KPMG, Deakin University, and SEB all chose supervised learning.

At KPMG, all of the use cases used supervised machine learning. A human expert interacts with Watson through a natural language interface using a keyboard to 'talk' to Watson and a monitor to 'listen' to Watson. Watson indicates, on the monitor, when it cannot confidently interpret a phrase so the human can provide feedback, thus adding to Watson's capabilities.

For Deakin University's application, Watson's 'ground-truth' was based on the newly written answers by staff to the first 2,000 questions. Deakin University decided humans would supervise all of Watson's learning in the future as well. The university did not want Watson to assimilate unverified facts or to adjust its affinity weights based on conversations and response feedback with students or staff. One interviewee explained: *"We didn't want Watson to serve up popular answers rather than accurate answers."* Deakin University reviews the logs of Watson's conversations to ascertain whether Watson needs retraining. Retraining could be as simple as adding a question variation or rewording a response, to more complicated revisions such as reorganising the intent clusters.

At SEB, the bank did not want Aida to assimilate unverified facts from conversations with customers, so SEB decided to guide Aida's learning with human intervention: *"For the queries Aida cannot resolve, she observes the employee-agent interaction, dynamically learning from her colleagues how to deal with similar variations. Once **her new learnings are approved by her human supervisors** she can answer these queries herself in future."*[42] SEB controlled the conversations from which Aida was allowed to learn; SEB only wanted the software to learn from 'good' customer service conversations. SEB updated Aida with new information every three hours as of 2016.

(26) Decide optimal time to escalate calls to humans

As part of managing cognitive applications, there are other unique development decisions to be made, such as deciding when to have humans take over the service. This was a decision SEB had to make for both its internal and external services. As noted above, Aida was initially able to resolve about 50 percent of the calls without human intervention. Why didn't the software resolve a higher percentage? Part of the reason was because

SEB deliberately designed Aida to quickly escalate calls to a human, rather than frustrate their employees and customers. Thus, SEB restrained Aida by design.

Other organisations will need to make a similar determination: How many levels should cognitive virtual agents deal with before escalation to a human? For some consumer applications, organisations might decide to *never* escalate calls to a human. For example, consumers seem to accept that if Apple's Siri or Amazon's Alexa cannot help them, they will NOT be connected to the Apple or Amazon support desk.

(27) Keep subject matter experts continually engaged in curation

To participate in CA curation, subject matter experts (SMEs) have to learn how to train the machine, as it's a different process than training another human. It's fun – at first. But the sheer volume of training can fatigue SMEs who may decide they prefer their day job, particularly for highly educated SMEs like physicians and lawyers. Subject matter curation of content is an ongoing process after implementation, meaning that SMEs must be continually engaged in curation.

At Deakin University, the SMEs across campus are responsible for Watson's content. Traditionally, the SMEs were responsible for managing web-based content, which has its own particular structure and editorial style. For Watson, SMEs needed to write content in a form that a virtual system would provide, rather than what students would read on a web page. Thus, the SMEs had to be educated on how to write and structure content for Watson ingestion, which most did so enthusiastically. Chris Williver, Technical Project Manager for Deakin University explained: *"When we implemented Watson, that was an exciting time for the subject matter experts."*

After the exhilaration of Watson's launch, time marched on, and some SMEs were forgetting to inform the Watson support team when content needed to be changed. Chris Williver, Technical Project Manager for Deakin University continued:

> *"Some people starting to take their eye off the ball a little bit, forgetting that what they wrote 12 months ago needed updating. People naturally go back to their old ways of doing things. Ongoing engagement with the community is important."*

Chris predicted that over the next three to five years, the vast majority of student interactions with Deakin's online content will be via bots and virtual agents like Watson, rather than reading web pages.

8.9. Maturity Action Principles

Initially, organisations typically focus deeply on a new technology, such as creating a dedicated Centre of Excellence (CoE) or Innovation Lab. There's a lot to learn at first, so a concentrated effort makes sense. Once a proof-of-concept moves to a pilot and then to a full-blown enterprise application, the next step is usually pollenating the innovation broadly across the enterprise. As time passes, the organisation has deep expertise with the innovation and can step back to see how the technology can be integrated with other innovations to deliver even more business value. Eventually, innovations become institutionalised – part of the fabric of the enterprise architecture – and new cycles of innovation begin. For CA innovations, we found three compelling action principles:

(28) Move to a federated model to broadly infuse CA

New technologies that require a significant amount of resources in terms of investment and learning are often managed centrally, at least initially. Once the core team has gained expertise and proven the technology with initial deployments, a new management structure may be needed to more broadly diffuse the innovation. Zurich Insurance has been moving to a more federated model to accomplish this. It views CA as a general-purpose technology that can be applied to many business contexts that use text-based data. Going forward, the centralised group will serve as in-house consultants to help business operations pick the right tool for the task, but the business unit will lead and run the automation. Gero Gunkel, Program Manager of Innovation and Business Development at Zurich said: *"It's a bit like a supermarket; you come and tell us what you want, and we say, use this and this."*

(29) Continually innovate because today's 'cool' is tomorrow's 'yawn'

Consumers have an insatiable appetite for new technologies, particularly for tools that enhance their ability to access services anytime, anywhere. However, the thrill prompted by the newest technologies wanes quickly – today's 'wow' innovations fade into the background and become part of the minimum expected technology toolkit. This pattern of waxing and waning exhilaration is evident across many of our cases, but really stands out at Deakin University.

William Confalonieri, Chief Digital Officer for Deakin University, described student expectations as: *"expecting a digital world to be highly fast and functional, beautiful and usable, optimised for mobile, and consistent and seamless."*[43] Students were initially very excited by the Watson application, but as time went on, their technology expectations rose. One interviewee said,

> *"When we started, students were amazed it could answer a question. Within a year, they ceased to be impressed and some stopped using it because it lacks speech to text capabilities."*

Indeed, in 2016, Google reported that 20 percent of mobile queries were voice searches.[44] Student expectations are massive; students want their universities to at least match the technical capabilities of their own personal devices.

(30) Integrate service automation programs

"The bank's deployment [of IPsoft's Amelia] provides a strong example of the productivity improvements that can be achieved by combining cognitive and autonomic solutions. It highlights the potential of integrating digital labour, autonomics, people, processes and technology into a single system that increases performance levels."[45] **Executive from SEB Case Study**

How might service innovations be integrated? By mid-2017, some organisations were coordinating their CA and RPA initiatives. A common first step was to bolt CA as a feeder to RPA. As organisations began to address the difficult, dark, and dirty data issues for CA, CA was used to structure inputs for RPA processes that Optical Character Recognition (OCR) technology had missed, increasing the number of transactions that RPA could handle. With more structured data available, organisations can better deploy analytics to describe and predict events (see Figure 8.6). As noted in the previous chapter, 80 percent of Zurich Insurance's claims data is text-based and unstructured. By using a CA tool to structure claims data, it could more effectively use predictive analytics to reduce claims costs and shorten time to close. We also saw in Chapter 2 that RPA can be used to feed cognitive automation on the backend.

Integrating, or at least coordinating, RPA and CPA programs is just the beginning. Increasingly, organisations will create competitive advantage by connecting various innovations such as: **S**ocial media; **M**obile technologies; **A**nalytics and Big Data; **C**loud services; **B**lockchains; **R**obotics; **A**utomation of Knowledge Work (like RPA and CA); the **I**nternet-of-Things (IoT); and **D**igital Fabrication (i.e. 3-D printing) – which we call '**SMAC/BRAID**', for service delivery (see Figure 8.7).

Deakin University integrates many of its innovations. It's most recent application is called 'Genie'. It's actually a platform made up of chatbots, CA

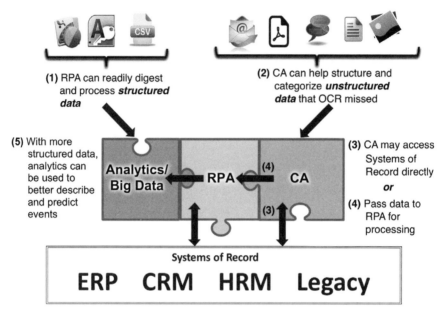

**Figure 8.6: Service automation integration –
CA, RPA, and analytics**

(e.g. Watson), voice recognition, and predictive analytics,[47] presented to users as a proactive, virtual personal assistant launched on their mobile devices. William Confalonieri described its potential uses:

> *"Genie is a proactive agent. So if you have an exam in two days and you haven't been reading the material, Genie is going to remind you that the exam is coming up and you haven't touched your material."*

In order to deduce that situation, the application accesses the learning management system to determine the last time the student opened course materials. William Confalonieri offered another example:

> *"If you have been studying in the same place for ten hours, it's going to tell you that's not good for your health, you should go and walk for a bit."*[48]

Figure 8.7: Service automation's building pieces
(Source: Lacity and Willcocks (2017))[46]

In order to deduce that situation, the student would need to grant the application permission to track his or her location. The platform went live in March 2017 as a pilot for some business and law students. Deakin University will incorporate feedback from the pilot to improve Genie, before a broader launch scheduled for Fall 2017.

How else might service automation's building pieces be integrated? Organisations like LO3 Energy and Moog Aircraft are integrating 'SMAC/ BRAID' to produce secure, trusted, point-of-use, 'just-in-time' supply chains. Such a supply chain needs a trusted record of data provenance, from the asset's origin to a time-stamped history of events related to that asset. All parties in the supply chain need to verify their identities and authorise and validate transactions. If digital fabrication is involved, the supply chain needs to know the 3D printing instructions have not been corrupted. Such a supply chain integrates IoT, blockchain, cloud, mobile, digital fabrication, analytics, RPA and CA technologies. The possibilities are endless.

8.10. General Action Principles

In reviewing the four case studies, we became clear that two other Action Principles needed to be highlighted, of a more general nature.

(31) Prepare for a lot more effort than you think

The media can be highly misleading about cognitive automation capabilities, and frequently underplays the amount of work it requires to get tools to perform proficiently. Zurich Insurance's experiences reinforce those we found at KPMG, SEB, and Deakin University. Therefore, any organisation adopting cognitive automation technologies will have to overcome inflated hopes and set realistic expectations. In particular, it is clear that cognitive automation tools are not, as of 2017, 'plug and play' in the sorts of organisational contexts we are examining. There is plenty of human work required. For example one Zurich executive told us:

> *"There are limits. Do you have enough training days? Is the data clear and understandable, and do you actually have a clear reference point? Especially if you talk to a subject matter expert and you say, 'explain me how to do it, what kind of features are relevant?' A lot of people think machine learning and AI have few human elements, but in fact they need a lot of domain knowledge and, to attack the domain knowledge, you need to synthesise that knowledge – you need to do process engineering. One of the least understood elements in all of these projects, whatever tool you use, is that it's everything **but** taking a machine, putting data in there, getting the result and going home."*

(32) Plan for more work and jobs than many predict

Some studies have predicted considerable job losses arising from automation. As we point out in some detail in the last chapter, such studies frequently offer no timeline; do not factor in job creation; focus on whole jobs rather than activities that make up jobs; underplay how long it can take a technology to become fully deployed into 50 percent to 90 percent usage; do not consider demographics – such as ageing populations; and do not factor in productivity shortfalls being experienced across many major economies now and across the next thirty years. They also assume the rapid perfectibility of automation technology. In addition they do not factor in the impact of the exponential data explosion, and the dramatic increase in audit, regulation and bureaucracy that increases greatly the work a company, like Zurich Insurance, has to process[49].

On jobs and work volumes, we can report that KPMG, Deakin University, SEB and Zurich Insurance were all reporting significant increases in work to be accomplished. Their experiences of automation are much more consistent with the more complex and nuanced picture we will develop in the final chapter of this book. Zurich Insurance is a more typical exemplar of what we have been finding both with robotic process and cognitive automation deployments. According to one senior manager:

> *"We will see reducing headcounts but it will be much smoother than most of the general predictions. It's rather that we will not reduce the headcount directly, but as people retire, we may not hire again. The company has already said that. Because the cognitive automation market is still very immature, one can see deployment being much slower than many have been suggesting. We will automate bits and pieces everywhere, but people will still be needed to work with the technology in many roles. New skills sets will be required, translating into new jobs."*

In the next chapter, we elevate the discourse from our empirical research base, to address the implications of all of this on the **'Future of Work'**.

Citations

1. Talk at IPsoft's Digital Workforce Summit, 1st June 2017, New York City.

2. Quote from IPsoft Panel Perspectives, Digital Workforce Summit, 31st May 2017, p. 3.

3. Willcocks, L. and Lacity, M. (2016), *Service Automation: Robots and the Future of Work*, (SB Publishing, UK). p. 246.

4. *WellPoint and IBM Announce Agreement to Put Watson to Work in Health Care*. Press release, 12th September 2011. https://www-03.ibm.com/press/us/en/pressrelease/35402.wss.

5. *In year two, MD Anderson Moon Shots Program begins to spin off innovation.* MD Anderson News Release, 30th October 2014. https://www.mdanderson.org/newsroom/2014/10/in-year-two-md-anderson-moon-shots-program-begins-to-spin-off-in.html.

6. *Memorial Sloan Kettering Trains IBM Watson to Help Doctors Make Better Cancer Treatment Choices.* 11th April 2014, https://www.mskcc.org/blog/msk-trains-ibm-watson-help-doctors-make-better-treatment-choices.

7. Gaudin, S. (2014), 'Cleveland Clinic uses IBM's Watson in the cloud to fight cancer'. *ComputerworldUK*, 29th October 2014. http://www.computerworlduk.com/news/it-vendors/cleveland-clinic-uses-ibms-watson-in-the-cloud-to-fight-cancer-3583302/.

8. *IBM and LifeLearn Tap the Power of Watson to Transform the Veterinary Industry*, 6th October 2014. http://www.lifelearn.com/2014/10/06/ibm-watson-lifelearn-sofie/.

9. Picton, G. (2014), *Study shows promise in automated reasoning, hypothesis generation over complete medical literature.* https://www.bcm.edu/news/research/automated-reasoning-hypothesis-generation.

10. Willcocks, L. and Lacity, M. (2016), *Service Automation: Robots and the Future of Work*, (SB Publishing, UK); Lacity, M. and Willcocks, L. (2017), *Robotic Process Automation and Risk Mitigation: The Definitive Guide*, (SB Publishing, UK). Available from www.sbpublishing.org.

11. SEB 2015 Annual Report http://sebgroup.com/siteassets/about_seb1/who_we_are/ar15_strategy_en.pdf.

12. Willcocks and Lacity (2016) reported on the ROIs for 13 RPA adopters, which ranged between 30 percent and 200 percent.

13. Op. cit. Inglebrecht, N., and Lowendahl, J.M. (2016),

14. Lacity, M. and Willcocks, L. (2017), *Robotic Process Automation and Risk Mitigation: The Definitive Guide*, (SB Publishing, UK).

15. Pisano, G. (2012), *Creating an R&D Strategy*. Harvard Business School Working Paper 12-095, available at http://www.hbs.edu/faculty/Publication%20Files/12-095_fb1bdf97-e0ec-4a82-b7c0-42279dd4d00e.pdf.

16. Quote from IPsoft Panel Perspectives, Digital Workforce Summit, 31st May 2017, p. 3.

17. Lacity, M. (editor), (2008), *Major Currents in Information Systems: The Management of Information Systems*, Volume 4 - series editors: Willcocks, L., and Lee, A., (Sage, London); Nelson, R., (2007), 'IT Project Management: Infamous Failure, Classic Mistakes, and Best Practices'. *MIS Quarterly Executive*, Vol. 6, 2, pp. 67-78.

18. Miles, C. (2013), *The Project Champion: A Management Best Practice*. Available at http://smallbiztrends.com/2013/12/what-is-a-project-champion.html.

19. Burns, K. (1997) Lewis & Clark: *The Journey of Discovery*. Four hour documentary that can be watched online at http://www.pbs.org/lewisandclark/.

20. Quote from Willcocks, L. and Lacity, M. (2016), *Service Automation: Robots and the Future of Work*, (SB Publishing, UK), p. 244.

21. Lacity, M. and Willcocks, L. (2017), *Robotic Process Automation and Risk Mitigation: The Definitive Guide*, (SB Publishing, UK).

22. Quote from Willcocks, L. and Lacity, M. (2016), *Service Automation: Robots and the Future of Work,* (SB Publishing, UK), p. 245-246.

23. Cortana is Microsoft's personal assistant software that uses voice recognition; it competes with Apple's SIRI and Google Now.

24. In 1988 the roboticist, Hans Moravec, created what has subsequently been called 'Moravec's Paradox' suggesting the strengths and weaknesses of cognitive tools: "It is comparatively easy to make computers exhibit adult level performance on intelligence tests or playing checkers, and difficult or impossible to give them the skills of a one-year old when it comes to perception and mobility". Quoted in Kasparov, G. (2016) Deep Thinking: Where Machine Intelligence Ends. (John Murray, London).

25. Lacity, M., and Willcocks, L. (2016), 'Robotic Process Automation at Telefónica O2'. *MIS Quarterly Executive*, Vol. 15, 1, pp. 21-35.

26. We have many cases that cover the issue of transparency in client-provider relationships reported in: Lacity, M., and Willcocks, L., (2015), *Nine Keys to World-class Business Process Outsourcing*, (Bloomsbury, London). For survey results pertaining to transparency, see: Lacity, M., and Rottman, J. (2011), 'Building a Better Outsourcing Community', *Globalization Today*, March, pp. 29-31.

27. Quote from IPsoft Panel Perspectives, Digital Workforce Summit, 31st May 2017, p. 4.

28. Adhikari, S., 'ANZ, Deakin University set to harness Watson', 8th October 2014, *The Australian*. http://www.theaustralian.com.au/business/latest/anz-deakin-university-set-to-harness-watson/news-story/3b35da14a4571bb30406a fab0cdf7a45.

29. Standard Bank example from Lacity, M. and Willcocks, L. (2017), *Robotic Process Automation and Risk Mitigation: The Definitive Guide*, (SB Publishing, UK).

30. HfS Webinar: Standard Bank Case Discussion. https://www.youtube.com/watch?v=Fl-6NKdmltE .

31. Quote from IPsoft Panel Perspectives, Digital Workforce Summit, 31st May 2017, p. 5.

32. Davenport, T. (2015), 'Lessons from the Cognitive Front Lines: Early Adopters of IBM's Watson', *The Wall Street Journal*, 3rd December 2013. http://blogs.wsj.com/cio/2015/12/03/lessons-from-the-cognitive-front-lines-early-adopters-of-ibms-watson/.

33. *IBM Watson Hard At Work: New Breakthroughs Transform Quality Care for Patients*. Press release, 8th February 2013. https://www-03.ibm.com/press/us/en/pressrelease/40335.wss.

34. Pioneers Panel. http://www.ipsoft.com/wp-content/uploads/2016/12/Pioneers_ Panel.pdf.

35. Lacity, M. and Willcocks, L. (2017), *Robotic Process Automation and Risk Mitigation: The Definitive Guide*, (SB Publishing, UK).

36. Quote from IPsoft Panel Perspectives, Digital Workforce Summit, 31st May 2017, p. 6.

37. Pioneers Panel. http://www.ipsoft.com/wp-content/uploads/2016/12/Pioneers_ Panel.pdf.

38. Watson @ Deakin University. Video posted 18th March 2015. https://www.youtube.com/watch?v=MK9gakgPDoc.

39. Flinders, K. (2016), 'How a Swedish bank prepared robot Amelia to provide customer services', *ComputerWeekly*, 8th - 14th November.

40. Machine learning is a way to program computers so that computers perform tasks competently based on prior examples, not just based on logic rules.

41. Hern, Alex (24th March 2016), 'Microsoft scrambles to limit PR damage over abusive AI bot Tay', *The Guardian*.

42. IPsoft case study, *Amelia in Action: IT Service Desk Agent for SEB Bank*.

43. William Confalonieri, *Creating effective and personalized digital experiences.* Presentation for the Connect Show, Melbourne, 22nd April 2015.

44. Sterling, G., *Voice search growing as virtual assistant market heats up.* Posted 18th May 2016 on: http://searchengineland.com/google-reveals-20-percent-queries-voice-queries-249917.

45. IPsoft case study, *Amelia in Action: IT Service Desk Agent for SEB Bank.*

46. Lacity, M. and Willcocks, L. (2017), *Robotic Process Automation and Risk Mitigation: The Definitive Guide*, (SB Publishing, UK).

47. Coyne, A., *Meet Genie, Deakin Uni's virtual assistant for students.* Posted 3rd March 2017 on https://www.itnews.com.au/news/meet-genie-deakin-unis-virtual-assistant-for-students-453230.

48. Ibid.

49. See Willcocks, L. and Lacity, M. (2016), *Service Automation: Robots and the Future of Work*, (SB Publishing, UK), Chapter 10.

Chapter 9

Automation and The Future of Work Revisited

By Leslie Willcocks

> *"We are ourselves creating our own successors....we are daily giving them greater power and supplying by all sorts of ingenious contrivances that self-regulating, self-acting power which will be to them what intellect has been to the human race. In the course of ages we shall find ourselves the inferior race."*
>
> **Samuel Butler, 1863**[1]

> *"Within 30 years we will have the technological means to create superhuman intelligence. Shortly after, the human era will be ended."*
>
> **Vernor Vinge, 1993**[2]

9.1. Introduction

The word 'robot' first appeared in 1920, but we have long been fascinated by the idea of creating a higher intelligence. Ancient mythology is full of references: For example Hephaestus, god of mechanical arts aided by two assistants made of gold *'living young damsels, filled with minds and wisdoms'*; Pygmalion, king of Cyprus, crafted his ideal woman out of ivory and brought her to life; and the Jewish legend of Golem, built from clay by a rabbi to protect his community from persecution. But while robots captivate us, we also seem to be highly suspicious of them. And with the development of Artificial Intelligence (AI) in recent years, we are increasingly seeing a rising tide of opinion warning us that the place that robots – physical and software –

could really hurt homo sapiens is not on some post-apocalyptic 'Terminator' battlefield, but in the workplace.

These anxieties are not new. And, quite rightly, automation has invariably been accompanied by health warnings. If the Luddites rebelled, famously, against early 19th century English factory automation, then, in 1874, Samuel Butler charted a more comprehensive, prescient dystopian future with work taken over by the rise of the machines:

> *"There is no security against the ultimate development of mechanical consciousness, in the fact of machines possessing little consciousness now."*

His book *Erewhon* uncannily points to the self-producing, conscious, all-controlling machines of our own worry point – the 'Technological Singularity' envisaged by Vernor Vinge in 1993, and by others since.[3] The fictional Erewhonian citizens destroyed most of their machines to stop this from happening. What should, and will, we be doing?

Initially confined to the most basic and process-driven tasks in the modern workplace, physical and software robots are becoming enhanced by the collection of tools we call 'cognitive automation', to infiltrate all aspects of our lives. In 2017 we found Amazon promising to deliver our all-important purchases by drone in the near future. Uber was pressing ahead with the idea of driverless cabs, despite some embarrassing failures to date. A hotel in Japan had android receptionists, as well as porter, cloakroom, service and cleaning robots. And a company in California was attempting to automate the world's oldest profession, which will enable robots with the capability for the most intimate of services. So are humans rapidly heading for history's work scrap heap? The accumulated evidence, as well as our own extensive research into the actual and likely effects of robotic process and cognitive automation (see Chapters 2 to 8), portrays a much more complex and nuanced narrative than the hype or fear stories we read every day.

9.2. 'Hype or Fear' – Deconstructing Automation Narratives

Looking at the bigger picture, it is not easy to pick your way through the media representations of the debate around automation, robots and the future of work. Sources and multiple studies are very variable in quality, evidence and rigour, but they seem to polarise around two storylines – hype or fear. We have met these before in Chapter 8, as a typical early stage response to technology adoption. In the case of automation, 'Hype' tells us that it is largely going to be fine and most of us are going to live in a well-run, technologised world – let's call it 'Automotopia' – with more than enough goods, services, and leisure. Technology will create jobs and provide solutions to multiple problems. There are many symbols for this, but a typical one is a service robot deployed in service or care settings, for example in Japan, to solve elderly care problems and labour shortages – a country, as we have seen, also sporting the fully-robotised Henn-na show hotel. The assumptions embedded in this narrative are that technology will be a panacea; there will be massive benefits; the technology is perfectible; there will be few barriers; and adoption will be quick and pervasive.[4]

Meanwhile the other, 'Fear', vision is essentially dystopian, with sample headlines or article titles being: *'Who Owns The Robots Rules The World'*; *'How The Robots Will Take Your Job and Kill The Economy'*; *and 'Robots could displace 10 million British workers'.*[5] This polarised narrative – let's call it 'Automageddon' – also assumes quick and pervasive adoption of the technology, but sees it as displacing a huge number of physical and cognitive-based jobs across industries, geographies and at most levels in the organisation. Here the assumptions are that automation means job displacement; there will be little job creation; that societies, organisations and individuals will be ill-placed to respond to the rapid deployment of automation; and that human capabilities will have little role to play in the future of work.

Interestingly 'Automotopia' is not well represented by detailed studies of, as opposed to speculations, about this optimistic scenario.[6] But 'Automageddon' does find more underpinning in fine, detailed, sober studies such as Richard and Daniel Susskind's *The Future of the Professions* and Martin Ford's *The Rise of the Robots*.[7] Both provide much detail on the tasks that could be automated in multiple sectors and across most occupations in the relatively near future. But other accumulating evidence, and our own work since 2016 when we last examined these issues[8], suggest a more nuanced and complex narrative than the headlines shout at us on a daily basis – and less pessimistic conclusions than Ford and the Susskind's arrive at. We also suggest a future shaped, as much by human will and imagination and ability to absorb change, as by any specific technology, however heavily invested in.

The studies since early 2016 have tended to be richer in data, and more fine-tuned in their analysis than the polarised debates in the media. Nevertheless, media reportage of these studies still tends to follow the 'Hype' or 'Fear' models, downplaying qualifications and counter-evidence actually often in the studies themselves to favour a dominant, simpler, certainly more seductive, storyline.

That said, as a note of general caution, we have also become increasingly skeptical about the more macro studies on the technology and future job numbers. The problem with all too many is that they are projections going forward, with not necessarily good data sets, often carrying questionable, even tacit assumptions, and few make their methodology transparent. Even if you take the best of the studies, the limitations start to become clear quite quickly.

For example, the still most quoted study in the media – and one of the most rigorous and admirable of its time – is by Frey and Osborne (2013).[9] Looking at 2010 data for 702 occupations in the US, they found that 47 percent of occupations were under high risk of being computerised (the figure for the

UK in their later study is 35 percent). However, the researchers do not try to specify the speed of technology development, nor a time period for the loss of jobs. They say: *"some unspecified number of years, perhaps a decade or two"* (page 38). Nor do they attempt to predict the number of jobs lost.

Three further limitations we would point to. Firstly, the study, like many others in this area, does no analysis of jobs likely to be created by changes in work and technology. Secondly, it focuses on job and occupations but not on activities, nor the amount of work that needs to be done, which seems to be increasing exponentially – more of that later. Thirdly, the study largely factors out the key bottleneck of how commercially feasible, viable and organisationally adoptable the emerging technologies are, i.e. the long road to diffusion of innovation dilemma is ignored. The researchers do, however, point to three engineering barriers to computerisation, i.e. tasks that humans do that are not easily automatable. One block is 'complex perception and manipulation tasks' (manual, finger, cramped workspace). Another barrier is 'creative intelligence' (involving novelty and value, originality, fine arts production). The third barrier is 'social intelligence', including social perceptiveness and recognition of human emotion, (e.g. negotiation, persuasion, care). As we discuss below, the three concepts are not adequate for fully describing the multiple valuable human qualities that will continue to apply at work. Geoff Colvin wrote a recently published book called *Humans Are Underrated* and one entitled *Only Humans Need Apply* was written by Tom Davenport and Julia Kirby. Both are salutary reading on this subject.[10]

We will move on to demonstrate that these are important, in some cases game-changing omissions, if you want to arrive at a balanced view of what job losses are likely to be as a result of automation. However, media everywhere continue to quote the headline figure of 47 percent job loss as a result of automation, often without stating any of these critical qualifications to the storyline – in fact certainly always downplaying most of them. Another media case, perhaps, of 'too good to be false'.

You will recall that the work by Frey and Osborne (2013) is one of the more rigorously arrived at studies of automation and the future of work. It becomes highly necessary, therefore, to examine the studies, reports and research that have been produced more recently to find a way through them, and see if we can gain better insight into the more likely scenarios concerning automation and the future of work.

9.3. Automation and Job Loss: A Cross-Study Analysis

The first key point is that there is little agreement on the overall figures for job losses as a result of automation. The studies are best seen as a starting point rather than definitive statements. All have some flawed assumptions and data weaknesses, hidden often by seemingly precise figures. There are many reports quoting statistics on automation and jobs, and we can only draw upon them selectively here, but, collectively, they provide a complex picture rather than a straightforward one of job displacement.

As we have seen, Frey and Osborne suggest that on an unstated time horizon, 47 percent of current US occupations (35 percent in UK) are under high threat from automation. The converse point, of course, is that 53 percent (US) and 65 percent (UK) are not. In a follow-up study the researchers found 25 percent of UK occupations (21 percent in US) have a creativity component too high to be automated.[11] Forester Research (2016) estimated that 16 percent of US jobs would be lost by 2025 (23 million - about 11 percent of the present US workforce), but also job gains of some nine percent, leaving a net loss of seven percent. Their revised figures in 2017 suggested that, by 2027, robots would take 24.7 million jobs, but create 14.9 million new jobs, leading to a net loss of 9.8 million jobs, again about seven percent of the US workforce.[12]

A 2016 study by Arntz, Gregory and Zierahn for the Organisation for Economic Co-operation and Development (OECD) came to different figures. Re-running the US data using a task-based rather than an occupation-based approach (see below) they found that only nine percent of US individuals (not 47 percent) face high job automatibility (i.e. in excess of 70 percent automatibility). Using different, European data from 2012, it analysed the tasks within jobs (see below) and suggested that an average of nine percent of OECD jobs (10 percent in UK) would become highly automated within a decade.[13]

Assessing the methodologies used in the Frey and Osborne and Arntz et al. studies, PricewaterhouseCoopers (2017)[14] attempted to reconcile these figures, and concluded that up to 30 percent of UK jobs could potentially be at high risk of automation by the early 2030s (comparisons are 38 percent in US, 35 percent in Germany and 21 percent in Japan). However, the report suggests that not all such jobs may actually be automated due to a variety of economic, legal and regulatory reasons and also makes the point that these studies do not factor in job creation.

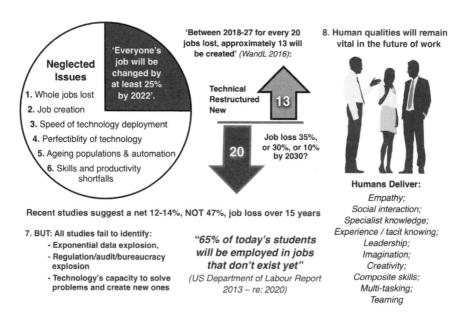

Figure 9.1: The impact of automation on work 2018-2027

In practice, we would argue, there are important qualifications to the headline figures. We see eight major such qualifiers, that individually undermine the usefulness of many job loss estimates, and collectively produce quite a compelling alternative, complex picture (see Figure 9.1).

9.3.1. Jobs versus tasks and activities

Are whole jobs lost as a result of automation? Of key interest is not the job as a whole, but the percentage of the job or activity that is automatable. Chui et al. (2015) picked up this point.[15] From their study, for example, 80-100 percent of a file clerk's work, 25 percent of landscaping and grounds keeping work, and more than 20 percent of a CEO's work is automatable in the near future. McKinsey suggest about 73 percent of work done by staff preparing and serving food in restaurants (three million in the US) could be done by robots – but ask: will 73 percent of those people really be replaced?

Studies that look at work activities as a better unit of analysis than whole jobs suggest job restructuring will be the more normal pattern. McKinsey Global Institute, in 2017, estimated that only five percent of jobs could be completely displaced by automation tools currently available. They suggest that, in the US, 60 percent of workers could have 30 percent or more of their jobs automated, while 30 percent of US workers are in jobs where 50 percent or more of the work could be automated. In their view, the consequences will be considerable role redefinition for many, and it is not just low wage, low skill jobs being impacted by automation.

Supporting this view, OECD data suggests that while, on average, nine percent of jobs are highly automatable, anything between 10-35 percent of jobs (depending on country) face a medium risk (50 -70 percent) of changes in task as a result of automation.[16] Certainly our own organisational-level research suggests every person's job is likely to be changed by at least 25 percent on an 8-10 year time horizon, as technology increasingly permeates task performance.

9.3.2. Job creation

What impact will job creation have? Unlike Forester Research (2016), all too few studies focus on job creation from new technology, though job creation has inevitably happened in the past. One pattern has been that process innovation enabled by technology has seen jobs lost, while product innovation has seen job gains. One study estimated that around six percent of all UK jobs (10 percent in London) present in 2013 did not exist in 1990. The new jobs related mostly to digital technologies. PricewaterhouseCoopers (2017) suggest that, by the 2030s, five percent or more of UK jobs may be in areas related to new robotics and AI of a kind not currently existing. Additionally, the report sees the productivity and income generated from these innovations being recycled into additional spending, so creating demand, that will generate extra jobs in less automatable sectors, for example healthcare and personal services.[17]

New jobs, historically, also come from new services, business models and innovations that are made possible by changed technologies. It is difficult to calculate what the effect might be, but one study of the impact of the Internet in France between 1996-2011 found for every job lost, 2.4 jobs were gained.[18] ATMs introduced in the US, to replace bank tellers, in the 1970s actually increased the bank teller numbers by the 1990s. More lower-cost branches were opened needing more tellers, and tellers moved to customer interaction tasks that were beyond ATM capabilities. For the UK, Deloitte (2016) estimated that over the previous 15 years technology contributed to 800,000 job losses but also helped to create 3.3 million new, higher skilled jobs.[19] Reviewing the recent history of jobs and technology, Stewart, Debapratim and Cole (2015)[20] argued that the present debate is skewed towards job destruction. In practice technology has substituted for labour as a source of energy; jobs have been created for the drivers of technological change; technology has created jobs in knowledge intensive industries; and technological change has lowered expenditure on essentials, creating new demand and jobs. Machines replacing humans has resulted paradoxically in faster growth, and, in time, rising employment.

Is this time different? Stewart and colleagues believe not. Those who argue that it is, for example Brynjolfsson and McAfee (2014)[21], tend to focus on the technological possibilities, rather than the many other, more shaping, non-technological factors that have affected the speed and pervasiveness of technology adoption in the past, and will continue to do so in the future. However, McKinsey (2017), PricewaterhouseCoopers (2017), and Forester Research (2016)[22] tend to support our own research that this prior pattern, if not the exact figures, is likely to repeat in the future as new work and new products and services are enabled by the technologies.

Arntz et al. (2016) put more detail on the possibilities for job creation. Using OECD data, they point out that labour-saving technologies have to be produced, and this has already created a demand for labour in new sectors and occupations, along with jobs complementary to the new technologies. New technologies can boost a company's competitiveness and thus customer demand, thereby generating new demand for labour. They cite a study by Graetz and Michaels (2015), of industrial robots in 17 countries having no negative impact on the total working hours at the sector level. They also cite Gregory et al. (2015) finding that computerisation generated 11.6 million net jobs across 27 European countries between 1999 and 2010. In past waves of technological innovations, Mokyr et al. (2015) reviewed many studies and suggest that workers, at least in the long run, benefited from past technological advances in terms of higher wages and income, although there is also evidence that there was at least a temporary increase in income inequality related to some technological innovations.[23] At the same time, as in the past, automation and digitisation are likely to be associated with large shifts within occupations and industries, pressuring workers to adjust to changing economic and working environments and skill needs.

Looking across the studies, and at our own projections within organisations we have researched, it seems that across the next ten years at least, for every

20 jobs lost another 13 jobs could be created. These will not be just in technology, design, implementation, operating and fixing, and the creation of future technology and software. In our own studies we are seeing new jobs developing around the technologies and its delivery within major business organisations. There are new, more technical jobs, but there are also a range of managerial and administrative jobs around maintenance and keeping the new technologies going. In business operations, automation also frees up people to focus on what people do well, and on work they could not previously have had the time to do. A lot of recombination of tasks is already taking place, while technology can be, and is most frequently being, used to complement and augment human strengths rather than substitute for them. Newly configured jobs emerge from this process of transition through work redesign. Automation also needs oversight. As yet we have not come across an automated system at work that does not need human attending and intervention. New jobs are also emerging from doing the things machines are just not able to do and that require human attributes (see below). During 2016-17 we also saw new work arising from new products and services enabled by automation deployment in banking, insurance, education, utilities, and manufacturing. These may be 'early days' phenomena, but the patterns are familiar to us from our studies of other digital technologies.[24]

Taking into account job loss and creation effects, the studies we have reviewed up to this point suggest an average net job loss of 12-14 percent across the top 20 economies of the world within the next 15 years. But this is before looking in more detail at six further factors that need to be considered.

9.3.3. Speed of technology deployment

How fast will automation technologies be deployed pervasively in work organisations? A typical feature we have observed at the technology 'Hype and Fear' stage is how technology is portrayed as being very quickly deployed in a seamless manner across multiple sectors. But does this bear up to scrutiny as the likely trajectory?

289

In studies of e-business and cloud computing technologies, we found key antecedents that affect technology diffusion. Two seem significant in the context of automation technologies.[25]

The first is **attributes of the technology itself**:

- Does it give relative advantage?
- Is it compatible with existing ways of operating?
- What is the risk level?
- Is it too complex or not administratively feasible?
- Is it easily trialable with tangible outcomes?
- Is technical support given?
- Is there potential for re-invention?

While e-business and cloud computing technologies had many positive attributes, we still found slow widespread diffusion of innovation in specific major organisations taking often 4 to 5 years. Our own research suggests a similar pattern for robotic process and cognitive automation.

The second antecedent is **the innovation implementation process**. This includes a range of practical factors that support or slow an innovations progress from design to adoption, diffusion and usage, through to exploitation and further innovation. Key issues here are:

- The sectoral structure, absorptive capacity for new knowledge, and sectoral receptiveness to change
- Adopter attributes
- Organisational readiness for innovation
- How easy the innovation is to assimilate – or is it a complex, non-linear process with many 'soft' elements?
- The quality of the organisation's implementation processes

Our own research for this book suggests that the implementation challenge is very real in the context of automation, especially for large organisations with a legacy of IT investments, infrastructure and outsourcing contracts. There are also cultural, structural and political legacies that will shape the speed of implementation, exploitation and re-invention. In particular, by late 2017 we were finding organisations running up against what we would call 'silo challenges' – in respect of technologies, processes, skill bases, culture, and organisational structures – that slow adoption considerably.

Manyika, Chui et al. (2017) also raise this point in their McKinsey Global Institute study.[26] They suggest five factors that affect the pace and extent of automation: technical feasibility; cost of developing and deploying; labour market dynamics – will labour continue to be cheaper or comparable?; economic benefits – does the technology deliver notably superior outcomes?; and regulatory and social acceptance.

In practice, we have found getting a digital technology to a workable, safe, commercial level, and then engineering the technology for specific use cases, can take several years.[27] The same is likely to happen to cognitive tools, ranging from digital personal assistants to driverless cars. Modelling cognitive automation tools, Manyika, Chui et al., (2017) found solutions development taking one to nine years, depending on human capabilities being automated, with social and emotional capabilities having the longest time frames. Cognitive automation is costly to develop: the area saw at least $45 billion invested during 2016-17. Deploying service automation tools also incurs expenditure often, we have found, three to six times the cost of the actual software. For example, we found one cognitive solution in organisations costing $1.5 million to get to proof-of-concept, and $12 million to fully implement. These figures are not typical of every solution by any means, but, as earlier chapters have demonstrated: data has to be collected and proven; software adapted to organisational processes; people trained; stakeholder buy-in achieved; governance structures established; projects undertaken; and technical and organisational change managed.

On labour market dynamics, these can be complex, and just because a task can be automated, it does not follow that it is cheaper or better to replace a human in that role. Humans possess degrees of flexibility and composite skills application that cognitive automation tools will not exhibit any time soon, and, on some estimates, not for 35 years. There is quite a lot of evidence that humans prefer human interaction and presence in many situations, for example on airplanes, in service contexts, and when being judged in legal cases, even where machines may seem safer, faster and/or more objective. On economic organisational benefits from automation, these may well be very promising, as we have seen in earlier chapters, but much depends on not just attributes of the technology, but also of the innovation implementation process, as described in this section. It is also early days for considering regulatory and social acceptance. As automation becomes more pervasive, the regulatory burden and social concerns are likely to mount, even though, as with all previous technologies, they operate in catch-up mode. A 2017 report by the International Bar Association warned that legal frameworks regulating employment and safety were becoming rapidly outdated. It suggested that 'AI' will test employment law safety and insurance, and human quotas could be needed for certain jobs.[28] By 2018 we were already seeing some regulation, and certainly rising concerns, on privacy, safety, dangers of excessive control by big providers, and exacerbation of social divisions through differential access to work, education and the benefits from automation.

To bring this together, Manyika, Chui et al., (2017) reviewed the historical rate of adoption of 25 previous technologies. Once commercially available, technologies still took between eight to 28 years to achieve 90 percent adoption (the range for 50 percent adoption was between five and 16 years). Fast adoption included airbags, TVs, on-line airline booking; relatively slow adoption included dishwashers, pacemakers, mobile 'phones and personal computers. These figures are consistent with our own findings on the adoption of customer relationships management systems, ERP systems, e-business and cloud computing technologies.[29] Manyika, Chui et al., (2017) suggest that hardware-based automation technologies, like driverless cars/lorries and physical service robots, could lengthen the time for adoption, as they need capital and physical production. Meanwhile, they still expect software/cloud-based automation technologies to fall within the range of eight to 28 years for 90 percent adoption. They, together with all commentators, see speed of adoption varying, sometimes dramatically, across occupations, sectors, and countries. Health care, transportation, accommodation, food services, administration and financial services feature as early adopting sectors, along with jobs focusing on repetitive physical activities, data collection and processing. On the other hand, jobs requiring higher education qualifications and non-automatable skills will attract pay premiums. Japan, US, France, Germany, Italy, Spain and the UK will see faster adoption than emerging economies, while cost and relatively lower wage levels in India and China will likely slow adoption.[30]

9.3.4. Perfectibility of technology

How perfectible is the technology? Historically, the IT industry has done a good job of convincing their customers that the story is one of continuous technology innovation and improvement, often conflating this with the reality of upgrades, and new versions frequently needed due to early releases of limited and/or imperfect technology and software. In practice, workplace technology products and services are rarely 'plug and play' or 'fire and forget', despite our more user-friendly experiences as consumers of products like the iPhone or video games. This trend continues into the design and development of automation tools. Under the umbrella term of 'AI', we are now regularly presented with the narrative that automation technologies, quite quickly, will match and supersede, by huge margins, human capabilities. In practice, as we have seen in earlier chapters, the application of robotic process automation has been limited so far, though set to grow to a potential market of $22 billion by 2025.

On conservative estimates, the cognitive automation market may exceed this some ten times by 2025, but by early 2018 applications were discrete, small in impact, and the overall market still quite immature.[31] A lot of this points to attributes of the technology being less than as represented – even by quite well informed technical sources.

To assess the perfectibility of current and future automation tools, Manyika, Chui et al. (2017) developed a highly useful (though not exhaustive) framework of 18 human capabilities needed at work, and likely to be needed in the future.[32] These divide into sensory perception, cognitive capabilities, natural language processing, social and emotional capabilities, and physical capabilities. They found that automation could perform seven of the capabilities at medium to high performance, but their modelling suggests that automation tools are nowhere near able to perform 11 capabilities to an above human level – and it would be anything between 15 to 50 years before many tools could. Furthermore, humans tend to use a number of capabilities in specific workplace contexts, and machines are not (and will not be any time soon) good at combining capabilities, let alone being integrated to deal with complex real life problems. These conclusions are consistent with the workplace research of Davenport and Kirby (2016) and the AI research reported by Alexander (2017).[33]

By way of summary, we are already seeing rapid growth of automation across sectors in the areas of repeatable, physical activities, data collection and data processing. The more automatable capabilities at work include: information retrieval; recognising known patterns; optimisation; planning; natural language generation; sensory perception; and gross motor skills. However, many other capabilities are much less automatable, as are tasks that require composite skills such as: managing people; applying expertise in decision-making; planning and through creativity; interfacing with stakeholders; and performing unpredictable physical activities. Assumptions about the perfectibility of automation tools any time soon need to be heavily qualified.

9.3.5. Ageing populations and automation

Many recent studies reassess the role of automation in the light of changing demographics across many countries.[34] Having said that, several major reports into IT, AI, automation and the US economy/workforce, choose to ignore altogether the issue of ageing populations.[35] Is this wise? Ageing populations in the G19+N (the G19 plus Nigeria) – producing between them some 80 percent of the world's GDP – may well lead to significant global shortfalls in labour and skills over the next thirty years. Further automation may be one way of coping with such shortfalls.

Let us put some detail around this proposition. One cannot assume that the 1.7 percent annual growth in employment, between 1964 and 2014, will be maintained over the next 35 years. Declining birth rates and ageing populations across the G19+N may well see employment growth decline to 0.3 percent a year, leaving workforces too small to maintain current economic growth, let alone meet espoused aspirational targets. Manyinka, Chui et al. (2017) estimate that the G19+N gap in economic output needs to be filled by the productivity equivalent of 130 million FTEs (Full-Time Equivalents) to maintain current GDP per capita for the next 35 years. However, to meet projected targets, this figure rises to 6.7 billion FTEs by 2065.[36]

The McKinsey Global Institute study projects 11 ageing developed and emerging economies having labour pool shortfalls of between two percent (e.g. China, South Korea) and nine percent (Germany) by 2030. Some 14 of the 20 economies will have shortfalls of between two percent (e.g. Turkey) and 16 percent (e.g. Canada) by 2065. By 2017, Japan's workforce was already shrinking, while China's workforce is projected to decline over the next ten years. By 2026, without productivity improvements, China may well be short of some 600 million FTEs to meet its projected economic growth targets. The United States already faces a shortfall of about 15 million workers by 2020, just to maintain its current GDP per capita figure. Clearly there are strong demographic pressures inhibiting economic growth in countries with high shares of ageing populations such as Germany and South Korea. These could benefit, quite quickly, from any productivity boost automation could give, while other countries with shrinking populations – the US, UK, Australia, Canada, Japan, France Germany Italy – will need significant productivity gains by 2030 to offset labour shortfalls.

This inclusion of demographic changes is important, as a corrective to the studies of job loss that either downplay these factors (e.g. Ford (2015), and World Economic Forum (2016)) or choose not to look at demographic changes at all (Frey and Osborne (2013) and Bowles (2014)).[37]

9.3.6. Automation, skills and productivity shortfalls

Are there skills and productivity shortfalls that inhibit organisations and countries from reaching their economic targets? Most recent studies recognise skills shortages and mismatches now and into the future, with increasing automation. At a macro-level, across the G20 countries, by 2020, there is likely to be a surplus of 95 million low skill workers (58 million in India, China and young developing economies). But there is also likely to be a shortage of some 45 million medium and 40 million high-skilled workers.[38] Skills security is eroding across sectors and geographies. Organisations will need to tap new talent pools abroad and at home. Technology can be designed to make the more of the skills workers actually have. As we have seen in earlier chapters, redesigning work and reconfiguring what constitutes 'jobs' can complement emerging technological capabilities. Clearly, major issues are reskilling, continuous education and redeployment of labour forces. The automation effects mainly, certainly over the next ten years, will be in the low skill areas – concerning repetitive physical activities, data collection and data processing – and on the other more automatable capabilities discussed above (see 9.3.1., 9.3.2. and 9.3.4.).

There is an irony here in that, while many studies are predicting large job losses as a result of automation, we are also seeing skills shortages reported across many sectors of the G20 countries. These shortages are not necessarily just in areas relating to designing, developing, supporting or working with emerging digital, robotic and automation technologies. The complexity is caught nicely where Deloitte (2016) reported that 114,000 jobs in the UK legal sector would probably be automated within 20 years. The research also pointed to an overall increase of some 80,000 jobs in recent years, mostly in higher skilled and better-paid jobs such as barristers and solicitors. At the same time the study points to a Warwick Institute of Employment Research study suggesting that 25,000 extra workers with technical competence, plus broader skill sets, were needed in the legal sector between 2015-2020.[39] There is a double irony here in that there is already an income and employment opportunity gap between high-skilled and college educated workers and those with low or medium skills. Automation may well exacerbate such skills gaps as it becomes much more pervasive across occupations.

Demographic changes, plus skills mismatches and shortages, feed into productivity issues at macro and organisational levels. In practice, it is increasingly likely, despite the lack of attention given to the issue by most studies, that major economies are going to experience large productivity shortfalls – even to maintain their present economic growth rates, let along achieve their espoused growth targets, over the next twenty years. Automation and its productivity contribution may turn out to be a coping, rather than a massively displacing phenomenon.

Looking across the 20 biggest global economies, the projections of Manyinka, Chui et al. (2017) point inexorably in this direction. As we saw above, workforce size will be too small to maintain even current per capita GDP growth over the next 50 years. Over the last fifty years productivity growth has been 1.8 percent per annum. If this rate is maintained then the rate of GDP growth from 2015 to 2065 will fall by some 40 percent. To achieve required aggregate GDP per capita growth of 2.9 percent, acceleration is needed to some 2.8 percent compound annual productivity growth from 2015 to 2065. This productivity gap is most obvious in fast growing countries like India, Indonesia, China, and Nigeria, China. But it also occurs in countries experiencing shrinking or slower growing working populations, such as Japan and Germany. Many countries, for a variety of reasons, are also experiencing a slowdown in productivity growth.

Against these trends, the McKinsey Global Institute (MGI) estimate that:

> *"By 2065 the productivity enabled by automation could potentially increase economic growth by 0.8 percent to 1.4 percent annually – the equivalent of 1.1 billion to 2.3 billion FTEs."*

Different countries will need different levels of such a productivity boost, but the McKinsey modelling suggests that, assuming the earliest adoption scenario, 15 out of the 20 countries – eight aging developed economies, three aging emerging economies, together with Nigeria, South Africa, Saudi Arabia and Turkey – would close the gap between growth targets and actual economic output by 2030. On the latest adoption scenario, nearly all will be in economic deficit by 2030. Interestingly on either early or late adoption scenarios, South Korea, China, and India as well as Indonesia and Mexico will, despite automation, have economic output deficits by 2030.

There are historical precedents for such productivity boosts as a result of technological development. Looking at robots at work in IT and manufacturing, Graetz and Michaels (2015) estimated that these accounted for annual productivity increases of 0.4 percent in manufacturing and 0.6 percent in IT from 1993 to2007. Crafts (2004) estimated that the steam engine led to annual productivity growth of 0.3 percent per annum from 1850 to1910.[40] As the MGI researchers suggest, there are also precedents for large-scale structural shifts of the sort that automation could bring about if fully adopted, for example the shift from agriculture in the US from 40 percent to 2 percent total employment from 1900 to 2000, and in US manufacturing from 25 percent to 10 percent between 1950-2010.

In summary, many studies have underrated the impact of skills and productivity shortfalls across multiple sectors and economies over the medium and long term to 2065. Automation will undoubtedly add disruption to the existing skills shortages and require new skills profiles. However, on the macro-level estimations presented in this section, automation and its productivity contributions may create considerable transitional disruption – depending on the speed of deployment – but may well be more of a coping, than a massively displacing phenomenon.

9.3.7. Dramatic increases in amount of work to be done

Will the amount of work to be done remain stable? Most studies of automation and the future of work tend to have a black hole in their analysis when it comes to not allowing for several major developments, discussed in this section, that have massive implications for the future amount of work to be done. As background, work intensification would seem to have been increasing for at least a decade, but especially since the financial crisis of 2008. Organisations have sought to increase productivity and the amount of work done by 'sweating the assets', and attempting to do more with less, using the same labour base and partly through applying digital technologies. As background, this phenomenon is very under-researched – people seem so used to work increase and work intensification, it is as though it is part of the everyday work climate and not worth remarking upon. However, some studies are indicative.

Thus Willcocks, Cullen and Craig (2009) record the 'sweat the assets' strategy being adopted in many organisations they researched following the financial crisis.[41] Felstead, Gallie et al. (2013)[42] found that the percentage of UK jobs needing hard work moved from 31.5 percent in 1992 to 45.3 percent in 2012. Since 2006 both the speed of work has quickened and the pressures of working to tight deadlines have also risen to record highs. Korunka and Kubicek (2017) collect a range of research papers recording work intensification over the last ten years across several economies.[43]

In our own research for this and two previous books, we very frequently found that, apart from the many other benefits, a major reason for automation was a range of stakeholders experiencing a rising tide of work to be done. The limits to working smarter and high performance practices were being tested, and the practices often found wanting. In the context of automation, our findings are supported by a 2017 multi-country survey of some 1,874 corporate respondents.[44] Of these executives, 70 percent said that the pace of work grew by at least 10 percent in 2016, and nearly half said it grew by 20 percent or more. Only 15 percent said that the pace of work had decreased or stayed the same. It found that, by 2018, 46 percent of companies needed greater automation to handle the volume of tasks being generated. By 2020, without more automation, 86 percent of organisations believed they would reach their break point and dealing with the increased volume of work would no longer be sustainable. The survey found that adoption of automation was still very slow, but that financial benefits from deployment were significant.

But where is this dramatic increase in the amount of work coming from? We have identified, through a close reading of the studies to date, that almost all routinely leave out three factors that, in our view are already, and will be, sources of considerable work growth over the next ten years.

The first is the **exponential data explosion**. The 2017 survey mentioned above found, for example, that nearly 80 percent of respondents reported that data from mobile devices and the Internet of Things was accelerating the pace of work. Some estimates suggest that 90 percent of the world's digital data that we try to process, was created in the last two years, and that the amount of digital data grows by 50 percent a year. Even if these figures are only ball-park, they still raise the fundamental question: How are we going to collect, store, process, analyse, and use data arriving in such colossal volumes? It implies a massive explosion of work, especially as data seems to create more data. Maybe we really do need more automation just to cope.

In the automation and future of work studies, the other largely unheralded source of work growth is **the cross-sectoral explosion of audit, regulation and bureaucracy** – amplified themselves by the data explosion and the application of modern information and communication technologies. We have been creating, we would argue, a veritable witches brew of data, technology and bureaucracy. Our LSE colleague David Graeber, in his excellent book *The Utopia of Rules*, would seem to be one of the few to have latched onto the importance of this development for the future of both work, and the capitalist system itself.[45] But even he probably understates the degree to which audit and regulation inevitably accompany high levels of distrust, the likelihood of market failure and increased demands for transparency. Such work may not be seen as particularly productive, but it is dramatically increasing across government agencies, business sectors and economies almost everywhere.

A third source of more work is **technology's double-edged capacity to provide solutions that also create additional problems**. For example, if you create more data, how do you process it, store, and analyse, then use it? A particularly good example is how the Internet has created cyber security issues. The cost of cyber attacks has been estimated at $445 billion in 2013, and continued to rise dramatically to beyond $600 billion into 2018. This has led to further technology solutions, of course – with the cyber security market being $75 billion in 2015 and also growing much faster since then to reach potentially $170 billion by 2020.[46] More technology is the all-too-often touted answer to our personal, social and business problems, but then we find ourselves on an endless treadmill of technological solutions and the new problems they also generate.

By way of summary, the dramatic increase in the amount of work to be done is one of the least analysed and considered factors in the automation and future of work debates, but may well be one of the more impactful. If one considers many organisations, self-reportedly at breaking point despite work intensification, working smarter, and the application of digital technologies to date, then consider how the exponential data explosion, the rise in audit, regulation and bureaucracy and the new technologies will then interact. Far from the headlines, a huge if under-analysed work creation scheme may well be underway, to which automation may only be a part solution.

9.3.8. The abiding relevance of distinctive human strengths at work

Will human qualities have any future role in work? In section 9.3.4 above we looked at this issue from the point of view of the perfectibility of technology, and found the technology both impressive and wanting. However the argument is too often cast in the frame that human qualities are all eventually replaceable by machines, and too little consideration is given to the human qualities that are distinctive, not easily replaceable, especially in combination, and that are likely to remain vital at work.

Multiple studies give examples of where human capability is being eroded by automation but certain human capabilities remain vital at work. Consider for example: leadership; empathy; creativity; sense-making; intuition; judgment; tacit knowing; influencing; insight; imagination; humour; social interaction; peer judgment; motivation; teaming; taste; worry/anxiety/concern; happiness; consciousness; and 'knowingness' ('a happy resonance between imagination and perception')[47]. This list is indicative rather than exhaustive, and is derived from our own casework, supported by Colvin (2015), Davenport and Kirby (2016) and Madsbjerg (2017).[48] These human capabilities are not at all that easy to replicate in specific contexts, and humans also have a facility to combine any or all of these in ways that machines are unlikely to master. In practice, automation may well free up humans to bring these qualities much more into their work, with positive impacts on productivity. In our own studies of automation, we have found plenty of cases where this was already happening – health care, insurance, utilities, banking, manufacturing, service providers, and legal services as just some examples.

9.4. The Bigger Picture

This final chapter has provided eight major qualifiers to the argument that robotic process and cognitive automation will create massive job loss in the next phase of what the World Economic Forum, amongst others, has called the 'Fourth Industrial Revolution'. Our objective has been to provide a more complex and nuanced picture of the future than has been emerging from the headlines and many of the earlier studies of automation and the future of work. That said, we recognise two 'big picture' issues that will shape the future impacts of automation. The first is that robotics and the automation of knowledge work – as represented by robotic process and cognitive automation – are only part of much bigger technological developments. As noted in the previous chapter, we call these SMAC/ BRAID (see Figure 8.7).

As we have argued elsewhere, the dramatic effects on the world of work will be from these nine major technologies employed combinatorially, and not just from the application of automation and robotics.[49] For organisations, differentiation and competitive advantage will come from their ability to connect these various innovations. But all these technologies are likely to have to pass through similar filters for robotics and automation, as we have pointed to in this chapter. We are also finding that the integration challenges being experienced in most organisations are considerable, and it may well take many years before these technologies can be fully optimised individually, let alone working in combination. Just looking at how RPA and CA are being deployed, we were finding, as of 2018, some examples of them being used together (see Chapter 2) but this was still a very underdeveloped area, while very few organisations had advanced to having a service automation strategy, let alone a strategy that links automation with other digital technologies. However, it is certain that this is precisely what organisations will be seeking to do, in the next phase. The second 'big picture' issue is that RPA and CA effects will play out within social, political, economic, legal and regulatory contexts (see Figure 9.2).

Figure 9.2: New technologies and their contexts

Historically, it is just not the immediate technology stakeholders who shape the long-term trajectory of technologies. Political, economic, social, legal and, increasingly, environmental concerns, players, institutions, and regulations have all played catch-up with technological developments, given the increasing speed and pervasiveness of digital technologies demonstrated over the last 30 years. But one only has to take a much touted new technology like driverless cars, and the social, regulatory and ethical, as well as legal, questions already surrounding it by 2018, to start to recognise the challenges a technology, or set of technologies, faces even if all too often, as Martin Ford argues, very late in the day.[50] For examples, biased algorithms received much attention during 2017, and the European Union was set, in 2018, to introduce a new law giving everyone in member states a right to an explanation of any decision affecting them that had been reached algorithmically. The year 2017 also saw calls for robots operating driverless cars, or as care givers, security guards and customer assistants to be fitted with 'ethical black boxes' to keep track of their decisions and enable them to 'explain' their actions when accidents happened. Economic factors also come to bear – automated heavy trucks may be technically feasible, but in the US the fleet of several million vehicles each with a 20 year life-span would cost about $320 billion to replace. Social factors may impact on whether care and service functions will be automated, whether humans will prefer social interaction with other humans. Political factors may militate against fast automation deployment, if citizens register dissatisfaction with job dislocation, or lack of benefits and educational support. In some countries regulations are already inhibiting what automation tools, together with big data, can be used for.

Our point here is that at least two big picture issues shape the degree to which the technical feasibility of automation tools will be converted into optimised pervasive usage. For SMAC/BRAID, integration bottlenecks could emerge that slow automation potential. On the other hand, fast convergence between RPA and cognitive automation and the Internet of Things and business analytics - as one increasingly emerging scenario - could see high-perceived business value from adoption convert into widespread usage. Social, political, regulatory, legal, economic and even environmental factors will also increasingly shape and be shaped by the pace and pervasiveness of workplace automation. How this proposition plays out in practice across societies and organisations is difficult to predict, but as automation begins to touch many more lives, – especially where automation has adverse effects – the influence of these factors, on technological trajectories is likely to increase rather than decrease. There are likely to be limits to the power of the rhetoric of unstoppable, all-embracing, all-giving technology when it comes up against the realities of how people, societies and organisations are set up, and being materially impacted by the technology and its consequences.

At this point, however, we need to register the serious concerns and potential perils of digital technologies described in our earlier book. These relate to five major areas: acceleration, employment, security, privacy and environmental sustainability.[51] Keen (2015), Greenfield (2017), Morozov (2011) and Zuboff (2015)[52], amongst many others, have also seriously questioned ownership and industrial structures, and how the use of technologies will play out and potentially exacerbate existing disparities in power, wealth and access. It is worth recalling Postman's perhaps timeless warning on technology: *"We always pay a price for technology; the greater the technology, the greater the price".*[53] As one example, Aiken (2016), Alter (2017) and Gazzaley and Rosen (2016)[54] chart the increasing evidence of the massive adverse impacts of internet and digital technologies on people's health and psychological well-being. As they suggest, we may be living through the largest uncontrolled social experiment of all time, with no real understanding of the consequences. Postman also pointed out that there are always winners and losers and the winners always try to persuade the losers that they are really winners. In addition, Postman, saw technology as not additive but ecological, and so potentially pervasive and transformative. Technology also *"tends to become mythic – that is perceived as part of the natural order of things, and therefore it tends to control more of our lives than is good for us".* Postman was speaking in 1998, and it would seem that the relevance of his words has only increased since then.

9.5. Conclusion

Our examination of dozens of major organisations found that RPA and cognitive automation are set to be very big game changers for businesses in the coming years. In the case of RPA, the necessary technology is, in many cases, mature enough to be cheaply, easily and non-invasively adopted. Immediate benefits can include costs savings, faster and higher quality processing, less error and better regulatory compliance. We are often seeing a triple-win for shareholders, customers and employees. We are still, however, not seeing RPA being used to replace humans, leading to large-scale layoffs, though the future looks less secure for outsourcing provider staff on this. Business operations staff has, on the whole, not felt threatened by RPA, but have tended to embrace it as a solution to a number of work problems. At the same time we have not been seeing RPA deployment bring back many jobs onshore - but neither have we seen RPA replace entire jobs.

In practice, the cognitive automation market is still quite immature, despite recent heavy investments made into cognitive automation tools and AI. Our studies suggest that more advanced forms of service automation, through software moving into more cognitive non-routine work, are less advanced than the hype suggests and will be mostly be small-scale, discrete projects within businesses until the back end of 2018.

However fast they develop, we think that RPA and CA will rarely see workplace use in the next phase to 2027, for a number of human skills and attributes. These are: fine motor skills/dexterity; mobility; social/emotional sensing; reasoning and output; natural language understanding; multiple agent coordination; creativity; problem solving; generating new categories and patterns; and activities requiring composite skills. What is also clear from our research is that the new technology works best **where it is guided by human intelligence**. And, at least for now and the foreseeable future, AI does not have the capacity to deliver the necessary will, imagination and similar intelligence and qualities – no matter how impressive the achievements of DeepMind and IBM Watson.

Instead of reducing the need for humans, RPA and CA may end up transforming the workplace into a more productive and stimulating arena. As RPA, in our words: *"takes the robot out of the human"*, it will certainly eradicate many tasks. Likewise for cognitive automation tools, as they replace discrete cognitive, socio-emotional, natural language, sensory and physical task accomplishment. At the same time RPA and CA will also create new tasks and jobs and restructure others – looking across the studies and our own work suggests over the next five years around 13 new technical and operational positions for every 20 eliminated. We see most jobs being changed at least 25 percent, but very few eliminated in the period 2018 to 2027. We find much countervailing evidence against predictions of massive, rapid or long-term job loss. Most organisations we research are experiencing work intensification and dramatic increases in the work to be done. They are looking to do more – a lot more – with the same or less. Our view is that this is a product of the exponential data explosion, the rise of audit regulation and bureaucracy, technology creating problems, and unanticipated increases in work to be done. Far from taking over, automation will be, most likely just helping us to cope.

Meanwhile, the new human roles are likely to be ones which will offer more day-to-day job satisfaction, because they will be based on those human skills that robots cannot readily duplicate in the next 15 to 50 years. Thus, ironically, with more automation, human qualities like empathy, social interaction, specialist knowledge, experience/tacit knowing, leadership, imagination, creativity, composite skills and teaming will become even more vital in the workplace. Experts talk about the need for STEM (Science, Technical, Engineering and Mathematic) skills in the future, but there will also be a critical need for these other sorts of skills that cannot be replicated satisfactorily in the next 20 to 50 years by machines, and these human skills will become massively valuable. Our research suggests that organisations need to adopt a strategy that sees technology augmenting, complementing and amplifying human skills rather than being seen as a replacement technology. The ideal mix depends on the job level and type. Technology will need skilled technical people to work on current technologies and make it function, but also technologists focused on designing tomorrow's technologies. Automation technologies will enable jobs to be assembled that play to the strengths of humans supported by machines. These may be at higher levels – big picture analysis and judgmental work – or involve knowledge specialisation, or may well involve doing work requiring a combination of skills that really only humans do have.

In this context, perhaps the biggest challenge facing any manager is how to prepare and train their people for this brave new world. Governments and individuals themselves also have key roles in education and continuous skill updating. Accepting that physical and software robots are here to stay, the opportunity is there to build a future workplace, which is both more productive and more satisfying, and, perhaps, a lot more interesting. The fundamental question is whether major stakeholders – including governments, managers and technologists – will have the imagination and will to shape contexts and seize the opportunities as they present themselves.

Citations

1. Butler, S. (1863), *Darwin Among The Machines*. To The Editor of The Press, Christchurch, New Zealand, 13th June 1863.
2. Vinge, V. (1993), *The coming technological singularity: How to survive in the post-human era*. In Landis, G. (ed.) *Vision 21: Interdisciplinary Science and Engineering in the Era of Cyberspace*. NASA publication, CF-10129, pp. 11-22.
3. See for example, Vinge, V. (1993), op. cit. Also Kurzweil, R. (2005), *The Singularity Is Near*. (Penguin, New York).
4. An example is Kelly, K. (2016), *The Inevitable: Understanding the 12 technological forces that will shape our future*, (Viking, New York).
5. See Freeman, R. (2015), *Who owns the robots rules the world*, IZA World of Labor, 2015, May; *How The Robots Will Take Your Job and Kill The Economy*, Fast Company, 26th February, 2015, Futures Forum; 'Robots could displace 10m. British workers', *The Guardian*, March 2017.
6. But one example is Nowak, P. (2015), *Humans 3.0: The Upgrading of the Species*, (Harper Collins, London).
7. We are not suggesting that these authors subscribe to the polarised media version of 'Automageddon'. These are distinctive studies, but their tone and conclusions lean towards more pessimistic scenarios.

8. See Willcocks and Lacity (2016) op.cit chapter 10. The present chapter builds on 20 months of further research by the authors, together with more recent empirical reports by other researchers in the field.

9. Frey, C and Osborne, M. (2013) *The Future of Employment: How susceptible are jobs to computerisation?* Oxford working paper, September 17. At time of publication the paper was the first, much-needed, rigorous study to quantify, using empirical data, the meaning of recent technological progress for the future of employment. It covers much ground, and is on the whole clear about what its assumptions are, and what it does not try to do.

10. Colvin, G. (2015), *Humans are Underrated*, (Nicholas Brealey, London). Davenport, T. and Kirby, J. (2016), *Only Humans Need Apply,* (Harper Collins, New York).

11. Bakhshi, H., Frey, C. Osborne, M. (2015) *Creativity Versus Robots: The creative economy and the future of employment.* Nesta Report, London, April.

12. Forrester Research (2017), *The Future of Jobs: Working side-by side with robots.* Forrester Research, USA. The report updates, and includes details of an earlier September 2016 report.

13. Arntz, M. Gregory, T. and Zierahn, U. (2016), *The Risk of Automation for Jobs in OECD Countries: A Comparative Analysis*, OECD Social Employment, and Migration Working Paper: No. 189.

14. PricewaterhouseCoopers (2017), *UK Economic Outlook: Will robots steal our jobs?*, March. Article by Richard Berriman and John Hawksworth. Reviewing these methodologies makes one realise how small changes in assumptions or adjustments in formulae can make very big differences in the figures produced.

15. Chui, M., Manyika, J. and Miramehdi, M. (2015) 'Four Fundamentals of Automation'. *McKinsey Quarterly*, November.

16. OECD (2016), *Automation and Independent Work in A Digital Economy*, May, Policy Brief on The Future of Work. The briefing is based on the work of Arntz, Gregory et al., 2016 op. cit.

17. Price Waterhouse Coopers (2017) op. cit.

18. McKinsey and Co., (2011), *The Internet's Impact on the French Economy: How the Internet is transforming our country*, McKinsey, Paris, March. The report records 500,000 jobs being destroyed and 1.2 million created.

19. Deloitte (2016) *Transformers – How machines are changing every sector of the UK economy*, (Deloitte, London).

20. Stewart, I., Debapratim, D. and Cole, A. (2015), *Technology and People: The great job creating machine*, (Deloitte, London).

21. Brynjolfsson, E. and McAfee, A. (2015), *The Second Machine Age*, (Norton, New York).

22. See McKinsey Global Institute (2017), *A Future That Works: Automation, Employment and Productivity*, January, McKinsey and Co, San Francisco, Chicago, Brussels, New Jersey, London. Arntz, M. Gregory, T. and Zierahn, U. (2016), *The Risk of Automation for Jobs in OECD Countries: A Comparative Analysis*, OECD Social Employment, and Migration Working Papers, no. 189.

23. Mokyr, J., Vickers, C. and Ziebarth, N. (2015), 'The History of Technology Anxiety and The Future of Economic Growth: Is This Time Different?' *Journal of Economic Perspectives*, 29, 3, 31-50.

24. See for example, Willcocks, l., Venters, W. and Whitley, E. (2014) *Moving To The Cloud Corporation*, (Palgrave Macmillan, London). Willcocks, L. Sauer, C. and Associates (2001), *Moving To E-Business*, (Random House, London).

25. The other two are that, in pursuing adoption of novel technologies, organisations, providers and their partners need to become much more collaborative than ever before; and the speed with which diffusion through informal, unplanned communication and influence moves to formal planned dissemination. See Willcocks, Saur and Associates (2001) op. cit. chapter 6. Also the comprehensive review by Greenhalgh, T., McFarlane, F., Bate, P. and Kyriakidou, O. (2004), 'Diffusion of Innovation in Service Organizations: Systematic Review and Recommendations', *Milbank Quarterly*, 82, 4, 581-629.

26. Manyika, J., Chui, M. Miremadi, M. Bughin, J. Goerge, K., Willmott, P. and Dewhurst, M. (2017), *A Future That Works: Automation, Employment and Productivity*, January, McKinsey and Co, McKinsey Global Institute, San Francisco, Chicago, Brussels, New Jersey, London.

27. See Willcocks, Sauer and Associates (2001) op. cit.; Willcocks Venters and Whitley (2014) op. cit.

28. Bowcott, A. (2017) 'Robot revolution will be a legal minefield, report says. Reported in *The Guardian*, 4th April 2017.

29. See Finnegan, D. and Willcocks, L. (2007), *Implementing CRM – From Technology to Knowledge*, (Wiley, Chichester); Seddon, P., Shanks, G. and Willcocks, L. (eds.) (2003), *Second Wave Enterprise Resource Planning Systems: Implementing For Effectiveness*, (Cambridge University Press, Cambridge); Willcocks, Sauer and Associates (2001) op. cit.; Willcocks Venters and Whitley (2014) op. cit..

30. See also Willcocks,L. and Lacity, M. (2016), *Service Automation, Robots and The Future of Work*, (SB Publishing, UK). Also PricewaterhouseCoopers (2017), op. cit.

31. See Fersht, P. (2017), *The robotic process automation market will reach $443 million this year*, HFS Research, June. www.hfsresearch.com. See also our chapters 1 and 2.

32. See Manyika, J., Chui, M. Miremadi, M. Bughin, J. Goerge, K., Willmott, P. and Dewhurst, M. (2017);

33. According to Manyika et al (2017) integrating capabilities to create a technical solution can take a further one to nine years of development time. The longest times were for integrating social and emotional capabilities. See also Davenport, T. and Kirby, J. (2016), 'Just How Smart Are Smart Machines?', *MIT Sloan Management Review*, 57, 3, Spring, 20-25. Aleksander, I. (2017), 'Partners of Humans: A realistic assessment of the role of robots in the foreseeable future', *Journal of Information Technology*, 32, 1-9. The 11 not easily automatable capabilities identified by McKinsey Global Institute are cognitive - generating novel patterns/categories; logical reasoning/problem-solving; creativity; coordination with multiple agents; socio-emotional - output, reasoning and sensing; natural language – understanding; physical – fine motor skills, dexterity/mobility; and, to a degree, navigation.

34. See for example Dobbs, R., Manyinka, J.and Woetzel, J. (2015), *No Ordinary Disruption*, (Public Affairs, New York). PricewaterhouseCoopers (2017), Manyinka, Chui et al., (2017) op. cit., Forester Research (2017) op. cit.

35. National Academies of Science, Engineering and Medicine (2017). *Information Technology and the US Workforce: Where are we and where do we go from here?*, (National Academies Press, Washington). Also Executive Office of the President of the United States of America (2016), *Preparing For The Future of Artificial Intelligence*. Executive Office of the President and National Science and Technology Council, Washington, October, Executive Office of the President (2016), *Artificial Intelligence, Automation and the Economy*, December.

36. Manyinka, Chui et al., (2017) op. cit.

37. World Economic Forum (2016), *The Future of Jobs: Employment, skills and workforce strategy for the fourth industrial revolution*, WEF, January; Ford, M. (2015) op. cit.; Frey and Osborne (2013) op. cit.; Bowles, J. (2014), *The Computerization of European Jobs*, Breugel, July.

38. Dobbs, R., Manyinka, J. and Woetzel, J. (2015), *No Ordinary Disruption*, (Public Affairs, New York), see chapter 8. The researchers suggest China will have a high skills shortage of 23 million by 2020 while young developing economies will be short of some 31 million medium skilled FTEs.

39. Deloitte (2016), *Developing Legal Talent: Stepping into the future law firm*, (Deloitte, London). Also Croft, J. (2016), 'Machines set to take over 114000

law jobs', *Financial Times*, 16th March, page 4.

40. Graetz, G. and Michaels, G. (2015), *Robots At Work. Centre for Economic Performance*. LSE discussion paper, 1335, March. Crafts, N. (2004), 'Steam as a General Purpose Technology: A growth accounting perspective', *The Economic Journal*, 115, 495, April.

41. Willcocks, L. Cullen, S and Craig. A. (2009), *The Outsourcing Enterprise: From cost management to collaborative innovation*, (Palgrave Macmillan, London).

42. Felstead, A, Gallie, D, Green, F and Inanc, H (2013), *Work Intensification in Britain: First Findings from the Skills and Employment Survey 2012*. Centre for Learning and Life Chances in Knowledge Economies and Societies, UCL Institute of Education.

43. Korunka, C. and Kubicek, B. (eds.) (2017), *Job Demands In a Changing World of Work*, (Springer, New York).

44. Servicenow (2017), *Today's State of Work: At the breaking point*, Servicenow, The on-line survey was fielded between 20th March and 7th April 2017, in Australia, France, Germany, Mexico, Singapore, the U.K. and the U.S.A.

45. Graeber, D. (2015), *The Utopia Of Rules: On technology, stupidity and the secret joys of bureaucracy*, (Melvilel House, Brooklyn).

46. Bank of America Merrill Lynch report detailed in *Cybersecurity Investing News*, 9th September 2015. Other figures from composite news sources.

47. Aleksander, I. (2001), *How To Build A Mind*, (Wiedenfield and Nicholson, London). As one of the major AI researchers, Aleksander still points to the fundamental mindlessness and 'unknowingness' of computers and artificial intelligence.

48. Colvin, G. (2015), *Humans are Underrated*, (Nicholas Brealey, London); Davenport, T. and Kirby, J. (2016), *Only Humans Need Apply*, (Harper Collins, New York); Madsbjerg. C. (2017), *Sensemaking – What makes human intelligence essential in the age of algorithms*, (Little Brown, London).

49. See Lacity, M. and Willcocks, L. (2017), *Robotic Process Automation and Risk Mitigation: The Definitive Guide*, (SB Publishing, UK).

50. See Ford, M. (2016) 'We are completely unprepared for the robot revolution'. *Financial Times*, 2nd May.

51. See Willcocks and Lacity (2016) op. cit. chapter 10.

52. Keen, A. (2015), *The Internet is Not The Answer*, (Atlantic Books, London); Morozov, E. (2011), *The Net Delusion: How not to liberate the world*, (Allen Lane, London); Zuboff, S. (2015), 'Big Other: surveillance capitalism and the

prospects of an information civilization', *Journal of Information Technology*, 30 (1), 75-89; Greenfield, A. (2017) Radical Technologies. Verso, London.

53. Postman, N. (1998). *Five things we need to know about technological change*, Talk in Denver Colorado, March 28. The fifth thing he pointed to was: 'There is imbedded in every great technology an epistemological, political or social prejudice. Sometimes that bias is greatly to our advantage, sometimes not.'

54. Aiken, M. (2016), *The Cyber Effect*, (John Murray, London); Alter, A. (2017), *Irresistible*, (Random House, London); Gazzaley, A. and Rosen, L. (2016), *The Distracted Mind: Ancient brains in a high-tech world*, (MIT Press, Boston).

Service Automation:
Robots and The Future of Work

Service Automation
Robots and The Future of Work

Leslie P. Willcocks & Mary C. Lacity

Hardback, 304 pages (Pub. 2015)
(ISBN: 978-0-956414-56-4)

The hype and fear, globally, that surrounds service automation, robots and the future of work need to be punctured by in-depth research. This book, by Professors Leslie Willcocks and Mary Lacity, captures a year's worth of learning about service automation based on a survey, in-depth client case studies, and interviews with service automation clients, providers, and advisors.

The authors cleverly embed today's empirical lessons into the broader history and context of automation, as a vital key in understanding the fast-rising phenomenon of service automation. They also present a balanced, informed and compelling view on gaining the many benefits, as well as managing the downsides, of present and future technologies.

This title can be purchased from

www.sbpublishing.org

Email: sales@sbpublishing.org
Tel: +44(0)1789 267124

Worldwide shipping is available

SB Publishing

Robotic Process Automation and Risk Mitigation: The Definitive Guide

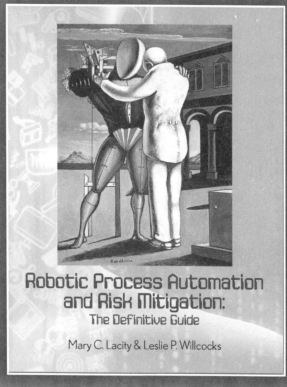

Robotic Process Automation and Risk Mitigation:
The Definitive Guide

Mary C. Lacity & Leslie P. Willcocks

Softback, 108 pages (Pub. 2017)

(ISBN: 978-0-995682-03-0)

This pioneering guide offers the first comprehensive analysis to Robotic Process Automation (RPA)risks as actually experienced and dealt with by organizations. The authors present analysis and findings from a two-year study. As more organizations adopt RPA, they find that best practice companies are able to gain a 'triple win' from RPA: a win for shareholders, a win for customers, and a win for employees. But while such results are impressive, they are far from guaranteed.

Service automation, like all organizational initiatives, is fraught with risks that need to be mitigated. The RPA risk mitigation framework reveals the significant RPA risks, and identifies 30 key risk mitigation practices that the research found to be successful. Whether an organization is just beginning its RPA journey or has reached maturity, this definitive guide serves as a key source of knowledge.

This title can be purchased from

www.sbpublishing.org

Email: sales@sbpublishing.org
Tel: +44(0)1789 267124

Worldwide shipping
is available

SB Publishing

This is an invitation to join us on our new website:

www.RoboticandCognitiveAutomation.com

Despite the massive hype surrounding robotic process automation, cognitive automation and artificial intelligence (AI), these emerging technologies are becoming more real, relevant and impactful every day.

Our objective on this website is to dispel myths and misinformation about risks and effective practices, through insightful, researched-based commentary that is independent, objective, rigorous, ahead of the learning curve, and highly practical.

We are also focusing on the bigger picture consequences of automation. This will lead us into interactive discussions on major issues as they arise such as:

- The future of work
- Technology and ethics
- Physical & psychological health
- Quality of work

- Automation & the economy
- Automation & the environment
- Political & social challenges
- Emerging technologies

We will also be connecting up service automation technologies with the broader digital transformation ongoing over the next ten years or more.

We will also be running discerning and sceptical eyes and brains over emerging technologies in business and work contexts to find out their capabilities, limitations and likely diffusion, using our customary, searching, evidence-based assessments.

There is a plethora of information available on the website, including free, downloadable research papers; regular blogs; links to RPA & CA advisors and providers; and video interviews where we answer questions on robotic process and cognitive automation.

"Robotic process automation takes the robot out of the human; cognitive automation complements and amplifies both the human, and RPA. Service automation technologies can deliver a triple-win of value for shareholders, customers and employees – but only if managed well."

Whether you are an existing adopter of RPA & CA; thinking of moving in that direction; or just have a keen interest in where the technology is currently at, you can join us on the adventure that is: 'Automation and the future of work.'

Professor Leslie Willcocks
London School
of Economics

Professor Mary Lacity
University of
Missouri-St Louis